For Moral Ambiguity

For Moral Ambiguity

national culture
and the politics
of the family

Michael J. Shapiro

university of minnesota press

minneapolis — london

Published by the University of Minnesota Press
111 Third Avenue South, Suite 290
Minneapolis, MN 55401-2520
http://www.upress.umn.edu

Library of Congress Cataloging-in-Publication Data

Shapiro, Michael J.
    For moral ambiguity : national culture and the politics of the family / Michael J. Shapiro.
      p.   cm.
    Includes bibliographical references and index.
    ISBN 0-8166-3853-5 (hardcover : alk. paper) — ISBN 0-8166-3854-3 (pbk. : alk. paper)
    1. Family—Political aspects.   2. Family—Moral and ethical aspects.
  3. Family in literature.   4. Family in motion pictures.   I. Title.
    HQ515 .S5 2001
    306.85—dc21

                                              2001001898

Printed in the United States of America on acid-free paper

The University of Minnesota is an equal-opportunity educator and employer.

12 11 10 09 08 07 06 05 04 03 02 01   10 9 8 7 6 5 4 3 2 1

To the memory of Lena Lopiansky Miller

Contents

Acknowledgments

This book is dedicated to the memory of my aunt Lena Lopiansky Miller, one of my mother's older sisters. Lena, who lavished affection and generosity on her family, lived for almost ninety-two years, forty of which were spent working as an auditor for one of the Internal Revenue Service's New York City offices. A Phi Beta Kappa in math from Brown University early in the twentieth century, Lena was employed during a period when women had trouble finding work that called upon their intellectual capacities. She briefly held one job that did—tracking the trajectories of missiles in New Mexico. But she quit because, as she put it, although she loved the job, "New Mexico was no place for a Jewish lady."

After she moved east, Lena had a full and rewarding life. She lived briefly in Washington, D.C., but then permanently in New York. In middle age, she was married for a short while to Aaron Miller, a self-taught socialist intellectual who was very far to the left of Lena's conservative views. In any case, Lena's primary passions were travel, baseball (she was a dedicated fan of the man to whom she referred as a perfect gentleman: the great Washington Senator pitcher Walter Johnson), and Gilbert and Sullivan operettas.

Fiercely independent, Lena lived by herself in an apartment in the Chelsea section of New York until she died, even though she was legally blind for the last fifteen years. She had many impressive accomplishments, but one in particular stands out for me. At age eighty-eight she won the prize for the best costume at the annual costume party of the New York Guild for the Jewish Blind. She wore a Hawaiian hula outfit consisting of a grass skirt and a coconut-shell bra.

I am grateful for the criticism, advice, and encouragement of many who solicited, criticized, and/or suggested elaborations of my chapters in their various stages of development: Jane Bennett, Bill Carroll, Bill Chaloupka, David Campbell, Robert Caserio, Bill Connolly, Jodi Dean, Mick Dillon, Jenny Edkins, Rainer Eisfeld, Kathy Ferguson, Jorge Fernandez, Dilip Gaonkar, Robert Gooding-Williams, Sankaran Krishna, Sakari Haninnen, Bonnie Honig, Neal Milner, Deane Neubauer, Cindy Patton, Manfred Steger, Rob Walker, and Sarah Winter. I owe a very large debt of gratitude to the staff at the University of Minnesota Press, especially my editor Carrie Mullen, her editorial assistant Robin Moir, production manager Amy Unger, and to an excellent copy editor, Robin Whitaker. And, finally, I am infinitely grateful to my wife, Hannah Tavares, for her love, support, and encouragement, and for the inspiration I get from her exemplary political and intellectual passions.

Introduction

The "Family Values" Campaign

Under the banner of "family values," a discursive campaign, in the form of a diverse set of closely associated conservative reactions, is being waged.[1] At stake is control over contemporary national culture and the consciousness of succeeding generations. Articulated in political speeches by public personae as well as in trade and academic publications, the family values discourse is aimed at redeeming an imagined past and colonizing the present and future. The aim, specifically, is to install a commitment to the moral and political importance of the traditional family, a regulative ideal that is represented as both contractual and natural: It is centered in a legally and religiously sanctioned marriage; it is heterosexual; it is child-oriented; and, especially in recent decades, it is threatened by non-"family friendly" media representations of extrafamilial attachments, sexualities, and life styles. In pursuit of that aim, many contemporary neoconservatives are judging ideas, artistic genres, and institutions on the basis of a moral imaginary—a mapping of diverse conventions with respect to both family and civic relations within the assumption that those employed by some are more morally worthy than those of others. Indeed, rather than regarding the norms they approve as "conventions," neoconservatives tend to regard them as "virtues," as commitments that enjoy transhistorical validity.[2]

In contrast with moralization (and thus dehistoricization) of particular practices and commitments, C. Wright Mills recognized, in a meditation on the history of the judgments applied to motives before the mid-twentieth century, that the warrants for motive attribution are historically contingent. Wryly observing that the desire to do evil had seemingly disappeared, he provided a sketchy genealogy of discourses of motive: "Individualistic, sexual, hedonistic and pecuniary vocabularies of motives are dominant in many sectors of twentieth century America, while religious vocabularies of motives are on the wane."[3]

Focused on family values rather than a generalized motivational profile, the cogency of the discourses associated with the neoconservative, family values movement relies on a paramnesis, a seemingly willed forgetting of the kind of historical evidence that energized Mills's observations. Historically, the "family" is a contingent form of association with unstable boundaries and varying structures. As an object of appropriation in the contemporary culture wars, however, it is represented as a historically stable, noncontingent result of natural inclinations and morally appropriate choices. Best regarded as a reactionary politics of representation, the moralizing of the family features, among other things, moralistic attacks on contemporary popular culture genres (e.g., feature films and prime time television) and on a wide variety of official and vernacular practices as well as on aesthetic productions regarded as uncongenial to the neoconservative family imaginary.

This book displaces moralizing with political thought. The investigations I undertake are meant to elucidate the politics of the family. Beyond my desire to impeach the conceits of the neoconservative family values movement, my aim, more generally, is to think the political in the context of thinking "the family." There are, of course, diverse meanings attributable to the expression *the politics of the family*. A conventional one, employed by political thinkers, treats the forces deployed in various historical periods that constitute family life and public life as competitive venues of authority and attachment. For example, Hegel (whose position receives extended treatment in chapter 1) saw family life as both a foundation for and a threat to civic life. He states, in one of his most relevant remarks in this respect, that "the community . . . can only maintain itself by suppressing [a feminine] spirit of individualism," which he saw as centered in family life.[4]

In accord with much of the critical contribution of feminist theory, Kelly Oliver contests the Hegelian and post-Hegelian presumption of a sharp separation between private and public spheres, which has functioned largely to segregate women and family life in general from the domain of political relations.[5] More generally, feminist theorists have analyzed a wide range of texts in the political theory canon, treating especially the texts' spatial predicates, which are complicit with a male-dominant gender order. They have shown, further, that much of traditional political thought's idea of a "civil society" has required a neglect of a complex interdependence between private and civic life. In addition, feminist theorists have impeached the historical narrative of liberalism in which the contemporary (masculine) individual constitutes an unproblematic mode of liberation.[6]

Contemporary queer theorists have also played a significant role in engaging and disabling the "prevalent U.S. discourse on the proper relation between public and private, spaces traditionally associated with the gendered division of labor."[7] Among other things, they have shown how "queer culture . . . has almost no institutional matrix for its counterintimacies."[8] As a result, for example, city zoning schemes that constrain public sexual expression compromise the "right to the city" of gays and lesbians.[9] Although diverse aspects of a feminist and, more recently, a queer critique of the political theory canon, and of political institutions and processes in general, have provided important insights into relationships between spheres of intimacy and civic politics and have influenced my thinking, my investigation is focused on a broader set of issues than the relationships of gender and sexuality to a politics of the family. My primary concern is with the critical contributions of diverse genres, which contain counterpolitical articulations by diverse family members to the dominant discourses on such primary attachments as the nation and/or the state. And I am concerned especially with voices that contest conservative appropriations of historical and contemporary family values discourses as a weapon against a politics of multiplicity. Much of the contemporary contention involves the articulation of normative models within which the family is appropriated in support of various symbolic attachments. In addition to describing and criticizing the symbolic politics associated with such appropriations, I treat the ways in which family space, historically protean though it is, serves as a critical locus of enunciation, as a space from which diverse family personae challenge the relationships and historical narratives that support dominant structures of power and authority and offer ways to renegotiate the problem of the political. Moreover, by extending recognition to less heeded voices and genres of expression, I seek to frame the political within a democratic ethos (an ethicopolitical sensibility, which I address within various chapters as well as in the afterword).

Given that the discursive terrain I am entering involves contending representations, the primary domains of elaboration in my investigations are genres addressed to relationships between families and civic life. For those who do political theory, the primary genre is, of course, the canonical texts in the history of political thought and philosophy. As is well known, for example, Plato's Socrates regarded the family as a dangerous venue of attachment that threatens to diminish the pull of civic life. Ever since the Platonic attack on the family as a threat to civic life in *The Republic* (which is more or less rescinded in *The Laws*), much of the political theory canon has sought to reinstall the importance of the family and, at the same time, situate it as an abstract domain of attachment with varying but primarily congenial implications for civic life. The few texts in the political theory canon to which I address myself serve more as exemplary objects of analysis than as intellectual guides. The variety of perspectives they offer—for example, a Hobbes who saw the family as primarily a contractual unit and a Hegel who saw it as a natural/moral one—reflect dominant moments in the history of political contention. Although the texts often offer keen insights and serve to illuminate some of the historical forces at work at the time of their writing, they are usually obliquely polemical and unduly abstract and disengaged from their own context as well as from life-worlds in general. As a result, anthologies devoted to the place of the family in the political theory canon fail to provide a relevant political sensibility for the present.[10]

Thus, although I occasionally resort to the political theory genre, I also pay attention to many others. There is no way to access families without the mediating influence of genre; indeed, thought in general cannot escape such mediation. Even philosophical discourses, often regarded as exemplars of unmediated rational thought, function as diverse genres. As Jean-François Lyotard has noted, "The Treatise, the Manual, the Meditation, the Discourse, the Dialogue, the Lecture, the Manifesto, the Diary . . . " all mediate their objects and thematics through genre.[11] However, different kinds of genre mediation create different kinds of challenge to investigation. For example, the genres available to the investigator of ancient familial structures and relationships present special difficulties. In his investigation of the ancient Greek family and its relationship with political authority, James Redfield notes that there is little documentary evidence produced by the families themselves (there is an absence of diaries, household logs, and so on). As a result, he has to rely on fictional genres such as the tragedies and on abstract political treatises.[12] The situation with the ancient Israelites is similar. The biblical texts are ambiguous with respect to locating the influence and scope of the family. The boundaries of the Israelite family are fugitive in the texts, because, as Johannes Pederson has shown, they intermix designations for families, clans, and houses and do not clearly distinguish when they are speaking of individuals and when they are speaking of tribes. Moreover, the general sense of the Hebrew Bible is patriarchal; it is a story about

4

how one man (Abraham) becomes a people. It is therefore difficult to separate the rhetorically patriarchal text from the evidence of the actual degrees of patriarchal authority. Certainly there is some evidence in the text, especially in the legal codes articulated in Deuteronomy, that the patriarchal tendency of the Israelites was attenuated as a result of their encounter with a Canaanite monarchical structure and city culture.[13]

Similar difficulties afflict those who wish to analyze contemporary domestic life, which abounds in "direct" evidence (people's reports, court transcripts, letters, autobiographies, and so on). Contemporary family life is at least reflexively a prey to various fictional genres, which are always already articulating themselves through supposedly descriptive ones. Among other things, persons' self-understandings are shaped as much by the regulative ideals they receive from various media as they are by personal experience. People tend both to live in a family and to process information about families from diverse genres—novels, television dramas and sitcoms, and feature films, among others. And often the media trump face-to-face experience. As Don DeLillo has implied in his novel about the fictional Gladney family (and the consumer-oriented codes that dominate life by the 1970s),[14] the television set is the family's most influential household voice. But even in earlier historical periods, domestic fiction, as realized in novels, shaped idealized perspectives on family life: "Fictional representations of the modern household preceded other manifestations by about fifty years."[15] As a result, given the significant gap in which the fictional family precedes the actual one, in terms of both configuration and the quality of emotional exchanges, fictional forms dominate contemporary understandings of family life. And, more specifically, the conjugal, patriarchal, heteronormal family, which historical evidence shows to be more a "regulative fiction than a reality," is a mythical entity shaping the contemporary conservative, family values movement.[16]

From my perspective, two important considerations derive from the ineluctably mediating effect of genre on thought and analysis. First, any investigation of the significance of the family in the shaping of political relations must be deeply involved in analyzing the genres within which the family achieves status as a set of representations, and, second, it must be recognized that mediation is not necessarily a deficit. Given that diverse genres contain critical capacities, I will be identifying and exploiting these capacities as I make a case for theorizing rather than moralizing the family. And, inspired in part by Walter Benjamin's politics of writing, my approach is not didactic. Instead, I piece together diverse fragments,

5

a mosaic of genres, with the aim of encouraging "the reader to pause and reflect" rather than to adopt a particular moral code.[17]

Having addressed the concepts of theory, genre, and writing, some additional words about my approach, or for want of a better term, method, are in order. To put it simply at the outset, my treatment of the politics of the family is located somewhere between the vocation of political theory/philosophy, which is associated with social science disciplines (but primarily political science) and genre analysis, which is associated with diverse disciplines in the humanities. Insofar as my investigation proceeds by interpreting the texts in various genres—visual arts such as photography, film, and television, literature, political theory, public discourse, and mixed forms such as comic strips—my method is in part hermeneutic, a method that to a degree spans the disciplines of the social sciences and humanities. Certainly, however, much of my approach involves the enactment of political theory as well. Among other things, I treat historical and contemporary tensions between familial and civic attachments with concepts such as authority, equality, and sovereignty, which situate my analyses in the broad frame of political theorizing. At the same time, however, I make frequent use of a hermeneutic sensibility, for example, seeking to render a detail in a text intelligible by locating it in a larger meaning frame that is constrained by the text's genre, historical circumstance, or situation of emergence.

Nevertheless my "method" is post- or antihermeneutic in important respects. Rather than seeking to deepen allegiance to particular interpretive frames, I employ a genealogical sensibility within which interpretation is a subject matter rather than a strategy of epistemic closure. Because the genealogical perspective is treated in chapter 2, here I simply want to note that, within that perspective, the existence of a particular institutional arrangement or of particular meaning practices is historically contingent and best investigated by analyzing the peculiar arrangement of forces that give them their temporary stability rather than attempting to show how such institutions or practices validate fundamental human characteristics or privilege a particular narrative of human development. Thus, for example, Gertrude Himmelfarb's (pseudo)investigation of Victorian virtues, in which she seeks to prove that the Victorian age had a homogeneous moral code and, moreover, had morals worthy of contemporary emulation,[18] can be usefully contrasted with Robert Mighall's investigation of the geography of gothic fiction in the Victorian age. Rather than judging contemporary morals within a frame that privileges a Victorian hermeneutic, as Himmelfarb does, Mighall demonstrates the intimations of modernity in certain Victorian texts. He shows how, when gothic writings dramatize familial conflicts between a "father's dynastic ambitions and the children's romantic love," they reflect the tensions arising from a historical change in family values—a change from "the older Aristocratic model of 'alliance' (characterized by primogeniture, arranged marriages, and the entailment of property)" to a "model of sexuality (with its emphasis on romantic love, choice, and familial affection)."[19]

My approach to diverse textual genres also resists a simple hermeneutic sensibility. My purpose is not to respect the boundaries of genres and hence interpret details on the basis of this respect but to summon alternative genres as critical thought vehicles (the rationale for Mighall's use of gothic writings). Roughly speaking, a "genre" is a particular "codification of discursive properties" that functions within certain "horizons of expectation."[20] While those horizons are historically contingent, it is nevertheless the case that knowledge of a genre practice aids in interpreting its specific realizations. But more important for my purposes, it also provides an appreciation of critical, transgressive texts that question rather than reinforce the relationship between modes of intelligibility and political attachments.

A useful illustration is provided by the impact of Wagner's musical compositions on French symphonic music in the nineteenth century. David Michael Hertz has pointed convincingly to a parallel between Mallarmé's poetry, which obfuscates the "syntactic hierarchy of a poetic line,"[21] and the "fracturing of the musical period in Wagner" (17–18), which was influential in the subsequent departures from orthodoxy of the musical compositions of French symbolists such as Debussy. Influenced by the Wagnerian disruption of the musical period, Debussy's music disrupts familiar meaning conventions; his melodic ideas are not contingent upon a rigid tonal scheme" (117). Ignoring the norms of musical periodicity, resisting expectations of closure, and rejecting the authority of conventional tonality, Debussy's scales have no conventional points of beginning and ending (for example, they often have whole-note intervals, a practice that violates the tonality conventions through which musical spacing and narrative is commonly understood).[22] Instead of developing themes, Debussy creates musical fragments, a multiplicity or nonlinear set of musical associations that resist instead of moving toward a stable narrative or set of references.

The result is a disruption of conventional musical intelligibility and, by implication, the production of a system of counterintelligibility to conventional musical genres. And significantly, because nineteenth-century musical forms were being appropriated on behalf of a French republican national allegiance, Debussy's challenges to conventional musical intelligibility distressed French nationalists. Alfred Bruneau, for example, the inspecteur general des beaux-arts and a spokesperson for a republican musical aesthetic, was disturbed by having, on the one hand, an undeniably talented composer and, on the other, a music that could not be unambiguously appropriated to an espousal of genuinely French republican traits. Because "he could construe Debussy's innovations only within the narrow framework of his own aesthetic-political discourse," he, like other spokespersons for the Republic, was upset by the resistance of the compositions to a nationalist cultural politics.[23]

Influenced by such examples of meaning-disruption, much of my consideration of diverse genres is aimed at privileging counterintelligibilities and thereby at evincing a critical perspective on the politics of the family. However, in many cases, the critical perspective I summon inheres not in the transgressive nature of a particular genre I analyze but in the juxtapositions I effect. To evoke Walter Benjamin on writing once again, I want to note (as I have elsewhere) that much of my "method" consists not only in direct argumentation but also in what Benjamin referred to as "literary montage," a showing as opposed to a saying.[24] Hence, although more could be said by way of introduction to what is involved in my contrast between moralizing and thinking or theorizing the family-politics relationship, the remainder of my introduction reflects my interest in showing as well as saying, as I enact my argument that effective thinking requires engagement with the forces at work at particular historical moments. I begin with a contemporary and compelling juxtaposition, one that speaks to a clash of meanings and the implications that derive from a major preoccupation of family values activists: exorbitant sexualities.

Solondz versus Podhoretz

Todd Solondz's film *Happiness* (1998), which maps the dark yet humorous spaces of contemporary suburban family life, constructs a morally ambiguous character, Dr. Bill Maplewood. The doctor, a "family man" in seemingly unsuccessful therapy, is a secret consumer of child pornography and a child molester; he drugs his family's dessert in order to sodomize his son's sleep-over friend in the middle of the night. But it's hard to dismiss Maplewood as simply a moral monster, because his pedophilia does not exhaust his personality. He also shows great caring and sensitivity as he speaks to his coming-of-age son about male sexuality. As a result, rather than creating an object of contempt and moral obloquy, "Mr.

Dr. Maplewood (played by Dylan
Baker) talks to his son (played by Justin
Elvin) about male sexuality, in *Happi-
ness* (1998).

Solondz," as Janet Maslin puts it, "calmly draws the audience into sharing
the doctor's ordeal."[25]

In disabling the audience's ready-to-engage moral sensors, Solondz's
film effectively achieves a critical, semiotic displacement. Because he disrupts the inclination to apply unambiguous moral terms to Dr. Maplewood, he turns attention away from Maplewood as an object of scorn
and toward the discourse of sexual morality. To put it in a semiotic
idiom, the film turns attention from the signified to the signifier and,
"more precisely, from the conceptualization that transforms signifier
into signified to those unconceptualizable qualities of the signifier that
keep it unsettled in form and meaning."[26] Put thematically, Solondz's
film shifts the focus from the morality of a specific character to the ambiguities in moral perspectives.

In contrast with the implied attitude in Solondz's film, which achieves
a semiotic displacement, is Norman Podhoretz's heated attack on what he
sees as dangers to a fundamental American decency: child molesters,
Nabokov's *Lolita*, Larry Flynt's magazine *Hustler*, Milos Forman's film
about the trials of Larry Flynt, and the Marquis de Sade's writings (along
with all who take Sade seriously as a political thinker). The numerous displacements in Podhoretz's essay, written at roughly the same time as
Solondz's film was in its first run, exhibit a Freudian rather than a semiotic
mode of substitution. On the one hand, Podhoretz understands some of
the mechanisms of Freudian displacement. He says that the credence given
to "outbreaks of hysteria" in which teachers are falsely accused as child molesters "is the displaced and distorted product of an uneasy conscience."[27]

On the other hand, his stridency simulates that very hysteria. To avoid the application of a Freudian interpretation to his outburst, Podhoretz locates the moral passion in a surrogate. At the outset, after reporting on "a cache of child pornography on a computer used by a convicted pedophile in a Minnesota state prison," he displaces his own moralizing position with that of his mother-in-law, who is also from Minnesota:

> The only moral standards she recognized as valid were the rigidly puritanical standards prevailing in the St. Paul of her day. . . . So far as she was concerned, the rest of the country, and especially New York, was going to hell while St. Paul, and the Mid West generally, remained an enclave of purity and rectitude. . . . She withheld even de facto recognition from anything that disrupted or challenged the moral order in which she believed with all her heart. (24)

By displacing his moralizing onto his mother-in-law, Podhoretz gets to "have it both ways." With a patronizing tone in his treatment of his mother-in-law's midwestern morality and his references to his New York (or, more specifically, Brooklyn) upbringing, he implies that he has a more sophisticated moral discourse at his disposal. Before he exercises his own voice, however, he discredits—through the mouth of his rock-solid, middle-American mother-in-law—all but heteronormal, family-oriented forms of sexuality. He then goes on to exhibit the same moral certainty he had displaced on his mother-in-law. In behalf of "American morality," he chastises those (like Vladimir Nabokov, Milos Forman, Larry Flynt, and especially anyone who valorizes the thinking of the Marquis de Sade) who "try to sow moral confusion" (30).

Podhoretz's style is hyperbolic and his claims extravagant. He ends his analysis with the claim that Nabokov's *Lolita* is a "dangerous book," a conclusion he says he is now able to reach because of the epiphany he experienced when he read about "a ring of pedophiles in Minnesota" (35). But in the process of achieving his conclusion about the threat of Nabokov's book, he exhibits an anxiety about alternative sexualities that must certainly predate his discovery of the ring mentioned in the newspaper article. The extravagance of Podhoretz's claims (for example, that Weimar Germany was "sexually unbridled" [25], that Nabokov's Humbert "seduces his twelve-year-old stepdaughter [Lolita] and continues forcing himself on her until she turns away" [29], that in Sade "buggery is by so wide a margin his favorite activity that the term 'sadist' might more precisely have been used as a synonym for sodomite" [30], that "commentators" on Sade, "his apologists," are coyly silent about homosexuality in his texts [30–31], and that "one must indeed belong to the intelligentsia—or perhaps the *French* intelligentsia—to see moral value and wisdom in the abstract lectures about freedom and nature with which Sade surrounds . . . scenes" [30]) encourages a symptomatic reading.

Without treating all these claims and their implications, I should note that the seduction in *Lolita* could well be interpreted as Lolita's rather than Humbert's and that "buggery" is one of many sexual acts described by Sade and is less important in Sade's stagings than the venues and contexts in which sexual acts take place. Moreover, buggery has political significance for Sade. As a nonprocreative sex act, it is congenial to his antiheredity model of political authority. And, contrary to Podhoretz's perception, the "French intelligentsia" commenting on Sade devote considerable attention to the role of homosexuality, sodomy, and to all that Podhoretz finds abhorrent and without redeeming literary or political significance in Sade's writing.

It is readily understandable that Podhoretz, a minor intellectual and insignificant writer, would vent his anger on Nabokov (who, according to Podhoretz, merely dallies with his considerable skills—art for art's sake rather than for the reader's ease of understanding) and on a widely recognized intelligentsia. More interesting from a symptomatic standpoint is his perception of threat. Given that many of his extravagant claims do not ring true, it is appropriate to locate Podhoretz's displacements in a Freudian narrative: He misperceives a threat, then misrepresents it, and then responds aggressively to that misrepresentation.[28] The extravagance that the displacements reflect suggests that the trauma provoking Podhoretz's reaction must predate his reading of the newspaper; it is doubtless a repetition of an earlier trauma. His chain of displacements is telling. At one level, Podhoretz recognizes a threat, but at another, he perpetuates a misrecognition in which the threat is "unrecognizable because it consists of ever-changing cathexes that can be 'recognized' only by being displaced, dislocated, disfigured."[29]

This brings us back to Podhoretz's having it both ways. His essay manifests an obsession with homosexuality in general and sodomy in particular. He charges Sade's "apologists" with being protective of homosexuality, sees buggery as the main focus of all of Sade's writings,[30] and most significantly, after reading about one episode of pedophilia, evokes an extended signifying chain that includes his mother-in-law, Nabokov, Milos Forman, Larry Flynt, the French intelligentsia, and the Marquis de Sade. It's tempting to side with Christopher Hitchens, who, after noting the obsession with anal intercourse exhibited by Podhoretz (and other "neoconservatives"), suggests that it requires "professional attention."[31] However, the attention here is critical, not therapeutic.

Rather than becoming concerned with his fixation on sodomy, I am interested in Podhoretz's opposition to moral ambiguity (which Solondz so powerfully conveys in *Happiness*). And, rather than concerning myself with a particular case of manifest anxiety, I am interested in a more general cultural anxiety. At various historical moments, changes in technology, in systems of exchange, and in space-time of interactions produce reconfigurations of collective modes of existence and, as a result, challenge the dominant understandings and representations of personhood. Inasmuch as modern conceptions of personhood are closely tied to the national imaginaries in which collectives recognize themselves, contemporary cultural anxieties associated with reformulations of personhood are articulated in discourses connecting persons with national cultures.[32] Podhoretz's outburst is but one instance of a more general reactionary manifestation in which the American nationhood is seen to be under threat from people who deviate from the common moral sensibilities of persons like Podhoretz's mother-in-law.

William Bennett, for example, a commander of the neoconservative army in the contemporary culture war, evokes the "common sense of the people" against "drug dealers, drug users, inner-city residents, Non-European immigrants, state bureaucrats, homosexuals, liberal church leaders, secularists, atheists, liberal arts academics and liberal journalists," all of whom deviate from those "individuals" who, taken as a whole, represent the American people.[33] For Bennett and other neoconservatives, the primary threats involve the link between nationalism and sexuality. They want to preserve the tenuous assumption that the American state embodies a coherent cultural nation, which is reflected in a family-oriented, heteronormal sexuality. Any deviation from this model in felt attachments or in sexual orientations, or even in representations of sexual orientations, is a threat to national coherence. For Bennett et al., "the modality of national culture in the United States," as Lauren Berlant has put it, "exists mainly as a negative projection, an endangered species, the shadow of a fetish called normalcy, which is currently under a perceived attack by sex radicals, queers, pornographers, and pop music culture."[34]

Berlant goes on to pinpoint the nationalist frame within which neoconservative cultural anxieties are manifested:

> The anxieties surrounding the process of making people into national
> subjects confirm that the hegemonic form of national culture is fragile

and always in the process of being defined, even when it appears as a thing with an essential character that can be taken prisoner, like the soul in fierce battles between rival gangs of angels and devils. (173)

Lending confirmation to Berlant's interpretation, academic moralists, commenting on the 1998 impeachment proceedings of the U.S. Senate, perceived a threat to national morality as a whole in the Oval Office of the White House rather than merely from the moral pluralism of popular culture and the arts. Decrying the morality of the Clinton presidency, they referred to "certain moral qualities" that are "central to the survival of our political system" and evoked a state of "crisis" that threatens "our children and our students." Seeking to protect "the integrity of both public and private morality," they, like Podhoretz, pointed to "the moral character of a people" and implied that "moral issues" can be unambiguously addressed.[35]

Leaving aside for the moment the issue of moral certainty, I want to note that there are complex conceptual issues and politically productive ambiguities associated with identifying a "people," much less attributing to them a fundamental character. As Giorgio Agamben has suggested, the figure of the people represents a fundamental "biopolitical fracture." On the one hand, it is a figure of inclusion: *the people* refers to "the total state of integrated and sovereign citizens"; but, on the other, it is a figure of exclusion, referring to "a fragmentary multiplicity of needful and excluded bodies"—"naked life" as a reality that pulls away from the more integrative concept of political existence.[36] And, as Agamben goes on to note, much of the shape of national political discourse derives from an attempt to finesse this fracture, to turn a multiplicity into a unity and a disjunctive set of political discourses into a single, legitimating representation of national unity.

Vaguely aware of the complexities of producing a unified discourse with unambiguous moral predicates, neoconservatives appropriate the figures of children, students, and peoples, all of whom are in need of protection from artistic productions that represent centrifugal forms of attachment and conduct. Once secured as moral foundations, these virtually defenseless moral entities will allow thought to evade ambiguity and allow moralists to displace politics with moral certainty. In this connection, Berlant has suggested that neoconservative moralizing, which harks back to precrisis episodes of a more moral national existence, "veils, without simply suppressing knowledge of, the means by which the nation's hegemonic contradictions and contingencies are constructed, consented to, displaced, and replaced by images of normal culture that 'the people' are said already to accept."[37]

Contrary to this mode of thinking, I shall be arguing that cultural texts, events, and productions that evince moral ambiguity are important political interventions. Moral ambiguity is what should be cultivated in a healthy and engaged polity, and it is a necessary predicate to critical thinking about the family-polity relationship. Interestingly, television, whose programming is also under attack by neoconservatives, is often the medium providing the most critical and politically perspicuous treatments of the contemporary family. Rather than evincing the regulative ideals central to the family imaginary of those involved in the family values movement, television programming in the past two decades has departed from its depiction of the conventional family ideal that characterized its programs from the 1950s through the 1970s.

By the 1980s, television's family became more a "loose, liberal, contractual affair between a miscellaneous number of big and little adults."[38] This portrayal accords with the changing familial structure, a "postindustrial family" with increasing numbers of men and women employed outside the family. Along with changes in ethos—an increasing recognition of alternative sexualities and attachments—the family unit in modern postindustrial societies has become, in the words of one analyst, more a structure of "elective affinities" than a "natural" (i.e., traditional) structure.[39] And, rather than promoting regulative ideals by sorting good and bad characters, television sitcoms, for example, *The Mary Tyler Moore Show,* avoided a simplistic didacticism that inheres in unambiguous personae. All the characters present different faces. For example, Mary herself hovers ambiguously between the docile employee trying to make it in a man's world and a politicized woman with feminist leanings, telling the truth to male power. As a result, "the viewer's attention and allegiance are shunted from one character to another. The narrative is less linear and the characters decentered, creating a world more relativistic and less clearly demarcated into good and evil."[40] And, more recently, the unruly Roseanne (of the family sitcom by that name), challenged a traditional wife-mother persona and habitus not only with her actions but also with her body, which violates the stylistic conceits of the modern bourgeois woman. Roseanne's body and behavior provide a pedagogy that disrupts and therefore politicizes the regulative ideals surrounding the traditional family.[41]

But perhaps more destructive of the power of regulative ideals is the way the forms of television programming produce a historical consciousness. Because contemporary viewers can tune in to reruns of programs from earlier decades, allowing them to compare past and present versions of the family, they can adduce a historical consciousness. The temporal disjuncture, a juxtaposition of the old and new, produces the impression that the viewer is "somehow more enlightened than the characters" and "that the past is absolutely central to the interpretation the network solicits."[42] This practice of juxtaposition locates television in a more critical position than, for example, many school curricula and museum presentations, which often mask their narrative selections and hence historical sensibilities. As a result, as Lynn Spigel discovered in her analysis of television reception by her students, "television serves as one of our culture's primary sources for historical consciousness" (25).

There are other contemporary genres supplying critical perspectives on the family. As Vivian Sobchack has pointed out, for example, some film genres speak to the contemporary situation in which the boundaries between family and public life are increasingly ambiguated by new processes of spatial and temporal exchange, which transform and redefine the boundaries of the family. For example, the contemporary genres of horror, science fiction, and family melodrama converge in the dramatization of these processes that "test and represent the coherence, meaning, and limits of the family as it has been constructed in patriarchal culture."[43] As figures from the outside world—the past and future, for example— invade the family, a more general recognition is evinced: The social world can no longer be conceptualized and dramatized by a strict separation of public and private spheres. And, most important for purposes of my concern with a critical perspective rather than a moralizing didacticism, the film genres of which Sobchack speaks play out without attempting to resolve the scenarios of the family's current dilemmas.

The genres in Sobchack's analysis reflect dynamics peculiar to "now-time"; they are genres of contemporary popular culture that invite us to reflect on the complex interactions and reconfigurations of familial and civic space. Like these genres, which adduce ambiguities rather than moralizing about regulative ideals, others, from ancient times to the present, are effectively addressed to transformational episodes in familial relations and configurations. They help create the conditions of possibility for a critical politics of the family. Accordingly, in chapter 1, I provide a broad historical range of such genres, with the aim of displacing moralizing with a historical and genre-sensitive mode of theorizing. Thereafter, subsequent chapters demonstrate the ways in which diverse genres provide critical loci of enunciation that contribute to a critical politics of the family.

1. Resisting Resolution: Genre and the Family

Eteocles Loses His Cool; Aeschylus Holds On to His

It has been frequently noted that in Aeschylus's tragedy *Seven against Thebes*, the main character, Eteocles, undergoes "an abrupt transformation" (at line 653), changing from "a man who is 'cool and at ease, ready-witted and concerned for the morale of his people'" to a man driven and out of control, seemingly finally overcome by the curse imposed on his lineage in the Oedipus saga.[1] The elaborate mythological background to Aeschylus's story is outside the scope of this chapter. My concern is with the political implications of a philosophical trajectory running from Aeschylus through Nietzsche to Foucault and other contemporary writers and artists. And because the specific focus of my political inquiry is on a contention between moralizing and critical perspectives on relations between familial and public attachments, Aeschylus's *Seven* provides an auspicious place to begin.

Briefly summarized, the drama opens before dawn with the news that the Argive army, led by Eteocles' brother, Polynices, surrounds the walls of Thebes. In response, Eteocles, as the king, is preparing the city's defense. As he addresses his warriors, he begins with the injunction that saying the proper things, a discursive defense, is at least as vital a task as the military defense of the city: "Townsmen of Cadmus, speech must be fitted to the times."[2] Eteocles' remark about appropriate speech resonates with his subsequent attempts to quiet the feminine chorus. The women must remain silent and inside, leaving the action—verbal and military—to the men. Eteocles' attempt to muzzle the women is more than mere misogyny. It represents his attempt to maintain a masculine, civic order against a feminine attachment to a cosmology that privileges family and lineage. But inasmuch as Eteocles is part of a cursed lineage with fateful consequences, his attack on the female chorus represents as well his attempt at inventing a singular identity from what is an ambiguous or divided self: Eteocles the civic leader and Eteocles the son of a morally corrupted family.

With respect to the civic story, bound up with the preparation for the siege in the first part of the drama, Eteocles himself, after stationing his best champions at six of the city's gates, becomes the defender of the seventh. But the civic story cannot ultimately be separated from the family saga. Eteocles' decision to nominate himself as the last defender eventuates in his encounter with his brother, Polynices, the seventh Argive attacker. Neither brother has foreknowledge that they will oppose each other. Their encounter and the mutual killing that results, as each is pierced by the spear of the other, are a seeming fulfillment of their father's curse. But apart from this fateful outcome—Eteocles saves the city but loses his life—the conflict that the drama enacts is reflected in the change in Eteocles' demeanor. He is drawn into an event in which the righteous defense of the city also implies participation in what will be the enduring moral pollution of fratricide. At the crucial point at which he recognizes the dilemma, he flies into a rage, seemingly (to some commentators) leaving the cool effective leader of the city behind in exchange for an impassioned antagonist.

There are two basic alternatives to which commentators have turned to treat the disjuncture in Eteocles' personality. One is to attribute contradictory projects to Aeschylus's story by having his drama produce two Eteocleses: the mythological one who inherits a curse from the *Oedipodeia* and the historical one who defends the city. The other is to save the coherence of Eteocles' personality either by showing that he remains the effective leader throughout *Seven* or by showing that he knew he was accursed, even before his intemperate outburst.[3] Neither of these solutions preserves the spirit of Greek tragedy or the project that Aeschylus pursues in his dramas. Pierre Vidal-Naquet's response to these attempts at inventing a consistent Eteocles is compelling: "Eteocles is not a 'human being,' reasonable or otherwise. . . . He is a figure of a Greek tragedy. . . . The values that stand in contrast to each other on either side of line 653—that is to say the values of the *polis* and those connected with the world of the family, are not states of mind" (277–78). In short, Aeschylus's dramatic intent was not to represent emotionally coherent, believable human beings but to stage encounters between the conflicting forces at work in his time. The genre of tragedy he inaugurates is not a form of moral statement in behalf of particular, coherently developed protagonists. The tragedies dramatize conflicting values and social practices, connected to different cosmologies, which yield different normative systems.

The textual strategy of the contemporary novelist Don DeLillo warrants attention in this context, for it bears comparison with that of Aeschylus. His characters also "lack a consistent, coherent personality." They function as linguistic vehicles rather than as self-contained, plausible personalities.[4] As DeLillo notes in reference to the characters in his *End Zone*: "Some characters have a made up nature, they are pieces of jargon. They engage in wars of jargon with each other. There is a mechanical element, a kind of fragmented self-consciousness."[5]

Whereas one reviewer has complained that DeLillo fails to "render as faithfully as possible, the feelings his characters would be likely to have in the situations he has them in,"[6] it is clear that the primary actors in DeLillo's novels are codes, not personalities. DeLillo's text is an assembly of encounters among the conflicting codes of a divided sociopolitical order, a Kafkaesque system of clashing intelligibilities that defy coherence. And, more broadly, DeLillo's "America" is a world in which danger and death are dissimulated, mediated by placating and ambiguous codes. As one character in his *Players* puts it (reflecting a similitude between DeLillo's reading of modernity and the tragic disposition), "Behind every stark fact we encounter layers of ambiguity."[7]

There is a political pedagogy in DeLillo's failure to develop coherent characters. In his *White Noise*, for example, the plot focuses on the Gladney family and its failure to provide a "haven in a heartless world" (to use Christopher Lasch's romantic phrase).[8] The context for DeLillo's imaginative construction of the Gladney family is an epoch of modernity, a period of the triumph of consumer capitalism. Politically, it is a time in which a homology develops between the consumer and citizen-subject, as the coding of commodities converges stylistically with the coding of political events. Citizen-subjects and consumers merge into a single target of diverse economic and political media manipulation. Confusing and ambiguous codes evoke or dissimulate danger. And the family, far from being a reassuring unit of collective solidarity and protection, becomes instead a conflictual and susceptible collective that amplifies the symbolic manipulations of economic, political, and bureaucratic agents. Divided against itself, the family is less a collection of characters than it is a set of voices that relay different codes into the family's midst. Coherent or incoherent family characters are not what DeLillo fabricates. In *White Noise*, Gladney, his wife, Babette, and their children constitute diverse modes of susceptibility to media reports of danger. Their media-suborned articulations defy both individual and collective/familial coherence.

Unlike the modernity that provides the context for DeLillo's novels, the time period of Greek tragedy is brief and transitory. A "moment" rather than an extended epoch, it is situated between the "law as it was about to be born and the law as it was already constituted."[9] The ambiguity of tragedy's situation is mirrored in the discursive dualities that are its narrative vehicles. The collective figure of the chorus articulates, lyrically, concerns about the actions of the heroes rather than valorizing them. In contrast, the heroes and their interlocutors express themselves in dialogue. Reflecting a period of ambiguity in structures of authority and spheres of justice, the tragic writer is showing both stylistically and thematically the forces of the present, creating a distance from heroic values and ancient religion by creating encounters between heroes and the newly emerging legalisms of the city-state. As is the case with the modernity whose tensions occupy DeLillo's novel, the Greek order into which tragedy is a reflective intervention is also a prey to ambiguous and colliding codes. Specifically, although the rule of law is displacing the authority of lineage, and the polity, which is constituted on the basis of the emerging law of the city, is set against the *oikos,* or family, whose legitimacy is based on the traditional law of lineage, the order retains dualities and ambiguities. The tragic hero is not a character but a "strictly defined social and religious category."[10] And although the authority of the heroic age has been largely displaced by a legal structure, reflected in the obsessively legal discourse of the tragic writers, vestiges of that authority remain in the city's civic religion.

As a result of such conjunctural historical forces, the moment of tragedy, reflected in *Seven,* makes unambiguous right talking impossible. The conflict in the drama involves a struggle between the older gods affiliated with structures of kinship and the newer gods attached to public life. Because the different gods belong to different religious worlds, there are no actions that will produce a definitive justice and no words that will ultimately resolve ambiguity. Inasmuch as the emergence of the city's polis did not wholly displace the religious attachments, modes of behavior, and structures of familial and lineage solidarity associated with the *oikos,* there is no way to overcome the agonal aspects of word and deed. As a result, Eteocles' initial injunction about speaking properly is a vain hope. Speech cannot be simply "fitted to the times," because the order of the Greek city-state is riven by conflicting normative structures. Indeed, throughout the Greek tragedies, words have different meanings when delivered from different loci of enunciation. The word *nomos*, in *Antigone*, for example, "may be used with precisely opposed connotations by different protagonists."[11] Accordingly, Aeschylus's drama enacts encounters between conflicting and contradictory norms, associated with ambiguous articulations that reflect a clash between a religious tradition and a newly established legal code. The loci of the drama and the actions of the protagonists cannot be unambiguously judged within either set of norms.[12]

The collision between different and irreconcilable normative terrains or spheres of justice in *Seven* is dramatized by the way Eteocles' discursive defense of the city unfolds. After his initial injunction about the need for right talking, his emerging strategy, which involves selecting champions to defend each of the city's seven gates, situates him at the same time in an elaborate discursive war. Each Argive attacker carries a shield with "devices" (inscriptions and icons).[13] Although Eteocles nominates himself to meet the seventh attacker, his brother Polynices, it falls to him as leader to confront the rhetorical force of each shield. The shields, described in succession by a messenger (there are actually eight shields, but one is blank), have hostile devices foretelling the destruction of Thebes.

The succession of shields can be read in two ways: the divisions they reflect and the encounters they attract. First, their devices form two groupings, one group representing "the cosmos, the side of foreign war and the two fundamental forms of warrior activity" (i.e., those shields showing male warriors involved in fighting) and the other representing "the female world" (e.g., a woman is guiding the warrior on Polynices' shield) (296). One group, therefore, "is that of the *polis* at grips with the enemy," the major aspect of the story in the first part of the play, while the other is an extended reference to the curse associated with Eteocles' lineage, which dominates the consequences experienced in the second part of the play. In short, one set of shields is concerned with Eteocles the warrior, and the other is concerned with Eteocles "the son of Oedipus and Iocasta and brother of Polynices" (296).

Second, the shields are involved in an active collision of codes as Eteocles attempts to contest each hostile message and, especially, to resist the fateful effects of lineage by having the civic code of the polis dominate in each case. Eteocles' discursive defense of the city takes the form of turning the signs against their carriers. In response to each of the shields' devices, he exploits the ambiguities of language, which derive from the ambiguity involved in the collision of normative contexts within which the shields' hostile signs are being deployed. In response to the warrior signs, for example, such as that carried by the first attacker, Tydeus, he states that the violence of which the shield speaks will be visited on its bearer ("It does foretell violence—to himself": line 404) .

Nevertheless, despite the cleverness with which his discursive strategy unfolds, Eteocles cannot ultimately command the meaning of signs. The very ambiguity he seeks to exploit turns against him. Eteocles, who is both a warrior from the city and a son and brother from outside it, cannot hold language to his purposes of both saving the city and maintaining a singularity of self. He lacks a stabilized locus of enunciation, which is a necessary predicate for the stability of signs. That Eteocles is a divided body, both a civic and a familial personage, is reflected in two specific doubling effects that locate Eteocles both inside and outside the city. He has two "doublets" outside, one an opposing warrior with nearly the same name, "Eteoclos," and his brother Polynices, who shares the cursed lineage.[14] Ultimately, the divided Eteocles cannot locate himself ahistorically in his contemporary civic space and thereby control the discursive war. Despite his apotropaic gestures, when he hurls signs back at their perpetrators, the signs end up working against him. As Eteocles attempts to hold on to the meaning of signs at one level—reversing signs, one shield after another—another narrative is unfolding: "the family history which begins to operate upon the text with increasing insistence."[15] An implacable historical force haunts Eteocles' words, turning his attempt to maintain a civic detachment back toward his familial fate. As Froma Zeitlin has summarized it: "Against Eteocles' resistance to time and hence to inscription in the family's *history,* the narrative of the *story* presses forward to bring *back* the brother at the last" (49).

In what sense then does *Aeschylus* keep his cool? A clue is available at the end of the drama, when the two sets of codes, those connected to the civic order and those connected to family and lineage, diverge to indicate that the tension between them is maintained and that no reconciliation can take place.[16] In the final scene of *Seven,* a divided chorus makes clear that an irresolvable agon is at the center of Greek life. They divide into two groups, one following Creon and the corpse of Eteocles (in support of civic justice), and the other following Antigone, who in defiance of civic law (but in accord with the law of lineage) is going to bury Polynices. They act out what is in effect Aeschylus's aim, a dramatizing of the dilemma of justice in a Greek world torn between familial obligation and civic attachment.

From Fathers and Daughters to Fathers and Sons: *Njal's Saga*

After the ancient Greek tragedy, the genre of expression that perhaps most thoroughly explores relationships between familial attachments and civic duty is the Icelandic family saga. To analyze further the extensive and historically contingent forces that divide families and civic relations, I examine the best example of this genre, *Njal's Saga,* and to set up some contemporary familial-civic issues involving interactions between fathers and sons, I focus on a father-son dynamic that bears on the episodes with which the saga is concerned.

Njal's Saga, written in the thirteenth century about an event that took place in the tenth, is the longest and greatest of the Icelandic family sagas. Its two central characters, Njal, the wise man steeped in knowledge of the law, and Gunnar, a traditional warrior hero, form an alliance in an effort to keep the peace in a society riven by conflicting codes, especially one that prescribes blood revenge, which is opposed by one that stipulates the legal resolution of conflict. Closely allied to the conflicting codes are aspects of reputation. There are those who are known for manly deeds and those who are valued for their lawfulness and hospitality. The society moreover is at once extremely litigious and extremely violent, and at the center of the social world is a fateful set of contradictory forces. Extended kinship structures are welded together by obligations of reciprocity and support; "kinsmen" are expected to supply support in both feuds and law-suits. One's protection from violence is a function of the density of one's kinship/obligation network, because everyone allied to a chieftain-kin structure is obliged to aid others that are part of the network, both to protect them from violence and to ante up with money for compensation if one of them runs afoul of the law. Failure to observe one's legal obligations results in outlawry, and those who end up outside the law can be killed without the necessity of paying compensation.

At the same time, however, the more dense the network of one's kinship group, the more likely it is that one will be obliged to take a part in a dispute and thus become vulnerable in the cycle of revenge. As a result, knowing how to manipulate a complicated legal structure is at least as important as one's competence at violence. Njal excels at the former, and Gunnar at the latter. Although Gunnar tries mightily to avoid being goaded into violent encounters, and although Njal continually advises him on how to avoid dangerous consequences, the scheming of malevolent characters in the saga prevails. Ultimately, Gunnar is outlawed, and because he is unwilling to accept exile, he is killed by his enemies.

However, the personal drama of Njal is even more central to the story. Despite his legal and sociological sagacity, he and his family are attacked by their enemies. Their house is surrounded and set on fire, and the attackers prevent their escape from the flames. This outcome structures the entire story. The narrator orients all of the saga's episodes toward the death of Njal (the original title of the story is "Burnt Njal"). Unlike the modern novel, for example, the saga gives continued coverage to each character introduced only as long as that character contributes to the ultimate consequence. In the process of telling the story, the reader is apprised not of the depth of various personalities but of some deep structural contradictions within a society in which the rule of law and a relatively anemic, part-time civic life (there is a brief yearly meeting of all the clans to resolve disputes) cannot wholly displace violent means and cannot overcome the conflicts among families and clans. As a result, the saga offers an elaborate analysis of conflicts among familial and civic attachments and a more general analysis of the complex relationships between familial and civic space in a historical society with a unique spatial structure—the boundaries of that society were understood more legally than territorially.

While there are abundant dimensions of *Njal's Saga* that are edifying with respect to issues in the politics of the family, my focus for the rest of the discussion of the story is on a single father and son relationship. From the modern reader's viewpoint, an extraordinary exercise of indirection on Njal's part occurs when he addresses his eldest son, Skarp-Hedin, at an important juncture of the story. To appreciate Njal's remarks, one needs to know that despite the goodwill of Njal and Gunnar, their extended kinship structures become involved in a dispute. It begins with a confrontation between Njal's wife, Bergthora, and Gunnar's wife, Hallgerd, at a wedding feast. The dispute irrupts over a seemingly trivial issue of who is to sit where, but given the prestige-semiology of seating at feasts, it is not trivial to the parties involved. As a result of the enmity, both Hallgerd and Bergthora take it out on the other's family by sending obligated servants to kill the servants in their rival's household. As the cycle of revenge escalates, Njal and Gunnar keep exchanging compensation to contain the dispute, but it gets out of hand when Hallgerd has her servants begin referring to Njal as "old beardless" and his sons as "little dung beards," an insult related to the fact that Njal is beardless. The suggestion is that perhaps it is necessary to put fertilizer on the faces of Njal's sons to make sure that, unlike their father, they can grow hair and thereby become sufficiently manly.

Hallgerd's insult is flung thusly during an encounter with Njal's sons: "Go home little dung beards . . . that's what we're going to call you from now on; and we'll call your father 'Old beardless.'"[17] While Njal is above being goaded into a manly display of revenge, his sons are not. The conversation at the center of my analysis begins as Njal's most hot-headed son, Skarp-Hedin, is planning to lead his brothers, Kari and Helgi, in an attack on Hallgerd's allies. Waking to the sound of Skarp-Hedin's battle ax, which is bumping against a panel of the house as he prepares to leave, Njal calls out, "Where are you going kinsman?" Skarp-Hedin replies that he is going to look for sheep, to which Njal remarks, "You said that once before . . . but then you hunted men" (the time, it is explained in further dialogue, when Skarp-Hedin killed Sigmund the White, Gunnar's kinsman, in revenge for the killing of Thord Fremansson, Skarp-Hedin's foster father) (202). It is then reported in the saga that Njal simply goes inside while Skarp-Hedin prepares to continue his participation in a cycle of killing that ultimately destroys the entire family.

What is perhaps most striking about Njal's remark "Where are you going kinsman?" is the seeming formality of the remark to a son. And equally puzzling (to the modern reader) is Njal's passivity in the face of a son's imminently dangerous act. Indeed, his passivity is of a piece with his inaction as his wife, Bergthora, escalates her dispute with Hallgerd, provoking acts of killing that initiate the interfamilial and interclan hostilities. However, Njal's passivity reflects an Icelandic structure that, though patriarchal and clan-oriented, also accorded much independence to family members. While throughout the saga, Njal is represented as prescient, he cannot control the acts of his family members. When he refers to Skarp-Hedin as kinsman, he is letting him know that his actions have implications that extend well beyond mere personal responsibility, that whatever violent acts Skarp-Hedin initiates will involve the kinship structure as a whole.

The strange indirection of Njal's remarks makes sense on the basis of two aspects that lend coherence to the saga as a genre. On the one hand, the narrative in *Njal's Saga* is driven by its historical referents. Njal and his family were burned in their house, and many other characters in the story are based on historical personages (for example, Thangbrand, a Christian proselytizer). And, historically, medieval Iceland experienced violent events that can be attributed to the conflicting codes and attachments of which the saga speaks. On the other hand, *Njal's Saga* belongs to a genre of storytelling that creates a peculiar narrative universe, which is governed in part by the situation of the story's reception. The family sagas were meant to be read aloud in a way that would both entertain and edify an audience about its national past. Thus, while the sharp gendered emphasis of the story, which, like the nineteenth-century novel, has men abroad and women at home, does reflect the actual gendering of Icelandic family roles, much of the overseas travel that the story reports is mythic. For example, the failure of Hrut and Unn's marriage early in the saga is a function of Hrut's pursuit of his inheritance in Norway, which leads to a series of events that eventuate in the grievances that finally destroy many of the saga's heroes. Neither the particular personalities nor the events associated with men's movements in and out of Iceland and women's managing of homesteads are necessarily realistic (e.g., Hrut's marriage to Unn fails because he is cursed by the Norwegian queen with whom he has a sexual liaison, and Unn's son by her second marriage turns out to be an effectively malicious character who goads people into violence).

The actions of the characters both move the story along its prescribed path and, at the same time, help listeners anticipate events. For example, early in the story, Hrut tells his brother that his daughter Hallgerd, who is ultimately to play a malicious role in the cycle of grievances, has "thief's eyes" (10). In short, in addition to having an explanatory coherence in which it maps the forces that produced the historical event of Njal's burning, the saga also has a genre coherence. It mobilizes coincidences to alert its listeners to the roles each character will play in producing violent consequences. When characters are no longer significant to subsequent action, the narrator informs the audience that so-and-so now leaves the saga.

Ultimately, as is the case with the ancient Greek tragedies, the Icelandic sagas occupy a space in a particular historical moment. In Njal's saga, for example, Christianity comes to Iceland in the midst of the expansion of the cycle of grievances. As a result, different kinds of characters, different actions, and added attachments and commitments influence the story before it reaches its climax (for example, near the end of the saga it is mentioned that one character is outlawed for blaspheming). Inasmuch as *Njal's Saga* was written after Christianity had established itself in Iceland, it is likely that the original listeners consumed it within a culture of reception that privileged resolution over revenge. But like the Greek tragedies, the family sagas point to aporias within a society that combines heroic and civic values. Characters are described rather than condemned. The sagas place side by side virtues of courage, friendship, and respect for the law and show at the same time that diverse ways of being and diverse attachments, especially to familial versus civic space, cannot be easily reconciled. "Family structure and family life," as one analyst has noted, "were subject to an overpowering conclusion: that order was evanescent, that kinship could all too easily be mocked and defeated by the 'turbulent' individual, while the individual himself had to answer to an inscrutable and often malignant fate."[18] It is shown, finally, that moral ambiguity haunts the best of intentions and that, at both individual and collective levels, incompatible forces defy coherence.

Contemporary Fathers and Sons, Contemporary Genres and the Deepening of Moral Ambiguity

Ever since the development of photographic technology, photographs have played a role in the politics of representation of the family, just as the family has been instrumental in the development of photography. Pierre Bourdieu puts the matter hyperbolically: "[P]hotographic practice only exists and subsists for most of the time by virtue of its family function."[19] For Bourdieu, the family photo (the group portrait, wedding picture, and so on) serves principally to represent the family's "image of its own integration" (26). As in the case of the development of other genres, this aspect of photography took on its significance at a key historical juncture. As the family became "progressively dispossessed of most of its traditional functions, economic as well as social," it began asserting itself "by accumulating the signs of its affective unity, its intimacy" (26). In sum, the emergence of domestic photography coincides with the historical development of "a more precise differentiation between what belongs to the public and what to the private sphere" (29). There are, however, complications to this story of mutual emergence. As photographic practice develops and becomes increasingly differentiated, it continues to be involved in demarcating a separation of public and private spheres, but it does so with a differentiation between types of photographs: the "memorial," which recalls the domestic scene, and the "emulatory," which is focused on significant public personages and serves to articulate "the widening distance of domestic scenes from the political sphere of action and belief."[20]

Nevertheless, while photographic images have served historically to demarcate and consolidate the private sphere of intimacy, distinguishing it from public life, like all genres, photography (and visual images in general) also operates within a critical perspective. Thus some photographic albums, for example, Sally Mann's *Immediate Family* and Jim Goldberg's *Rich and Poor,* explore, respectively, the ambiguities of the sexual boundaries of contemporary family life and the ways in which economic inequality affects familial structures and attachments in different ways for different classes.[21]

I turn therefore to an exploration of the ways in which a critical use of the image, in association with two biographical texts written about fathers by sons, provides perspectives on generational tensions afflicting one's participation in public life. Specifically, treating the tensions involving two families situated historically on two different sides of the Holocaust, I offer analyses of Peter Henisch's narrative challenge to his father Walter's role as a Nazi propaganda photographer during World War II and Art Spiegelman's comic-book-image challenge to his father's account of his experience as a Holocaust survivor. The contrast is therefore one involving alternative articulations of narrative and image as well as political positioning. Henisch imposes a written narrative on his father's photographic practice, and Speigelman imposes a narrativized set of images on his father's life story. In both cases, sons challenge their fathers' conduct and perspectives in ways that ambiguate the political significance of relationships between family life and public life.

Walter and Peter Henisch

Peter Henisch's *Negatives of My Father* belongs to a contemporary genre in Austria and Germany known as "*Vater-Literatur* . . . texts in which children expose and question the activities of their parents during the Nazi era. . . ."[22] Henisch's text politicizes family space not only by questioning a parent's role in a public, political event but also by reflecting generally on the ethicopolitical issues involved in judging the political actions of a parent. As in the case of Solondz's above-noted characterization of the father and pederast, Bill Maplewood, in his film *Happiness,* deep ambivalence is evinced in Henisch's text, as he attempts

> repeatedly . . . to strike a precarious balance between Walter Henisch as a nurturing parent and Walter Henisch as a Nazi war correspondent; between a father who instilled in his son a lively ideal of freedom and an Austrian citizen of Jewish descent who, without much question, went along with the dictates of fascism.[23]

Henisch articulates his ambivalence grammatically as well as through direct testimony. The narration continually shifts without clear markers between Peter and his father, Walter. It places the reader in the same ambiguous space as that occupied by Peter (who notes at the outset, for example, that he is guilty of a "slip," when he types a reference to *"my"* life story when he means to refer to his father's).[24] And whereas Peter begins his account as a "generational conflict" in which he has been wholeheartedly partisan" (12), he becomes increasingly tolerant of his father's schizoid tendency: Walter continually distinguishes his war correspondent self from his humanitarian self. Both father and son therefore have conflictual attachments. Throughout the text, Peter's shifting authorial presence reflects a conflict between a sense of familial loyalty and one of public responsibility. As he notes, he is hounded by the injunction "You have to condemn your father, otherwise you're defending him," but that injunction is countered by a contrary impulse: "On the other hand, Papa, I'm beginning to love you" (169). Peter recognizes that Walter's tutelage, at the hands of his proto-Nazi stepfather, who enrolled him in a precursor of the Hitler youth organization (the German Gymnasts), produced a volition-robbing structure of ideational coercion in the young Walter, from which he never fully recovered.

Nevertheless, despite his apolitical attachment to his photo journalism ("I did *my* work, what Goebbels made out of the photos was none of my business" [77]), Walter evinces considerable ambivalence, articulated as a sharp separation between his gaze and that of his camera. He refers often to a difference between his human and journalistic standpoints. For example, he mentions that he was both happy and bored to witness peaceful scenes when away from the war front: "As a *human being* I was happy to see that much peace in the midst of war. As a *war correspondent* I was getting bored" (78). Behind his Leica, he was simply fascinated by the war scenes and by both the ceremonial and methodical prosecution of the war by the German command. Indeed, his attraction to the Nazis was primarily aesthetic: "[C]ompared to the socialists and even more to the conservatives, the Nazis . . . did something for your senses, especially for your eyes, and therefore for the camera" (50).

Peter Henisch's narrative serves as a challenge to the politically anesthetizing effect of Walter Henisch's Leica. His "experiential novel" contains, at the same time, struggles between biography and autobiography ("Whose story is this, yours or *mine*?" Walter complains at one point [126]) and between photography and narrative. Craig Decker summarizes this struggle succinctly:

> Peter Henisch's textual transposition of Walter Henisch's photographs and life functions to direct his father's attention away from the camera and to the events in front of it. . . . Instead of a series of individual photographs,

which depict a selective and static slice of reality, Peter Henisch insists on placing these images into a larger narrative context."[25]

Peter Henisch's juxtaposition between narrative and photography constitutes as well a juxtaposition between photographic and historical time. The family biography, represented in photos of, as well as by, his father, is located against a historical time that prescribes reflection on public events.[26] But the son's insistence on a narrative that raises questions of responsibility is not in service of a commitment to moral closure. He aims, rather, "to avoid the deceit implicit in a false sense of historical closure" (150), for at the same time as he is committed to reclaiming an ethicopolitical stance on the historical events in which his father was involved, he is also committed to what he calls "narrative freedom"; he senses that his father experiences a "*premonition* of freedom" as one who has survived and can now exit from the constraints of the imposed "restrictions of the documentary, which had previously been more or less obeyed."[27]

Similarly, Peter Henisch the author experiences a sense of narrative freedom. Having explored the conjunctures and disjunctures between family time and historical time, he responds to his father's reaction to his manuscript by stating that, rather than write for or against either himself or his father, he is writing "against Death and therefore in favor of life," and when his father asks, "What kind of end do you have in mind?" he responds that he is "still looking for one" (178). At a minimum, he accepts disjunctures in both his and his father's life narratives. One cannot retrospectively read either life as a whole against a model of public responsibility, because his father's last injunction about himself seems to hold true about everyone: "You're not the man you used to be" (182). Peter's story does not resolve the moral and political issues between him and his father because, among other things, neither is a simple, wholly coherent character either historically or as a family member. But the critically productive engagement between photographic and narrative perspectives (between the two as well as within each of them, for Peter tries camera work for a while, and Walter imagines himself in a story mirroring that of Hasek's *The Good Soldier Schweik*) demonstrates that reality-capturing though it may seem, the photographic eye requires a supplement and that a critical perspective on the family-politics relationship, which is ineluctably mediated by the visual and writing technologies through which it is perceived, requires a critical perspective on genre.

Vladek and Art Spiegelman

Art Spiegelman's autobiographical treatment of his father Vladek's experience as a Holocaust survivor constitutes at once a creative mixing of genres and a telling set of contrasts and comparisons with Peter Henisch's text. The two volumes, *Maus* and *Maus II*, are cartoon narratives. Spiegelman renders his father's account (and his own frequent interruptions in the form of questions and interjections) as a comic book story or, to use Spiegelman's designation, as a "commix," a mixture of images and language.[28] The most significant contrast between the Henisch and Spiegelman texts is the logic of the language-image juxtaposition. While Henisch challenges his father's image production with a narrative, Spiegelman does the reverse: His images reconfigure and disrupt his father's tale. Therefore, added to the primary situational reversal of the accounts (they treat fathers on opposite sides of the Holocaust) is a reversal in the critical mixing of genres. What unites the significance of the texts is their shared problematics: They both "traverse the breach between past and present, Father and Son, language and image,"[29] and they both reflect on the ambivalences and ambiguities that afflict one's attempt to reconcile or at least order one's familial and public attachments.

Thematically, Spiegelman's text traces Vladek's life story from Poland in the 1930s, through his liberation from Auschwitz in 1945, to his life in New York in the 1980s. But although Vladek's story is reported in the text as a virtually verbatim account, it is reinflected with Art's questions and interruptions, and, most important, with a visual text, which usurps the significance of the narrative. Spiegelman's commix both displaces the historical account and wrenches its context by locating it in an agonistic, father-son interaction. In addition, the story is inflected by the use of animals used to represent people. The Jews are mice, the Germans are cats, the Poles are pigs, the American troops are dogs, the Swedes are deer, and the French are frogs.

In terms of genre, Spiegelman's text is a composite of multiple narratives and modes of expression. In addition to the concatenated image-boxes and the accompanying dialogue and commentary in the language balloons, there are actual photographs from the family's past and maps (of the Auschwitz and Birkenau camps as well as of the Catskills and Rego Park, New York). And there is also a commix within the commix— Art's earlier cartoon-dreamscape, "Prisoner on the Hell Planet," which he produced in response to his mother's suicide. Of all the genres contained in the Spiegelman text, the comic book format is the most radicalizing.

The use of a genre ordinarily confined to superheroes or to mundane and humorous issues in family life forces one to reflect on both the controversies associated with representing the Holocaust at all and the powerful investments that invariably impugn the ethical sensibilities of any genre of representation. But, despite deeply entrenched prejudices, which consign comic book narratives to trivial forms of entertainment, the genre engages a well-developed culture of consumption.

Since the early part of the twentieth century, at least three generations have learned to consume comic strips that depict family stories. *Gasoline Alley,* for example, a saga of the extended Wallet family, which ran in many newspapers from 1918 to the 1990s, presented a family organized around the production and use of the automobile. Arguably, the strip, which articulated family life with industrial development and the production of consumer goods, was complicit with the work of advertisers in the molding of self-concepts congenial to the creation of a consumer culture and the economic changes that refashioned family life from a locus of employment to a locus of consumption.[30]

Spiegelman's *Maus* disrupts the culture of comic book consumption of family tales not only by locating the family story in a historically and politically fraught context but also through the use of animals to represent the various national and ethnic types. At a simple, hermeneutic level, Spiegelman's use of animals, beyond their ability to register difference in a visual mode, trades on a widespread, cross-generational familiarity with comic book conventions. Certainly, for example, a personified Mickey Mouse is a condition of possibility for the acceptance of mice/Jews; the Tom and Jerry cartoons constitute a familiar prototype for mice/Jews being pursued by cats/Nazis; and, of course, the best-selling Richard Scarry children's books (read by adults to preschoolers) thrive on personified animals—for example, whole towns full of vocation-differentiated piggy people. At a more critical level, Spiegelman enacts a modality upon which Franz Kafka's writing thrived, the suppression of the "as it."[31] Jews are referred to as dogs, and accordingly Kafka produces a story from the point of view of a dog.[32] And in response to the general global abuses of European nations, Kafka has a talking ape, who, through a mimetic capability, manages in a short time to achieve "the cultural level of the average European."[33]

Like Kafka's, Spiegelman's animals/people effect an ironic reversal of the Nazi denial of humanity to non-Aryan peoples. As Spiegelman notes, "My anthropomorphized mice carry trace elements of Fip's anti-Semitic Jew-as-rat cartoons for [the Nazi publication] *Der Stürmer,* but by being particularized they are invested with personhood; they give *specific* form to stereotypes."[34] While the reversal of the Nazi project and the humanizing of what has been dehumanized constitutes, in itself, a critical contribution to historical memory at the levels of both historicopolitical and familial-generational times, a far more critical capacity is evinced in Spiegelman's mix of language and image. His commix treatment of his family's disjunctive composition of Holocaust stories critically disrupts a documentary mode with a many-genred text that blurs the documentary-aesthetic distinction,[35] just as his angles on the story blur the boundaries between family space and historical civic space. The most subversive element of Spiegelman's text, in short, lies in the tensions it produces between language and image.

Much of the image-language tension that Spiegelman achieves inheres in the disruption that comic strips constitute for narrative sequence. Just as Art Spiegelman continually disrupts his father's narrative (with interjections, questions, demands for information, and so on) the design of comic books, which allow one to read alternatively horizontally and vertically, interrupts narrative sequence. Ultimately, as Spiegelman puts it, the comic book form allowed him to tell a story of a breaking down of the authority of a narrative with a medium within which simple narrative breaks down.[36] The genre-assisted breakdown of the narrative in *Maus* highlights what is at stake in a conflict among generations aiming to install an alternative politics of historical memory and in the disjuncture between generational and historicopolitical time. The disjuncture is played out in Spiegelman's text also through the juxtaposition of the narrative strip images in the commix and the occasional still photographs, inserted from the family photo archive, which create disruptive breaks in the visual narrative.[37]

The breaks, disruptions, and incoherences achieved by Spiegelman's mix of genres underscore his embrace of the ambiguity of identities and attachments. Art himself is only occasionally represented as a mouse in the strip; he is often represented with a mouse mask. And his wife, Françoise, has to convince him to allow her a mouse identity (for a converted Jew) rather than a frog for her French identity. As was the case with Henisch's text, *Maus* ultimately endorses a model of the self as irrevocably fractured. Art the mouse, Art the son, Art the obedient transcriber of his father's story, and Art the crafty mixer of genres and skillful creator of ambiguity cannot be assembled into a person who has resolved either familial or historicopolitical issues, just as his text can only activate rather than resolve the disjunctures between the past and the present. Art's tale of the recovery of a survivor's story is not, as he notes, an account of what happened in the past but a rendering of a son's understanding. The story therefore hovers continuously between the vagaries of a father's telling and a son's multimedia-inflected recording of it and his own reactions.

As is the case with the Henisch text, Spiegelman's "collaborative auto-biography" offers a powerfully politicizing juxtaposition of disjoint temporalities as well as familial tensions.[38] Exploiting the different narrative layers of his multiply-genred text, Spiegelman crafts a many-layered tale that redeems a historically traumatic period (which for many is unrepresentable) for contemporary political thought. He provides, at once, a disruptive and enabling intervention into the contemporary politics of the family as it bears on the negotiation of the meanings of the past for the present.

Daughters and Families: Epistolary Interventions

For purposes of expanding the range of critical genres and discerning the contingencies affecting family–civic life relationships, I turn to the expressions of women in epistolary novels, separated in time by two and a half centuries. As is the case with the previous examples, the artistic productions emerge during disjunctive historical moments. The first, Samuel Richardson's *Clarissa* (the first tragic novel), reflects the ambiguities in authority structure associated with the eighteenth century's emerging bourgeois society. As is well known, the rise of the novel in England parallels the rise of bourgeois culture; it begins as primarily a form of domestic fiction that first developed in the eighteenth century in the works of such writers as Defoe, Sterne, Fielding, and Richardson, the last of whom was the first to gain eminence solely as a novel writer. Social historians of the novel have emphasized the novel's articulation with, among other things, the rise of the "individual," whose sentiments constitute, in the moral philosophy of the eighteenth century (for example, that of David Hume and Adam Smith), the center of gravity of morals.

Although there are arguably some general trends in philosophy, epistemology, and political economy that help to situate the problematics in the themes of eighteenth-century English novels, what frames Richardson's *Clarissa* is a particular "family values" moment, which can be extracted from the archive of the historical forces shaping relations within families as well as between them and civic authority. Written shortly before the Marriage Act of 1753, which prescribed legal controls over marriage covenants, Richardson's *Clarissa* emerges near the end of the period in which "family lineage gave way to family life."[39] The vertical family, as

Sarah Maza's figuration describes it, was replaced by a horizontal one: "The synchronic family of love had displaced the diachronic family of bloodlines" (208).

To express it in the abstract language of social theory, this new family, which was still afflicted by the norms and expectations of the fading patriarchal and lineage-oriented past, was thought to achieve its coherence on the basis of exchanges of sentiment rather than through the mechanisms of contract. In addition, family life was increasingly under official scrutiny. A new "governmentality" had emerged in which governance involved not simply the maintenance of the power and legitimacy of the sovereign and the control over territory but rather the active management of things and people—of, in Foucault's words, the governance of "a sort of complex composed of men and things."[40] Governance had effectively shifted its focus from extracting submission through imposing law to "disposing things" (95).

More specifically, marriage, like other aspects of family relations, was a target of legal intervention because of its perceived relationship with economy. Although considerable moralizing accompanied the debate on the Marriage Act, as in other historical periods, there was an imbrication of moral economy and political economy,[41] so much so that the moral discourse evinced during the parliamentary debate operated with economic figuration, exemplified in the remarks of one defender of the act, who said that its purpose was "to restrain all commerce between the sexes except in marriage."[42] But ultimately, the controlling argument was unabashedly economic-utilitarian. As another of the act's defenders put it, "[T]he happiness and prosperity of the country depends not on having a great number of children born, but on having always a great number of well brought up and inured from their infancy to labour and industry" (236).

The novel is therefore situated at a historical convergence of changes in morality and economy. And its mapping of the spaces and treatment of the contentions of domesticity reflect a time in which the privileged places of estates and aristocratic families in the social order are falling victim to an accelerating commerce and an associated rise to prominence of bourgeois culture. Clarissa, whose story begins with a suddenly inherited economic independence and her refusal to accept her father's choice of a marriage partner, seems at first to be the main character in a novel that articulates the impact of economic changes and a moral shift toward privileging individual sentiments over the patriarchal structure of family authority. But *Clarissa* is not simply a story of the struggle of a noble young woman who pits her individuality against a father who demands unequivocal obedience. *Clarissa* is, rather, a novel that focuses on a clash of discourses. Both personalities and structural dynamics are mediated through the differing linguistic styles expressed in the novel's medium, an exchange of letters. The many voices in the novel's letters, which constitute clashing positions on the relationship of utterances to morals and to reality, reflect the diverse forces that ultimately determine Clarissa's fate as a suicide.

As a personality invented to reflect a historical moment in the clashing of codes, Clarissa is, among other things, a "union of opposites," as Thomas Beebee puts it: "a minor made independent by her grandfather's legacy, a daughter who claims a son's right to choose her spouse."[43] But apart from the disjunctures in Clarissa's situation and the disjunctures between language and feeling, there is a more central discursive paradox manifested in the differences between Clarissa's and the rake Lovelace's approach to language. As Terry Eagleton has pointed out, Clarissa's approach to language is traditionally masculine, while Lovelace, who seeks to bed and marry Clarissa and who uses linguistic guile in the form of a false earnestness before abducting and raping her, displays a more traditionally feminine approach to language:

> The paradox of *Clarissa* is that Clarissa's writing is "masculine," whereas Lovelace's is "feminine." It has been claimed that men and women under patriarchy relate differently to the act of writing. . . . Men, deeply marked by the "transcendental signifier" of the phallus, will tend to view signs as stable and whole, ideal entities external to the body; women will tend to live a more inward, bodily relationship to script. . . . [However,] Clarissa herself exerts the fullest possible control over her meanings. . . . Lovelace's writing is mercurial, diffuse, exuberant.[44]

The paradoxical is to be expected in a time of instability. Given the destabilizing shifts in legal, moral, and emotional perspectives and, accordingly, a "coexistence of the older order and newer definitions of marriage . . . whole new social and emotional grammars had to be learned, by men as well as women."[45] In choosing an epistolary form for his novel, Richardson was effectively locating his didactic purposes on the side of a new grammar of morality. But also paradoxically, the linguistic register that Richardson summons is ultimately at odds with his intent to cast Clarissa as an avatar of a Protestant Christian morality, as one whose virtue comes from the heart rather than from obedience to an external religious order. Indeed, the evidence is overwhelming that Richardson, a Protestant moralist, intended to provide a moral lesson.

He cast Clarissa Harlowe, a virtuous, wise, and pious young woman, as a victim, one who becomes a "fallen woman" because of assaults on her character, trust, and, ultimately, her body. Believing that art has a moral purpose, Richardson had absorbed his age's Puritan-inspired commitment to a subjective morality. Nevertheless, the novel form in general and the epistolary style more particularly militate against Richardson's didactic intent.

Throughout the novel, the theme of Clarissa's nobility and virtue is secondary to the conflicting acts of interpretation, conveyed in the novel's primary axis of epistolary exchange, that between Clarissa, whose words are thought to be clear expressions of her sentiments, and Lovelace, for whom words are unstable acts meant to provide strategic advantage. Ultimately, therefore, with its emphasis on a clash of linguistic philosophies, *Clarissa* functions like Ted Solondz's film *Happiness,* an exemplar of semiotic displacement, rather than as a moralistic, didactic text. Its conflicting interpretive glosses render reality and morality ambiguous and, as a result, encourage readers to reflect on their own interpretive activity. The readers' attention is shifted from persons as objects of moral sympathy or obloquy toward the language of morality.[46]

At the level of its thematic, *Clarissa* is a sentimental novel, the tragedy of a moral and deserving woman who is ultimately redeemed by her steadfast commitment to the transparency of meaning, because, as the story line implies, she dies a martyr. Through not only her rape by Lovelace but also her penetration by his dissimulating codes of communication, the manner in which Clarissa's victimization and death are received valorizes unambiguous emblematic codes and disparages the ambiguities to which she falls victim. This thematic is foregrounded when one follows the spatial trajectory of the novel. Clarissa's tragedy builds through a process first of increasing confinement within family space (kept from public parts of the household and cut off from outside communication), thence to exile from the family and confinement within a bordello, and finally to her ultimate confinement: the coffin as her last resting place.

But when one heeds epistolary exchanges rather than spatial history within the novel, linguistic oppression looms larger than spatial confinement. Lovelace's letter expressing contempt for women's words, evinced in reaction to the epistolary exchanges between Clarissa and her intimate friend, Anna, is an exemplary moment in the novel's politics of discourse:

These vehement friendships are nothing but chaff and stubble, liable to be blown away by the very wind that raises them. Apes! Mere apes of *us*! They think the word *friendship* has a pretty sound with it. . . . the word is a *mere* word, the thing a mere name with them; a cork-bottomed shuttle-cock, which they are fond of striking to and fro.[47]

The character of Lovelace's strategic linguistic attacks militates against a moralistic, Christian reading of the novel. Although Richardson's aim was to produce a Clarissa who is redeemed by her steadfast commitment to language's transparency, the epistolary exchanges manifest a hermeneutic ambiguity. What emerges is not a simple moral lesson but an appreciation of a struggle between alternative approaches to language, connected to a historical moment that witnesses a broader struggle between masculine and feminine approaches to familial authority and civic responsibility. Read within a political rather than a religious register, *Clarissa* reflects the last gasps of a dying patriarchal order. It describes a time in which family space was becoming more egalitarian—a domain for new expressions of erotic desire and an arena for the expansion of the range of qualified political voices. The reader's appreciation of the weakening of the grip of unquestioned paternal authority is reinforced by the weakening of the transparency model of language. In its displacement of authorial intent, the epistolary exchanges in *Clarissa* produce not a moral lesson but an understanding of the relationship between the authority of language and the authority of persons. Paralleling the diminution of the century's patriarchal authority is a breakdown in the referential authority of words.

The Family as a Resistant Locus of Enunciation: "Women's Time"

Hanan al-Shaykh's *Beirut Blues,* a contemporary epistolary novel, is also addressed in part to a breakdown in patriarchal authority. The novel's narrative voice, articulated in letters, belongs to Asmahan, the name of a famous Arab singer from the 1930s, who fled Syria, "a principality full of macho men,"[48] to live independently in Egypt. Al-Shaykh's Asmahan is a member of a family of strong women who seek to control their family's fate during a historical moment of both transition and violence. Like al-Shaykh, this Asmahan "comes from a feudal family who owned land. . . . They lost everything to the Palestinians and then, second, to the idealistic Lebanese fighters, and finally, to a bunch of thugs" (305).

Covering the year 1985, "when the two Shi'a militias, Hezbollah and Amal fight each other" (305), the novel is situated in a moment of instability in authority structures and reflects a disjuncture in perspective between geopolitical time and what Julia Kristeva has called "women's time." Contemporary geopolitical time is largely a state production. It is designed to produce a unity within the citizen body with narratives that maintain the illusion of a temporally coherent national culture, symbolically constructed as distinct from the cultures within other states. This form of time is realized in the narratives of official and complicitous cultural texts that promote nationhood as the primary locus of attachment.

In contrast with geopolitical time, which provides a legitimation for state boundaries and national attachments, women's time offers an alternative locus of enunciation. This form of time, as Kristeva has construed it, has different modalities, which have emerged from different moments in the history of the feminist movement. In Kristeva's story of women's political mobilization, the initial struggle was an attempt by women to gain a place in the linear time of national history, to become full citizens by operating within "the logical and ontological values of a rationality dominant in the nation-state."[49] At a later stage, however, women's political mobilization has concerned itself with women's specificity in time, in, among other things, their position in the cycle of reproduction. This drive toward specificity and difference often locates women in opposition to the dominant historical time of national culture, not only because they often tend to focus on other times, but also because they speak from a position of singularity that undermines the presumption of a universal language of political community. Exemplifying the contention between national and women's time, al-Shaykh's novel treats the destruction wrought by the Lebanese civil war from her location within familial and other interpersonal networks. Like many Greek tragic dramas, the novel is located within a historical contention between alternative domains of codes. Specifically, al-Shaykh's *Beirut Blues* reflects a conflict between a version of women's time and the historical time of a state involved in a civil war.[50]

It must be noted, however, that as a genre the novel assembles a different constituency than that of the tragedies. In the case of the Greek tragic dramas, an audience was encouraged to reflect on their own problems, the normative incoherences involved in their local attachments. They were encouraged to consider immanent and unresolvable forms of otherness within both self and community. However, both the tragic moment and the Greek political experience upon which it reflected are in the past. The contemporary novel assembles a remote audience of readers and situates itself among conflicting representational practices in a world whose political relations are more mediated than those that obtained when the tragedies were written. What the novel can disrupt is less modes of subjectivity than a dominant politics of representation.

Yet there is a parallel between the tragic drama and novelistic forms. Both stage encounters among contending voices. Moreover, like the tragedies, the novel opposes a Hegelian "chronotope" (space-time pattern) within which a progressive history allows signs to achieve their objects.[51] As M. M. Bakhtin points out, the novel is a distinctive chronotope. It articulates time-space with a "density and concreteness" absent in a Hegelian, epochal narrative. A diverse set of temporalities converges in the novel as biographical and historical time sequences juxtapose "the time of life" with "historical time," allowing for a view of diverse and conflicting forms of attachment (250).

Al-Shaykh's *Beirut Blues* fully exploits the novel's heteroglossic character (its assemblage of many contending voices) to oppose the representational practices through which Lebanon has been recruited into the temporality of geopolitical history (for example, in the discourse of "foreign policy").[52] Her view of the civil war, from the vantage point of women's and family time, constitutes a resistance to the claims of a system of state sovereignties to exhaust the boundaries of political space, and her enactment of that view in her writing disrupts and reconfigures geopolitical time in a way that allows contentious normativities and presences to emerge. Al-Shaykh makes use of letters to record the disturbances that war creates for dispersed familial and friendship networks. All of the narration is contained in a series of letters that al-Shaykh's novelistic alter ego, Asmahan, sends to absent friends, to relatives, to lovers, to her idol, Billie Holliday, and even to a personified Beirut.[53]

Despite the existence of only one letter writer, a plurality of voices are represented. Unlike the case of *Clarissa*, in which the epistolary form reflects a moment of a woman's confinement, in *Beirut Blues* the epistolary form reflects an aspect of contemporary nation-state history. Because many Lebanese have left their war-disrupted country (there are more living abroad than at home), letters are the appropriate medium for interactions between those who have left and those who have remained. Apart from the insights into the Lebanese diaspora, however, the letters play a role in representing Lebanon's disjointed temporalities. Each letter constitutes a momentary binding of relationships that the war is threatening to sunder. As a whole, they reveal the unresolvable tensions between the geopolitical time of a nation at war and the various times associated with bonds of familial and personal affiliation. The first letter in *Beirut Blues*, sent to Asmahan's friend Hayat, effectively plays the times of domesticity and friendship against the war's duration. Recognizing that her friend has been trying to get in contact after seeing the news of battles among various factions, specifically, Hezbollah and Amal, Asmahan notes that she is much more preoccupied with the "trivia of love and sex" and the state of her kitchen (which has a rat) than the state of the country.[54]

At the same time, however, Asmahan recognizes a complex inter-dependency between civic and family space. She notes, for example, that as the war fragments city space (she witnesses "Beirut changing hands time after time and gradually fragmenting into smaller and smaller pieces"), family space experiences a corresponding compression: "[W]e have grown accustomed to our house becoming like a refuge during the war. Men and women were no longer segregated. Everybody slept in my grandfather's room" (237). The war is therefore shaping family space and, accordingly, the conditions of possibility for the family's way of being. Among the most disrupted familial structures is marriage, for women are deprived of available husbands: "They're all crooks or fighters. The rest have left, or don't have a penny to their name" (8). And families change their priorities; for example, one family takes one of their least academic children out of school in order to be able to afford the education of the more academically talented ones (98).

The disruption of personal lives, which constitutes much of the novel's descriptive content, is doubled by the novel's style. The letter, its narrative vehicle, is an instrument aimed at maintaining personal bonds, the connections between friends and family members, at a time when the forces shaping the city tend to sunder them. Both the form and content of the letters emphasize another temporality. They show that bonds between relatives and friends, like war, have a duration; because their endurance or steadfastness is what distinguishes them, they are decisively temporal phenomena. In the case of friendship, as Derrida has noted (citing Cicero), friends are temporally omnipresent; they are "there" even when absent. Like the friend Hayat in *Beirut Blues*, they are always already there in the future, through "the anticipated citation of some funeral oration."[55]

The ordeal of war, when read from the point of view of the bonds of families and friends, constitutes a paradigmatic case for the temporal distinctiveness of familial and friendship relations. Friendship, as Derrida notes, also contains the possibility of survival. Drawing on Aristotle's discussion of primary friendship, he identifies its temporal imbrication: it "never presents itself outside time: there is no friend without time" (14), for to be steadfast, friendship must inspire a confidence, which takes time. It becomes stabilized "through an ordeal which takes time" (15); it is a "becoming steadfast" (16). Al-Shaykh's narrator, Asmahan, explicitly recognizes the trial by ordeal that the war and their resulting geographic separation represents for her friendship with Hayat: "Our friendship could not have survived as it was with the passing of time and the war. . . . Perhaps because in Belgium you can only establish marginal relationships, you've preferred to remain in our shared past, which we both began to draw on to preserve our friendship."[56]

Both the novelistic genre in general and its epistolary structure in *Beirut Blues* more specifically combine to oppose the temporalities of family and friendship as enduring presences to the presence-shattering time of war. Al-Shaykh explicitly sets up an agonistic relationship between war as a "chronotype" and the interpersonal connections reflected in her novel's letters.[57] Over time, the violence of war has the opposite effect of letters with individual addressees: It depersonalizes; it erases individual presences. After riding in a tank, Asmahan recognizes how such instruments of violence destroy human presence. The tank represents for her the spatiotemporality of war in general:

> Now I understand why when they are in tanks soldiers feel they can crush cars and trees in their path like brambles, because they're disconnected from every thing, their own souls and bodies included, and what's left is this instrument of steel rolling majestically forward. I feel as if I've entered another world. No destruction, no people, no long years of war; they're gone as if I have been in a submarine the whole time.[58]

While Asmahan's letters are attempts to remain connected, to be part of the times of family and friendship, their effects are uncertain. Letters written during wartime may be undelivered. As a result, it is primarily the anticipation of the future that is disturbed in *Beirut Blues*. The letters contain an ambivalence; death and destruction may render them undeliverable. It is unclear, moreover, whether the bonds they represent can survive the war. As Asmahan says, the destruction wrought by the war is, first and foremost, a destruction of her identity in time. "The war was like an express train hurtling along without a stop, taking everything with it. It had deprived me of the opportunity of using the past to live in the present and give shape to the future" (359).

Although Asmahan is expressing a desire to be one in time, al-Shaykh's novel does not imply that either subjects or collectives are inherently unified. Like the divided chorus in Aeschylus's *Seven*, the women in

Beirut Blues are divided subjects, at times identifying themselves with the partisan divisions constituting the civic space of war and at times opposing the war as a masculine project destructive of personal and family life. Asmahan represents herself as contemptuous of civil war, but at one point her grandmother, Fatima, adopts the local martial code and suggests that the family should have its own militia. After all, she notes, after reviewing all the families with their own militias that she is aware of, "even the Albino has a militia" (113).

As it turns out, Fatima's bellicosity reflects an ambiguous relationship between family life and warring violence. Although much of the thrust of Asmahan's laments is about the war's destructive effects on familial and other personal attachments, ironically, familial attachments also amplify the war. Because of the rivalries among families and the complexion of politics in wartime, it is both prestigious and financially advantageous for families to get involved in politics in a violent way. Thus, one family "became involved in politics, took hostages and kidnaped those who got in the way of their business activities" (114). And, as the scope of their participation in violence grew: "Bullies and vigilantes gathered around them, until eventually they had a militia protecting them, their routes, and their men, whose methods of communication with the outside world had begun to command the greatest respect" (114).

Conclusion: The Ironic and the Political

The ironies disclosed in al-Shaykh's *Beirut Blues* constitute, at once, a moment of ironic detachment and a political statement about the contingencies afflicting all attachments. Family life is shown to have an ambiguous relationship to civic-life-as-war. Richard Rorty, a philosopher of liberalism's quest for civic solidarity, has argued that "ironists" make no contribution to political thinking; "irony," he insists, "seems inherently a private matter."[59] Rorty's argument rests on a spatial predicate, a radical separation between public and private domains. Aesthetic life, in which ironic detachment supplies insights, belongs in the private domain, while public life requires avowals of solidarity with existing groups and widely recognized and articulated policy. Accordingly, aesthetic discourse and political discourse represent disparate projects.

What Rorty calls political engagement, Jacques Rancière regards as mere policing—expressed commitments to the order of the visible and the sayable, to the spaces within which bodies have their assigned places.[60] By contrast, "the political," for Rancière, makes an appearance when the distribution of bodies and spaces is recognized as historically contingent, when the policing function is challenged, and when the reigning "ethos" is disrupted by a recognition of a "gap experienced between the capability of the speaking being and any ethical harmony of doing, being, and saying" (101). In this sense, aesthetic discourse, which calls into question the gaps and ambiguities of enunciation, is manifestly political. It contributes to what Rancière calls subjectification, by which he means not the imposition of already recognized social identities but the introduction of new voices that are at once expressive and disruptive. Subjectification provides warrants for articulations from a part that has not been recognized in public deliberation. In al-Shaykh's case, the women's voices she expresses do not simply reinforce already recognized political spaces and politically qualified speakers. Her voices call into question the adequacy of any stabilized political discourse.

In regard to the issue that arose in Aeschylus's *Seven,* there is no unambiguous mode of intelligibility, no form of speech that can simply be fitted to the occasion. The substitution of multiplicity for a uniformity of codes constitutes a resistance to the entrenched forms of saying and manifests thereby a commitment to politics. This disposition toward the political accords well with the tragic disposition, which Michael Dillon formulates in a way that is relevant here: "In the tragic consciousness, the very formulas, norms and boundaries employed to establish order are themselves at issue."[61] A politics faithful to such a disposition, Dillon adds, prefers "contingency, liberty, difference and excess over mastery, order, identity and modesty" (147). In its contemporary guise, reflected in al-Shaykh's staging of the conflicting familial voices in their diverse dispositions toward a violent civic life, politics has no ultimate warrant other than a commitment to continual questioning of the discordances lurking in every attempt to impose the harmony of secure boundaries around selves and community, in every attempt to secure the bases of private versus civic space. Al-Shaykh, the ironist, does more than merely question the extant social identities and social spaces of her polity. She shows, among other things, that so-called public attachments configure domestic ones and vice versa. The ironies she discloses in a war-torn Beirut, in which familial attachments both resist and reinforce violent encounters, reflect an abiding bond between politics and the tragic disposition.

2. Contingency, Genealogy, and the Family

Prelude: Nosebleeds in Salt Lake City

Shortly after the turn of the century, my paternal grandfather, Benjamin Shapiro, a man of humble origin and limited means, sought to move up in the world. After emigrating with his extended family from czarist-held Vilna on the Russian pale at age ten, he had gone to work almost immediately upon his arrival in the United States in the factories of the Connecticut River valley. By the time I knew him, he read the newspaper with his eyes following his forefinger across the page, and his spoken English was in an unpolished idiom, not unlike the itinerant laborers in Dos Passos and Steinbeck novels. After brief service as a corporal in the U.S. Army (he was stationed in the Philippines during the Spanish-American War), he was reluctant to resume working as a machinist in the dark factories in which he had been intermittently employed before enlisting.

Reading a Yiddish-language newspaper one day, he chanced upon an item placed by a (self-described) "Wealthy Jewish family in Salt Lake City." They were looking for a young Jewish suitor for their daughter, who was recovering from her injuries sustained in a house fire. Ben went out to Salt Lake City, in his words, "to have a look." However, the look did not avail. Instead, he ended up marrying my grandmother Anna, also an emigré from Vilna and a Connecticut resident, introduced to him by a marriage broker. Nevertheless, Ben liked to tell the story of his brief western sojourn. Perhaps he was wistful, for his marriage to Anna was not a happy one. By the time they were elderly, they lived apart most of the time; I don't recall having ever seen them together. Ben was in and out of a veteran's home, and Anna was in and out of a mental institution.

Ben's story always began with a very brief account of his journey westward. First there was a long train ride, taking a number of days (which

45

Corporal Benjamin Shapiro (center), my paternal grandfather, in the U.S. Army during the Spanish-American War.

varied with each telling). Then there was his body's uneasy accommodation to the altitude of Salt Lake City; he told about getting nosebleeds in his sleep and discovering blood on his pillow in the morning. My brother Ed and I would become impatient with the travel narrative and beg for details about the western venue and especially about the courtship: "The girl, Grandpa! What about the girl?" The story always ended with the same cryptic line: "Dem hands; if dey coulda only done sumpthin about dem hands."

For years I have imagined Ben's western adventure, mentally filling in details. His version of the story was more or less biblical, in the sense in which Erich Auerbach characterizes Abraham's journey to fulfill Jehovah's command that he sacrifice Isaac. The Genesis story has a chronology but is bereft of descriptive detail: "The journey is like a silent progress through the indeterminate and the contingent, a holding of the breath, a process which has no present, which is inserted like a blank duration, between what has passed and what lies ahead, and which is yet to be measured: three days!"[1]

Auerbach explains that the absence of detail makes sense when one recognizes that the Hebrew Bible is a genre designed for a particular kind of reader. The text is meant not to dazzle and entertain with descriptive imagery but to summon continual interpretation: "Since the reader knows that God is a hidden God, his effort to interpret it constantly finds something new to feed upon" (15). The explanation of my grandfather's sparse treatment of detail is also genre-related. An old man was engaging in self-indulgent reminiscing; the story was about him, about a decisive moment in his life. It was not meant to enrich our understanding of the West, of wealthy Jewish families at the turn of the century, nor was it even about "how the other half lives."[2]

Nevertheless, I have been continually engaged by my recollections of Ben's story, in part because of my imaginative additions to it. And because I keep the story of Ben's western experience alive in my imagination, fantasies about Ben's trip were evinced again when I saw Jim Jarmusch's film *Dead Man*. Filmed in black and white, the story opens with a young man, William Blake (Johnny Depp), on a train, dressed in a plaid suit and bowler hat. The passage of days is indicated with fade-outs, and the monotony of the journey is maintained with a montage of shots that cycle and recycle images of Blake's bored expression, other dull-looking passengers, the movement of changing landscape from the train windows, and the moving train, shot from various angles outside it.

Although the repetition of camera shots and the black-and-white medium with which it is filmed lend Blake's journey a quality akin to the "blank duration" to which Auerbach refers in his treatment of Abraham's journey, the changing landscape and changing clothing styles of the passengers provide a directional cue; it is clear that Blake is headed west. Like Ben, Blake is an unattached young man, headed west in search of a new

William Blake (played by Johnny Depp) on the train heading west, in the film *Dead Man* (1996).

life, in this case an accountant's job in a steel mill in the Far West town of Machine. But Blake is moving away from a failed marriage prospect rather than toward one. When, upon his arrival, the job is no longer available, and a series of violent events makes him a (gravely wounded) fugitive, pursued by both bounty hunters and badge-wearing lawmen, he is picked up by a Native American, "Nobody" (Gary Farmer), also unattached, who, after dressing Blake's wound, leads him through a wilderness and toward the place where he will die.

The film has a variety of powerful themes, among which is Nobody's passionate interest in the poetry of William Blake's famous namesake. For him, this William Blake is a renewed version of the original but is already a "dead man" ("Some are born to sweet delight / Some are born to endless night," he quotes from *Songs of Innocence*). But it is one of the film's minor episodes that has captured my attention. Blake almost becomes part of a "family." When he and Nobody spot trappers by a campfire, Nobody orders him to join them, under the apparent assumption that being "white men," they will make compatible living companions. As the camera zooms in, the three men (Iggy Pop, Jared Harris, and Billy Bob Thornton) turn out to be a family unit with elements of traditional gender differentiation. One of the men (Iggy Pop) is wearing a dress and bonnet and is doing the cooking. Blake's arrival interrupts a domestic quarrel.

One trapper (Harris) is disparaging the evening meal, the transvestite cook (Pop) is responding with a lament about how hard he tries, and the third (Thornton) is intervening to contradict the complaint and praise

William Blake and two of the family of trappers (played by Iggy Pop, on the left, and Jarred Harris, on the right), before the argument erupts over who is to gain Blake's favor.

the food. As Blake approaches, the culinary issue is rapidly displaced by a sexual one. Blake's appearance constitutes a reconfiguration of the "libidinal economy" of the family. With a new object of desire, the prior structure of investments is disrupted.[3] As the group fondles Blake, paying particular attention to the fine texture of his hair ("Your hair is soft like a girl's"), an argument starts over who his sex partner is to be: "You had the last one; this one's mine." After the argument turns violent, with Harris shooting Thornton in the foot, Nobody, seeing that Blake's new living situation will not work out, rushes in and kills Thornton by cutting his throat, and he and Blake kill the other two in a shoot-out. Even as he is struggling to load his gun, Iggy Pop is muttering, "I cooked, I cleaned. . . ."

What can one make of this group of trappers, whom Jarmusch, in an interview, likens to "a trace element of a family unit"? Jarmusch supplies a brief discursive answer: "Because these guys live out in the fuckin' nowhere."[4] But Jarmusch's cinematic answer is more elaborate and compelling; it helps situate the relationship between my grandfather Ben's aborted family story and the ones developed in *Dead Man*. At a thematic level, *Dead Man* exceeds a simple biographical genre. While at one level the film is about William Blake's death, at another, it, like my grandfather Ben's story, is about *the radical contingency of the family*. And, as a film, it achieves the contingency thematic with its composition and temporal spacing of camera shots. It shows how a variety of forces and events, well outside "natural" inclinations and forces of attraction, create and dissolve familial structures. In the filmic narrative, the ties that bind are more the result of contingent circumstances than they are initiating forces.

Family Values

Jarmusch's expression *fuckin' nowhere* has special resonance with reference to his filmic story. None of the sex depicted is confined within the traditional nuclear family or the home. When Blake alights from the train in the town of Machine, where he expects to find his job waiting, one of the first things he sees as he heads up the main street is a cowboy getting a "blow job" in an alley. When Blake stops and stares, the man points his gun at him. Blake also interrupts another extrafamilial episode of sexual intercourse—one on the ground in the forest between Nobody and a Native American woman (she is fucking Nobody "fuckin' nowhere"!). And, perhaps most telling as regards the diremption of families and fucking, is a story about the bounty hunter Cole, told by one of his companions, pursuing Blake through the wilderness. When out of earshot of Cole, he tells the third companion, apropos of Cole being dangerous, that

Cole had "fucked his parents" and, moreover, had proceeded to kill them, cut them up, and eat them.

In various other ways as well, the Far West encountered by William Blake is anarchic. By the time Blake's train is in the West, the passengers are mostly buffalo hunters in buffalo skin robes, armed with long rifles. At one point, they leap up to shoot at buffalo from the train windows. Blake's letter with a job offer at the Dickinson Steel Mill turns out to have no value. Indeed, he is forewarned in a conversation on the train with the train's (illiterate) stoker, who says, "I wouldn't trust no words written down on no piece of paper written by Dickinson out in Machine." The West, as it turns out, is "wild" in the sense that words do not work conventionally.

As is the case with the written word (the letter's empty promise), verbal intercourse also turns out to be as vexed and anarchic as sexual intercourse. While hiring the bounty hunters, for example, Mr. Dickinson (Robert Mitchum) addresses many of his remarks to a stuffed bear in his office. And Nobody's speech is aphoristic, full of poetic and biblical references, and in various Native American languages as well as in English. At one point Blake says that he has not understood a single word Nobody has uttered. Even Nobody's most frequent, seemingly coherent utterance, which he directs to Blake ("Do you have any tobacco?"), makes no sense to Blake, who had told him early on that he didn't smoke. Blake fails to understand the semiotic significance of exchanges of tobacco in an other America, long effaced in Cleveland but still very much a part of the Far West.

Bullets, like words, have unstable structures of articulation in Jarmusch's Wild West. They are also either wildly aimed or fired with little provocation: "Every time someone fires a gun at someone else in this film, the gesture is awkward, unheroic, pathetic; it's an act that leaves a mess and is deprived of any pretense at existential purity."[5] Blake's wound results from a bullet aimed at someone else; Cole shoots one of the other bounty hunters simply because the man had said, "fuck you"; Nobody shoots one of the trappers without aiming at him; and Blake acquires deadly aim only after his world is a blur because Nobody has taken his glasses and traded them. Moreover, there are no clear fiduciary responsibilities for the use of deadly force. Dickinson is an unprosecuted captain of the local industry, despite being a homicidal maniac with several killings to his credit. And he sends off "lawmen" and bounty hunters ("the finest killers of men and Indians in this half of the world") alike in pursuit of Blake.

One concept, expressed by the young woman whom Blake meets in Machine, knits the episodes of the anarchic violence, of both representational structures and deadly projectiles, into a single text. When Blake asks her why she has a gun, which he finds under a pillow on her bed, she answers: "Because this is America!" Jarmusch's film is not complicit with the mythic story of America's West as the venue in which a people has fulfilled its pre-scripted destiny. Instead, it offers a series of disjointed individual stories that intersect as a result of arbitrary encounters among their protagonists.

As this incoherent America emerges in *Dead Man,* the film's cinematic structure resists a single biographical perspective. Benjamin Shapiro's story of his trip to Salt Lake City, which clung closely to his experiences (for example, his nosebleeds) was not cinematic; he offered no verbal montage of shifting scenes and alternative viewpoints or voices. The autobiographical genre of his story owed most of its character to his unwavering first-person narrative. Films approximate biography if the camera follows, quite strictly, the actions of an individual. In contrast, as Gilles Deleuze has shown, cinema's use of the "time image" constitutes a way of interpreting events that is more critical than mere perception.[6]

As long as the camera merely followed action, the image of time was indirect, presented as a consequence of motion. The new "camera consciousness" is no longer defined by the movements it is able to follow. Now, "even when it is mobile, the camera is no longer content to follow the character's movement" (23). The thinking articulated through a film whose shots shift among a variety of scenes and alter their depth of focus generates meaning not on the basis of the experiences of individual characters but on the basis of the way an ensemble of shots are connected. These practices of filmic composition resist the simple chronologies that are the basis of "organic film narration," a story line produced when the camera adheres to a linear action sequence (127). In contrast, in "crystalline film narration," which structures *Dead Man,* the filmic description creates its objects. Chronological time, that which is imposed by following the actors, is displaced by "non-chronological time" (129). Instead of composing movement images to treat the tensions explicitly acknowledged by William Blake, which would have restricted *Dead Man* to a fictional biography, Jarmusch's camera shots create an ensemble of time images that constitute a parody of America's heroic history in which, among other things, it expanded westward, thanks to the actions of frontier heroes.[7]

The film also challenges the political mythology in which the nuclear family is a stable moral foundation, which gives rise, contractually or otherwise, to the nation-state. Its cinematic narrative substitutes arbitrary events for this mythic narrative, representing collective groupings, familial among others, as consequences of encounters rather than as foundational causes. Similarly, at the level of discourse, the film stages encounters among different vernacular idioms and, through montage, allows a hybrid cultural world with several normative disjunctures to appear.

The film displays the centrifugal forces constituting "America" at the level of the image as well. It explores spaces that are as normatively vexed and noninstitutionalized as the cacophony of languages, idioms, and syntactic styles constituting western speech. More generally, in his cinematic mapping of "fuckin' nowhere," a space in which a gender-differentiated family composed of three male trappers could exist, Jarmusch produces the West as a place where violence is spontaneous rather than institutionalized. Compared with densely "striated spaces," in which governmental states have imposed a pattern of normativity (e.g., Cleveland, William Blake's place of birth), Jarmusch's West is "smooth."

As Deleuze and Guattari have suggested, striated spaces are heavily coded with normative boundaries. Movement within them produces a tightly controlled ascription of identity to those who enter and traverse them. Striating space, they assert, is one of the fundamental tasks of the state, a function aimed at preventing nomadism.[8] This function operates both physically and symbolically. When they say that the state "does not dissociate itself from a process of capture of flows of all kinds, populations, commodities or commerce, money or capital, etc.," they are not simply referring to border patrols, toll booths, and revenue collection; they also mean the function of coding. The state is in effect a "town surveyor," and it responds against everyone who tries to escape its coding operations by striating space (386).

In contrast, smooth spaces, such as Jarmusch's West, are places of contingency that the coding apparatuses of the state have yet to demarcate. Unlike striated spaces with sedentary routes that "*parcel out a closed space to people,* assigning each person a share and regulating the communication between shares," smooth spaces contain nomadic trajectories that "*distribute people (or animals) in an open space,* one that is indefinite and non-communicating" (380). In such spaces, people invent relationships rather than succumbing to the preexisting codes that constrain individual and collective identities.

In addition to its treatment of the arbitrariness of connections—

the eventualities through which solidarities and separations occur—Jarmusch's *Dead Man* is itself an important event. It constitutes a disruption at two levels of political mythology. At a larger level of collective organization, it produces an America that emerged from anarchic and violent encounters (e.g., the camera pans scenes of burned-out Native American villages during Blake's canoe trip toward his last stop with Nobody, which points to the more genocidal episodes that accompany the individual ones occupying the film's main story line). At a lower level of collective organization, it challenges two kinds of discourse on the family: the universalizing political discourse that valorizes the traditional family as a foundational and moral condition of possibility for national political coherence and the episodic eruption of "family values" discourses, which seek to restore a model of family structure that has been altered. I turn, therefore, to a characterization of the myth of the natural family, which is still perpetuated in the familiar, foundational discourses on the family–civic order relationship.

Hegel's Ethical Family

G. W. F. Hegel is doubtless the most influential thinker among those in the history of political thought who have seen the traditional nuclear family as the primary unit within the social domain and as the moral foundation of the state. Like John Locke, Hegel distinguishes between the state and "civil society," roughly that domain of association and structure of allegiances existing outside the purview of the state. For Locke, civil society precedes the state. It is a naturally constituted, prepolitical community that retains prerogatives that each individual exercises in the form of rights. Seeing the state as a contractual extension of the society, Locke views each individual's allegiance to it as an implicit agreement to forego a degree of autonomy in exchange for certain protections.

Hegel's departure from the Lockean model is owed primarily to his steadfast rejection of contingency. Although in Hegel's legendary narrative the state is an extension of both the family and community, that extension is not a contractual one. Neither the family nor the state could be contractual, because that would imply that associative connections were "the transient and utterly chaotic accidents of contingent agreement."[9] For Hegel, the family possesses a "natural unity" that is threatened when civil society "tears the individual from his family ties" and "estranges the members of the family from one another, and recognizes them as self-subsistent persons."[10] And, worse, civil society replaces that natural unity with contingency: "For the paternal soil and the external inorganic resources of nature from which the individual formerly derived his liveli-hood, it substitutes its own soil and subjects the permanent existence of even the entire family to dependence on itself and to contingency" (148).

Ultimately, however, the state, as the historical evolution of the Idea, constitutes the realization of the ethical life that begins in the family. Hegel's family is the first "ethical root of the state"; it contains an "objec-tive universality in a substantial unity" (154). Hegel's story of how the state emerges from the family and civil society is teleological rather than contractual. Because the universally emerging mind governs all levels, the state, as the ultimate level of organization, is "the end immanent within them" (the family and civil society) (161). At the same time, how-ever, the state creates the condition of possibility for the ethical life of the family. Hegel's teleological narrative, therefore, resists chronological time. The state is the beginning as well as the end; it is, in Hegel's terms, "not so much the result as the beginning" of the natural ethical life: "It is within the state that the family is first developed into civil society, and it is the Idea of the state itself which disrupts itself into these two moments" (155).

What can we make of Hegel's story of the family and state? At a mini-mum, it is a piece of fiction in which "nature" plays a paradoxical role. First, it is left behind (as the civil society substitutes contingency for the organic solidarity of the family), and then nature returns (as the state re-stores the ethical life that is dissipated in civil society). Hegel's resolution of the paradox is to substitute immanence for chronology; he locates the state both at the beginning, where it creates the conditions of possibility for the moral family, and at the end, where it embodies the enlargement of an ethical life begun within the family.

Hegel's family-state story is an exemplar of what Etienne Balibar calls a "fictitious universality."[11] Contending with earlier, religious construc-tions of personhood, Hegel's philosophical project is an attempt to re-place a religious universality with a political one. But the stories are ho-mologous; while religious and political modes of hegemony differ in terms of what they ascribe as being essential to human personality, both aspire to a universal community of meaning that unites the status of each unit within a common understanding (58–59). More specifically, the po-litical universality, which Hegel sees as a common historical destiny for all peoples (although some, he thinks, still reside in earlier temporal stages), is ultimately a historically inevitable world of state citizens, whose national allegiances are enlarged versions of those that structure the natural (and therefore ethical) solidarity of the family.

An antidote to Hegel's fictitious universality is achieved with a more finite treatment of history. *Finite history* is Jean-Luc Nancy's expression for an anti-Hegelian approach to characterizing "our time" in a way that ascribes to it neither a definitive past nor an expected future. History, in the finite sense, is a series of events in which people share a time without natural boundaries and share relationships without definite warrants such as "nature" or "reason." Finite historical events cannot "take place" because there is no prearranged space for them to occupy. They are happenings that make their place in time.[12]

In effect, Nancy's finite history accords well with a cinematic representation of events. Cinematic time images resist Hegelian and other modes of spatializing temporality that universalize the emergence of the state and expunge the contingencies associated with other ways of being-in-time. Yet Hegelian, fictitious universality continues to haunt contemporary discourses on the family, which attempt to moralize the nuclear family, valorize traditional parental authority, and locate traditional familial structures as foundational elements in the emergence of a democratic society and state. If we resist legendary narratives, however, and focus instead on the finitude of "our time," we can substitute a genealogical apprehension of familial structures, one which recognizes the character of families, at any historical moment, as events. More specifically, in order to reinstate the contingency that Hegelian philosophy seeks to expunge and therefore to recover, concretely, the arbitrary forces shaping familial structures and relationships, we must heed a genealogical perspective inaugurated by Nietzsche, elaborated by Foucault, and applied to the history of the family by Donzelot.

The Genealogical Perspective

Nietzsche, against a Hegelian historical sensibility in which normative existence is seen as a result of the historical progression of a rationality linked to a dialectical logic, offers a genealogical history. What exists as morality in a given epoch is a victory of one set of forces over others. Lacking intrinsic worth or historical affirmation, existing values are arbitrary instances of political domination. But they are represented otherwise; they are moralized by substituting a spiritual for a political supremacy.[13] However, a Nietzschean apprehension of the relationship between value and contingency does not prescribe mere ironic detachment. It encourages inquiry into the temporal emergence of what are taken to be values rather than seeking to find a unitary essence behind particular appearances. For Nietzsche, Hegelian dialectical thinking is precisely the vehicle for positing an essence behind existence. Whereas for Hegel, historical phenomena are particular manifestations of a transhistorical narrative, for Nietzsche, they have merely historical origins. More specifically, subjectivity is a shifting historical phenomenon for Nietzsche. He is attracted to the tragic disposition, manifested in the dramas of Aeschylus and Sophocles, because he sees it as an affirmation of an unstable and shifting multiplicity. Tragedy supplies a protohistory of a divided subjectivity;[14] it sets the tone for an appreciation of a series of unstable emergences, imposed interpretations of personhood that conceal multiplicity.

Traditional historical thinking since the tragic age, exemplified by Hegel, fails to appreciate struggles through which particular forms of subjectivity emerge. Instead, it interprets a particular mode of presence as an affirmation of a transcendent essence, and it preserves the Socratic delusion that morality is an achievement of a preordained destiny. For Nietzsche, morality is to be analyzed not as if it constitutes a claim to truth but as a sign of the results of the struggles of a particular age, as a dominant interpretation in need of a more detached, historically sensitive perspective.

Foucauldian Genealogy

Because Nietzsche's intellectual struggle was aimed at situating himself as an antagonist of the history of philosophical and religious thinking from Socrates onward—he constructs himself as "the anti-Christ" and as "the first tragic philosopher"[15]—his texts do not speak to particular political problematics, for example, the tensions between familial and civic attachments foregrounded in the Greek tragic dramas. The political pedagogy encouraged by Nietzschean genealogical thinking requires an elaboration, which is exemplified in some of Michel Foucault's historical investigations, particularly those concerned with the histories of punishment and sexuality. It is Foucault who has both addressed himself to the mode of historical inquiry that Nietzsche's thinking implies and has influenced the major, post-Nietzschean treatment of the family: Jacques Donzelot's *The Policing of Families*, which provides a powerful antidote to Hegel's naturalizing and moralizing of the family-state relationship.

For Foucault, Nietzschean genealogy is the essence of a politically perspicuous mode of inquiry. Accordingly, he begins his remarks on Nietzsche, genealogy, and history with the statement: "Genealogy is gray, meticulous, and patiently documentary."[16] Existing systems of intelligibility are for Foucault, as for Nietzsche, ambiguous achievements. Nietzsche saw his task, as the first tragic philosopher, to distance himself from imposed structures of harmony and intelligibility, discerning discord within every concord that philosophical thinking thought it had discovered. Foucault embraces this view of the arbitrariness of every age's practices of intelligibility and turns to history to make the arrangements of the present appear peculiar rather than a result of historically evolving wisdom. His investigations exemplify "thought from the outside," which, he notes, began when Nietzsche discovered "that all Western metaphysics is tied not only to grammar . . . but to those who in holding discourse have a hold over the right to speak."[17] Edified by Nietzsche's genealogical imagination, the task Foucault sets for himself is more a matter of patient inquiry than a matter of disqualifying post-Socratic philosophical complacency. He inflects Nietzschean discord within a linguistic register, analyzing discursive events to show how existing fields of enunciation allow political power to disguise itself as something else.

Treating instances of discourse as historical events to be viewed from the outside, Foucault struggles to find a language faithful to such thought (from the outside), because, he notes, "there is an irresistible tendency for thought to be repatriated to the side of consciousness" (21). He resists nevertheless, using, among other tropes, an ironic linguistic style, because he sees a political moment in the discourses of ironists, such as Maurice Blanchot. Their thought/language is "directed not toward any inner confirmation—not a kind of central, unshakable certitude—but toward an outer bound where it must continually contest itself" (21–22).

For the purpose of illustration, we can imagine how the continuing contestation Foucault invites applies to a specific commitment, expressed in an exchange over the value of individuality in different approaches to liberalism. Alan Ryan characterizes John Gray's "agonistic liberalism" as "the thought that a free society is a place where individuals and indeed the whole society work out their own particular fates."[18] Ryan's sentiments are deployed within a familiar discursive field. Contemporary liberal theory inherited the "individual" from canonical political thought, which, since the eighteenth century, has seen partisans of the prerogatives of persons contesting those with a more communitarian sensibility.

Within a genealogical perspective, one resists alignment with either of these partisan positions. What is encouraged instead is inquiry into the historical emergence of the problematic controlled by the liberal discourse on the singularity of personhood. As Foucault has shown, for example, the ordinary individual emerged as a describable personage in various writing genres (e.g., biography) in the eighteenth century as part of a more general development, to which he refers as "procedure[s] of objectification."[19] The modern "individual," in this reading, becomes part of a historical event of discourse. With this kind of historicizing, one resists what Foucault calls the "meta-historical deployment of ideal significations."[20] The sensibility it prescribes should not be seen as a resistance to political commitment. Foucault offers a politics of "irony" as an antidote to one of "infatuation" (143) with the unities immanent in the reigning system of intelligibility. It is a politics driven by the recognition that every set of rules and every mode of justice has no transcendent domain of legitimation; they exist as the result of an imposition. The (neo-Hegelian) hermeneutic, which turns what exists into the realization of a transcendent rationality, or at least into a reading of history as the relentless progress of knowledge, constitutes the kind of "injustice" characteristic of the "will to knowledge" (151), to the desire to consecrate existing arrangements rather than regard them critically.

The Emergence of the Modern Family

Although Foucault does not provide a specific genealogy of the family, he treats its significance as both a model and an object of intervention in his genealogical investigation of the "art of government." He notes that while the family provided a model of governance (as evidenced in political treatises through the seventeenth century), it was to be displaced by a concern with "populations" in the eighteenth century. The family's altered political significance—its change from a model of governance to an instrumentality relative to the population[21]—was part of a shift in approaches to the problem of governance (noted in chapter 1), the change from governance as the art of inducing submission to the law to governance as the management of people and things.[22] Picking up the story at this point, Jacques Donzelot's genealogical investigation of the family presumes a subsequent trajectory of governing the family as a part of a more general management of the social and economic order.

Donzelot's analysis of the production of the modern family, based on historical inquiry rather than moralistic fantasy, provides a counterstory to Hegel's fictitious universality and exemplifies a genealogical approach to discourse. Like Hegel, Donzelot recognizes that the family occupies a paradoxical position vis-à-vis the state. The family, he notes, is "both queen and prisoner."[23] But this paradox is not a result of a model that gives the family two incompatible places in a narrative. Donzelot's family is both "the strategic resultant of . . . diverse forces" and a mythical unity on which moralistic reactions to its transformations are based. It is, in effect, manipulated by nationalistic reasons of state and then moralized as being in crisis by nationalists (7).

What are the forces that have shaped the modern family? Donzelot's inquiry takes us back to the late seventeenth century to map the emerging forces that were operating both within and outside the family. Perhaps most significant were the changing structures of occupational recruitment. As work became increasingly supplied outside extended family structures, families continued to regulate marriages; previously, however, the purpose, beyond maintaining the family's reputation, was to preserve the family order as a working unit, although by the nineteenth century, the family became increasingly concerned with preparing children for a marriage that would facilitate achieving the credentials necessary for fitting into orders outside the family.

At the same time, states were intervening to transform families. With the development of nationally regulated economies, they sought to influence the way the family helped to produce a work force and to control the effects on families of fluctuations in the economy. This required increasing degrees of intervention in the health, education, and fiscal conditions of family members.

As a consequence of changes in economic structures and the related development of a state-manipulated social order, a "tactical collusion" developed between states and families: "What troubled families was adulterine children, rebellious adolescents, women of ill-repute—everything that might be prejudicial to their honor, reputation, or standing. By contrast, what worried the state was the squandering of vital forces, the unused or useless individuals" (25).

Ever since the altered conditions of an emerging modernity have imposed new pressures on familial structures and tactics, from within and without, there have been elements of collusion as well as degrees of opposition in the pattern of state-family relations. Moreover, the patterns of complicity versus resistance in these relations have differed for different classes, in part because they have had to cope with different kinds of intervening agencies (for example, social workers for the poorer classes and psychoanalysts for the wealthier ones). And, in general, various intermediaries (for example, doctors and therapists) have played different roles in the process of either reinforcing or challenging parental authority.

Whatever levels of pressure and blame various intervening agencies have leveled at the family, it has been in a context, encouraged by the state, of seeing the modern family as an institution whose responsibility is to qualify children to function outside the family's boundaries, within the state-managed, social milieu (225). Donzelot points out the bind of the contemporary family subject to such expectations. On the one hand, its ability to exercise its authority in relation to other institutions has been diminished; its "margin of autonomy" has been reduced. But, on the other hand, "its internal life is in demand"; it is ordered to strengthen its bonds, to maintain an affective hold over its members, which may have the paradoxical effect of lessening members' ability to function outside its boundaries (227). Yet, the ability of a young person to function within the social milieu—to find steady work, to maintain the bonds of affection with a partner, to effectively manage a parental role, and to qualify children to ultimately do the same—is increasingly determined by exogenous forces.

Moralizing discourses on the family are insensitive to the forces constructing the contemporary family's bind. They seek instead to bind the family-state nexus by evoking the kind of mythic normative family that emerged in Hegel's discourse. The high levels of surveillance of sexuality, to which Foucault referred in his analyses of modern governmentalities,[24] are aided and abetted in the activities of contemporary culture conservatives, who insist that high levels of surveillance of sexual and other practices are necessary for the maintenance of "decency." The nation's public sphere is a place where "decent" or "civilized" behavior must be maintained to ensure the nation's respect in the world of states.

Indeed, throughout modern history, nationalism and codes of decency have been significantly connected.[25] Their more recent interarticulations have been evident in campaigns of those associated with shielding "American civilization" from sexually explicit media. In a recent op-ed piece in the *New York Times,* for example, William Bennett and C. Deloris Tucker praised the Wal-Mart store chain for refusing to stock "compact disks with lyrics and cover art that it finds objectionable."[26] They make an appeal for "simple decency," which they claim has the support of "concerned parents and politicians of both parties" (A15). The evocation of decency has been articulated during the past decade with a more general family values, right-wing political initiative aimed at essentializing the conventional family and locating it in a mythic story in which the dissolution of traditional family structures is a threat to a previously vital national character.

Apart from the ways in which this story conjures away the impacts of changing economic circumstances on family structures—telling a mythic values story instead of a money story[27]—its crisis mode is belied by a history of nationalism's appropriation of issues of sexuality and codes of decency, which intensified throughout the nineteenth century as states increasingly used the idea of a unified national culture as part of the legitimation of their territorial sovereignty claims.[28]

The idea of decency, which has been part of nationalism's construction of a normative sexuality, has a historical trajectory that challenges a crisis model in which the present is understood as a qualitative change in the evolution of morals. Decency is a legacy of the concept of *civilité*, which in Europe was employed as a guide to behavior during the period of state formation. In the "age of absolutism," it was associated with the processes through which Western societies imposed domestic pacification. While the behaviors were being shaped, there developed a concurrent concept of civilization that was to become part of European self-appreciation, although in different states that civilizational discourse took on different qualities and was variously connected to antagonisms between different classes.[29]

Most significant, the norms prescribing constraints and codes of decency, which initially related primarily to within-society class dynamics as well as to state-sponsored aspects of pacification, eventually acquired a collective, ontological significance; they became part of a cluster of ideas about national distinctiveness. As George Mosse puts it, the norms constituting *civilité* needed a broader warrant; they "had to be informed by an ideal if they were to be effective. . . . In most timely fashion, nationalism came to the rescue."[30]

Although the idea of decency no longer has the official warrant it enjoyed at one time (it is a quaint anachronism when it appears in policy discourses), it has been central to the arguments of various factions in the right wing's continuing war on the arts and entertainment industry. While much of that war has been waged in academic publications and opinion journals, one of the more exemplary counterattacks has appeared in the form of a feature film written and directed by Paul Thomas Anderson. His *Boogie Nights,* a film about the pornography industry in the disco days of the 1970s and its move from theaters to videos in the 1980s, features a pornographic film production company organized as a family. The film is, among other things, an ironic reversal of the relationship between decency and family values; a part of an industry that produces "indecency" turns out to be a more effective "family" than the other, traditional nuclear families that are shown in the film.

Boogie Nights opens with shots of theater marquees, emphasizing part of the entertainment structure of Los Angeles in the 1970s. Porn film stars were marquee names, and drugs and discos were voguish parts of urban life. Jack Horner (Burt Reynolds), who plays the role of a surrogate father in his porn production company, adds young Eddie (soon to adopt the name Dirk Digler) to his "family." Upon meeting Eddie (Mark Wahlberg), who is a busboy in a nightclub, he exclaims, "I've got a feeling there's something wonderful in those jeans waiting to come out." Once Eddie becomes Dirk Digler and is acting in Horner's films, it comes out often and to much effect; Digler becomes a star with strong name recognition. Seemingly, 1970s porn star Johnny Wadd, known for his large sex organ, is the Digler prototype (Digler's qualifying attribute is also reminiscent of the sole qualification of Madame de Saint-Ange's gardener in the Marquis de Sade's *Philosophy in the Bedroom*, with which I compare *Boogie Nights* below).

But *Boogie Nights* is not itself a porn film. The sex scenes are few and are focused more on production than sex. Anderson's camera emphasizes the political economy of porn production—the recruitment and organization of the crew, the management of their relationships, and the actual work involved in setting and filming scenes, as Jack Horner tells Eddie/Dirk Digler: "You got your camera: You got your film . . . you got your lights, you got your synching, you got your editing, you got your lab. Before you turn around you've spent maybe twenty-five or thirty thousand dollars."

Horner's remark reflects a pervasive filmic strategy in *Boogie Nights*. Anderson's primary focus on the work of producing and staging pornography disrupts the usual spatiality of pornographic cinema. If we recognize two kinds of filmic space, "that included within the frame and that outside the frame,"[31] we can appreciate this disruption. It is accomplished by bringing the social organization of the pornography production ensemble into the same space as the action. The violation of this spatial separation reorients the film's thematic; it is more about families than about sex.

From the outset, shortly after Horner discovers that Eddie may be the talent he is seeking, it is evident that Horner is a surrogate father figure and his main female attraction, Amber Waves (Julianne Moore), is a surrogate mother. Thematically, then, *Boogie Nights* is a story of a surrogate family formed around the production company and located primarily in Jack Horner's home. The story opposes the family values stories emerging in a variety of genres with varying degrees of cultural authority,[32] for the heteronormal families depicted throughout the film are seriously impaired and/or fractured structures. Although they are aiming to qualify their children for survival on the outside, their disturbed interactions have the opposite effect (at least in the cases of Eddie and "Roller Girl" [Heather Graham], one of the younger porn actresses).

In this context, Jack Horner's family is a throwback. Unlike the modern family, whose major effort is to qualify its children to function outside its boundaries, Horner's is a premodern family from the point of view of the locus of work. Moreover, with the coming of the video age, which threatens the film star aspirations of Horner's children/actors, Horner acts to protect his family from the vagaries of economic change, prompted by technological change. And he does his best to protect his children from problematic consumers of porn as well as from outside forces (for example, even the drug use in his household is less excessive among his crew than among visitors at his parties).

Two external contexts bear especially on implications of the familial solidarity that Horner tries to maintain. First, the 1970s disco era is a period of challenges to social coherence. Not only are families being increasingly broken, but also the perceptual field as a whole is disintegrating into a pluralizing set of signs, all offering different styles of personhood. In the face of these changes, diverse moralizing responses are under way—efforts at symbolically binding relationships that are being sundered—which ultimately impact the fates of the various characters in Anderson's story. Second, the situation for women is being altered, for the 1970s marks the beginning of the process to which Nancy Fraser has referred as "the crumbling of the old gender order," an order centered on the "family wage."[33] Among the consequences of this alteration is a situation in which "needy women" have been increasingly subjected to an "exploitable dependency" (597).

The women and men in Jack Horner's film company are all ill-suited to the changing outside order. His film company and home operate as a temporary refuge from forces that are compromising the viability of traditional family structures, subjecting women to "exploitable dependency" and imposing rigid models of self-representation on men and women. And significantly, Jack Horner's substitute family is not a traditional patriarchy. Horner does not function as "the law"; indeed, he is more of a Sadean than a Freudian father. The sex scenes he directs are mostly boring and repetitious, and although the sexuality practiced within his films and household is all extrafamilial (from a conventional point of view), only one member of the film crew, "Little Bill," holds on to a traditional family model of sexuality. Upset at his wife's repeated adultery, he finally shoots her, a lover, and himself. However, Little Bill retains

The porn production family, as depicted in *Boogie Nights* (1997), with actors Mark Wahlberg at center, Burt Reynolds on his right, and Julianne Moore on his left.

his Horner family connection; one of the film's last scenes, a panning of the walls of Jack Horner's home, shows a photo portrait of Little Bill on a wall. Even his dramatic deviance fails to disconnect him from his surrogate family.

Like Sade's boudoirs, Jack Horner's home is less about sex than about singularity. He shows no personal interest in sex and, as a director in his films and in his home, is nondirective; his characters choose their styles. Roller Girl never removes her skates, even while nude for sex scenes. Dirk Digler, having invented his own name, is also allowed to invent plots and is permitted to select his moments of climax, even when they violate the script, and other members of the crew display diverse and even anachronistic styles (e.g., Buck Swope, a black, former stereo salesman, dresses in an outmoded cowboy style and is continually in search of an effective "look"). Horner shows himself to be completely nonjudgmental with respect to all the choices of individual style. In contrast, when the various members of Horner's family try to survive economically and socially outside the family—seeking bank loans, music careers, or visitation rights with children—the dominant social forces, ranging from the informal censoriousness of a society intolerant of pornography workers and alternative sexualities to the more institutionalized agencies of banks and judges, resist or batter them.

Horner is a Sadean father, therefore, in the sense that his management of space is aimed precisely at protecting the singularities of people who cannot operate comfortably within the normative climate of the outside life-world.[34] Like Sade, he rejects the naturalness of the traditional family. He sharply distinguishes the family and sexuality and sponsors a pluralistic idea of attachments. Although, unlike Sade, he encourages a familial style for his collective, he remains Sadean in the sense that familial structures for him are contingent and sexual acts are transient and insignificant with respect to the establishment of social or affectual bonds. Ultimately, however, Anderson's film neither valorizes nor disparages Horner's model of bonding. Its juxtapositions map a significant change in the forces that create the conditions of possibility for attachment and encourage critical thought about bonds, while recognizing the problematic claim any model of family structure has for political allegiance.

Conclusion: Binding Community

If we regard family structures and relationships as contingent after-effects of historically specific forces rather than as stable (natural or moral) bases for sociality and political commitment, what are our political options when it comes to seeking exemplars for the bonds of community? To approach the question I want to focus attention on the concept of binding, treating it as it is used by Jonathan Crary in his analysis of a Manet painting, *In the Conservatory*.[35] Among the aspects of the two figures in the center of the painting, which attract Crary's attention (a woman seated on a bench and a cigar-smoking man leaning on the bench from behind it), are each of their hands. Both are wearing wedding bands but seem to be an adulterous couple.

In his analysis of what he calls "the binding energy of the work," Crary argues that Manet's work was set against two aspects of fragmentation

In the Conservatory, by Edouard Manet (1879), now in the Gemaldegalerie, Berlin.

afflicting perceptual and social coherence in the late nineteenth century: The painting works to reconsolidate both a perceptual field being sundered by a breakdown in normative attentiveness, and a breakdown in the marriage bond reflected in adulterous relationships. In contrast with Manet's emphasis on binding, *Boogie Nights* explores a complex dynamic of binding and unbinding. This exploration is aided by the capacity of film, with its cuts, juxtapositions, and other spatiotemporal modalities, to enact a social bond without a normative fixity. Anderson's filmic story valorizes singularities while exploring alternative structures of being-in-common in ways that respect those singularities.

Finally, Anderson's film recognizes, without resolving, the tensions between singularities and affectual ties. As a result, his *Boogie Nights* aligns itself with Jean-Luc Nancy's suggestion that there are ways to be in common without foundational guarantees. Nancy's model of being-in-common eschews ontological grounding, because it rejects a "truth of a common subject" or a general model of sense, outside the "numerous singularity of each of the 'subjects of sense.'"[36] Collective identities have no coherent horizon behind them and no essence to be attained.[37] The social bond, for Nancy, is an unending process of tying and untying. Insofar as identity is involved in the process, it is provisional and contingent on the ties that are formed. And, insofar as there is a politics of the family one can endorse within such a contingency-affirming perspective, it is a politics that embraces and protects singularity while encouraging a plurality of ties that bind (familial and otherwise).

3. Families, Strategies, Interests, and Public Life

Narratives of the Public Interest

Of all the genres treating public life, explicitly political treatises have been among the most insensitive to changing circumstances. Political theorists persist, for example, in referring to private versus public interests as if the boundary practices constructing these domains are historically stable. A simple narrative has dominated influential, canonical political texts; "private life" precedes civic life, which, in turn, creates the conditions of possibility for the state as a political realization of popular will. In one version, inaugurated in the writings of John Locke, the state is a contractual extension of the civic order, which is composed of an aggregate of individual, private interests. In the Lockean narrative, civil society precedes the state; it is a naturally constituted, prepolitical community that has no public interests until the state, as a contractual extension of the civic domain, creates a public interest, associated primarily with the exercise of a domestic policing function. The state defends the interests of each (propertied) individual from predatory violence, and individuals reciprocate with allegiance in the form of an implicit agreement to forego autonomous violence in exchange for the state's protection.

As was noted in chapter 2, Hegel's model of the relationship is organic rather than contractual. His departure from the Lockean model is owed in part to his steadfast rejection of contingency. Although in Hegel's legendary narrative the state is an extension of both the family and the community and is the exemplary expression of the ultimate public interest, the ethical life, that extension is not the result of implicit contractual reciprocity. The state cannot be the result of a contract, because that would imply that associative connections are historically contingent. As is the case with Locke's version, however, Hegel's narrative tells us little about the vagaries of family-public relations in general or about the interests that emerge as a result of the specific forces shaping family life, civic life, and family-civic relationships at given historical moments. In what follows, I turn to two genres of popular culture, a detective novel and a feature film, in order to map the spaces of modernity as they exist in both a large urban area and a (fictional) small town and to treat the ways in which disparate and conjunctive interests, emerging from familial structures, generate actions within extrafamilial public domains. Unlike Hegel's approach, which concerns itself with "concrete universals" (e.g., the state), these genres address historically specific episodes and dynamics. They provide insights into what Walter Benjamin called the "uncanny" dimensions of modern life and address the ways in which people adjust to ambiguous and changing attachments and circumstances in order to pursue their interests: "The more uncanny a big city becomes, the more knowledge of human nature . . . it takes to operate in it. In actuality, the intensified struggle for survival led an individual to make an imperious proclamation of his interests."[1] Benjamin saw the detective novel as a particularly apt genre for understanding Paris, the world's most modern city in his estimation. Detective fiction is especially instructive, he thought, because of the way it maps the spaces of modernity (41). Edified by this insight, my analysis begins with a reading of a detective novel involving extraordinary personae, interacting primarily within the limits of the city of San Francisco.

Gypsies and Repo Men

The rationale for turning to detective fiction as a vehicle for mapping modern space is summarized succinctly by Tom Gunning, who elaborates Benjamin's basic insights into the genre:

> The narrative form of the detective story, rather than serve simply as an exercise in puzzle solving, depends explicitly upon the modern experience of circulation. While circulation relies on an evolving process of rationalization of time and space, the very intricacy and speed of those routes of transfer and exchange create a counterthrust in which stability and predictability can be threatened. The detective story maps out two positions in this dialectical drama of modernity: the criminal who preys upon the very complexity of the system of circulation; and the detective, whose intelligence, knowledge, and perspicacity allow him to discover the dark corners of the circulatory system, uncover crime, and restore order.[2]

Joe Gores's *32 Cadillacs* is an exemplar of these aspects of the genre, exercising all the dimensions to which Gunning refers. A crime novel version of an actual episode, the story pits a detective agency, specializing in auto repossession ("repo men"), against a group of Gypsies who have "ripped off" the Cadillacs: "Once upon a time a band of Gypsies really did rip off thirty two cars from a large Bay Area bank in a single day."[3] As Gunning's insight suggests, the story maps urban space; it treats spatiotemporal structures that define the modern city as an intricate and complexly normative system of circulation. Moreover, and also in accord with Gunning's remarks, it shows the way the criminal preys upon the very complexity of the system of circulation and how the detectives, whose intelligence, knowledge, and perspicacity allow them to discover the dark corners of the circulatory system, uncover crime and restore order. However, there are special features of this crime story. The personae occupy unusual positions in the normative order of the modern city. Since the emergence of both modern law enforcement and criminality, crime investigators and a "criminal element" have had an intimate relationship with structures of legality/illegality as well as with each other. The same enforcement structures that produce a surveillance of criminality have created what Michel Foucault calls "a delinquent milieu," a domain of "fabricated delinquency" or "controlled illegality" that produces the informants necessary to the function of policing.[4]

Ordinary private detectives lack the intimacy of police detectives with the system of legal norms but maintain it with the delinquent milieu. In this crime story, however, both the repo men and their targets, the Gypsies, operate largely outside this structure of intimacy with the legal system and mostly outside of the domain of delinquency connected to policing (although the repo men do make use of one Gypsy informant). As a result, their encounters provide insights into the spaces and tempos of the city—both public and private—that are not afforded by following the interactions between policing agents and criminalized personae who function within more recognized and normatively ordered city spaces.

Michel de Certeau's concepts are appropriate for identifying what is peculiar to the characters in this tale. Because they do not control their spaces of operation, Gypsies and repo men cannot employ what de Certeau calls "strategies," which involve

> the calculation (or manipulation) of power-relationships that becomes possible as soon as a subject with will and power (a business, an army, a city, a scientific institution) can be isolated. [A strategy] postulates a *place* that can be delimited as its *own* and serve as a base from which the relations of an *exteriority* composed of targets or threats (customers, competitors, enemies, the country surrounding the city, objectives and objects of research, etc.) can be managed.[5]

Instead, because they are "others"—people without the institutional-ized control of space from which strategies can be deployed—Gypsies and repo men employ "tactics": "The space of the tactic is the space of the other; it must play on and with a terrain imposed on it and organized by the law of a foreign power" (37). Because the field of this other is more temporal than spatial, "[i]t takes advantage of opportunities, and depends on them, being without any base where it could stockpile its winnings, build its position. . . . it must vigilantly make use of the cracks that particu-lar conjunctions open in the surveillance of the proprietary powers" (37).

Given their positioning outside the spheres of the proprietary powers, the Gypsies and repo men in *32 Cadillacs* employ a "mobile infinity of tac-tics" (41). At the same time, the novelistic genre within which their en-counter unfolds provides a perspective not only on the circuits of move-ment and exchange within the city but also on the disjunctions between the idioms and sites of enunciation of the different types involved in the circulation and exchange. Each word, as M. M. Bakhtin has put it, "tastes of the context and contexts in which it has lived its socially charged life."[6] And, more generally, as a genre the novel is distinguished, Bakhtin asserts, by its "heteroglossia"—plurality of contending voices. It is therefore well suited to resist the depluralizing political discourses that reference fixed and universal models of "private interests" and "the public interest."

Countering the depluralizing tendencies of official discourses, the novel is ideationally centrifugal; it maps a world of differences, which pull away from the verbal-ideological center of the social domain. As a result, the novel is stylistically suited to disrupt the political codes that deny difference and promote the fiction of a stable set of relations be-tween public and private domains. In the case of Gores's novel, the cast of characters adds to the genre's stylistically induced centrifugal tendencies. The culture of Gypsies is disjunctive with the boundary practices of pub-lic versus private characterizing their more mainstream, U.S. consociates. Gores is sensitive to the way the Rom radically distinguish themselves from outsiders, the *gadje.* They practice, among other things, a different relationship to consumption: "Buying . . . is a sucker's game, and no *rom,* ever, believes he is a sucker. For dealing with the straight world, the *gadjo* world . . . the motto is: *Gadje gadje, zi lai ame Rom san*—outsiders are outsiders, but we are *the rom.*"[7]

This boundary practice articulates itself in various ways. Gypsies maintain a separation between how they live and what they reveal. For ex-ample, the extreme cleanliness they practice in their daily lives—women will not speak to men in the morning until they have washed their faces, and all loners and outsiders are regarded as unclean—is belied by the clutter and dilapidation of the exteriors of their dwellings. And, in general, they avoid allowing what is seen or heard by outsiders to reveal what is practiced among insiders. They invent themselves and profit from the fabulous relationship they have with the outside world.[8]

The Gypsy practices of the exoteric versus esoteric reveal much more than the peculiarities of their culture. Historically, their use of some technologies and their resistance to others provide insights into the way those technologies have altered the public domain. In *32 Cadillacs* it is noted in passing, for example, that many of the Gypsies involved in the car scam don't read; designated readers among the Gypsies are required to manage parts of the theft. In general, some Gypsies have felt it distasteful but necessary to adopt some *gadje* practices and/or have various kinds of intimacy with outsiders whom they regard as unclean. Thus the car scam in *32 Cadillacs* is enabled in part by the sexual seduction of *gadje* men and women by Gypsies. The seductions require the crossing of a boundary that is constitutive of Gypsy practices of identity and attachment.

The Gypsy Family

The familial focus of *32 Cadillacs* is owed in part to the novelistic genre, especially the realist type, which, it is argued, places its acts and images in "a dynastic line that unites the diverse generations of the genealogical family."[9] In the case of *32 Cadillacs* the genealogical family that fulfills this imperative is an extended Gypsy family whose dynastic line is precisely at issue when the story opens. Because it is assumed that the Gypsy patriarch, or king, is about to die (he has staged an accident to give that impression), one of those vying to replace him in the dynastic line hatches the plot to steal the cars, because a long line of them will provide an appropriate funeral cortege and bring the necessary prestige to the one who supplies them.

The familial structure constitutes the basic social and political unit for Gypsies. Indeed, although they are exemplars of stateless people, at the same time, their approach to familial attachment exemplifies the "moral family," which Hegel saw as the ethical basis of the state. Interviews with Gypsies in the United States disclose this version of Gypsy philosophy: the good life, health, and happiness are functions of a clean and moral family life. Indeed, all bad things come from supernatural sanctions, which are activated when one violates familial loyalties. Intimacy with outsiders violates the laws of *marime*; it is a form of moral pollution that endangers all members of the *familia* or extended family, particularly the most vulnerable, which are the children.[10]

More generally, the Gypsy "nation" is made up of family units, large, extended families, protected by several exclusionary rules, for example, not allowing Gypsy children to have school contact with non-Gypsies after age ten. Marriages are generally arranged and are also familial in nature; for example, the California Gypsy families exhibit a preference for marriage between second cousins within the *vitsa* (a coalition of extended families).[11] Moreover, the historical story of the Gypsies is a story of resistance to the genealogy of the modern family, articulated in Jacques Donzelot's analysis (discussed in chapter 2). Rather than qualifying children to work outside the family, the Gypsy extended family is the source of employment. For the most part, family space and work space continue to coincide within the Gypsy nation.

Despite the importance of family genealogy in Gypsy society, written records of family blood lines are largely nonexistent, because Gypsies have an aversion to writing. To appreciate that Gypsy resistance to written language has been a survival strategy rather than a disability, we must understand the complicated spatial implications of writing technologies. On the one hand, the emergence of writing technologies helped to produce a public sphere outside the tutelage of former hegemonic institutions. Certainly, for example, the development of print in the fifteenth century was essential to the gains of a "critical humanism" and thus to the production of a vernacular language, which was instrumental in aspects of democratization that followed from the Reformation.[12] Writing technologies helped, in short, to dissolve the hegemony of a vertical model of space, based on a strict boundary between the domains of the sacred and the profane. And, as Benedict Anderson has argued, they helped to displace that vertical world with a horizontal one, a nation-state geographic imaginary.[13]

On the other hand, writing technologies in general, and in particular the written text as an extension of the self, became increasingly bound up with structures of proprietary control. Ever since the various struggles to establish copyright laws and install the author as a "proprietor," writing technologies have significantly altered the boundaries of the public versus the private sphere.[14] However, written documents have been enabling for some and disabling for others. In the form of property recordings, they constitute records that give propriety power a tangible warrant. In the form of stored dossiers, they have been part of the growing surveillance structures of state societies. Among other things, writing provides the normative codes through which modern space has been "striated," densely coded such that unauthorized movement can be tracked and contained.[15] Because the state "does not dissociate itself from a process of capture of flows of all kinds, populations, commodities or commerce, money or capital, etc." (385–86), it has attempted vigorously to sedentarize Gypsies (for example, with antivagabond and antivagrancy laws), and writing has been one of the primary instruments of surveillance.

As Foucault has noted in his analysis of the segmenting of space and the proliferation of technologies to fix identities and surveil them from centers of power, "an uninterrupted work of writing links the centre and periphery in which power is exercised without division."[16] Because the Gypsies' raison d'être has been the resistance to surveillance and sedentarization, they have been resistant to writing. They have always operated outside the state capture of space and, ironically, have found it easier to cross borders without passports and other written documents. Moreover, reflecting their aversion to written language, their language, Romani, has no words for *to write* or *to read*; they regard reading as a strange and idle practice.[17]

The disjuncture between Gypsy and *gadje* cultures becomes apparent early in the novel. The repo men speak constantly of working on the "Gypsy file," a dossier that they initiate and then continually expand in their pursuit. In contrast, insofar as Gypsies read, it is a matter of tactics— the exigencies of the moment. For example, in Gores's novel, while working a scam on a fortune-telling client, the Gypsies read the contents of his trash in order to create an impression that their intimacy with spiritual power is allowing them to know something about their client's destiny. And, because Gypsies are always moving, this kind of reading practice creates no paper trail; it is a tactic that articulates with the rest of their mobile practices, organized to live within the crevices and around the margins of the social order. Most significant, the differential relationships of Gypsies and *gadje* to writing technologies reveal the ways in which writing has organized the contemporary spatial order, the domains of public versus private.

The central scam of the story, the ripping off of the thirty-two Cadillacs, involves the tactical use of written documents. A Gypsy, Rudolph Marino, manages to dress in expensive clothes, book a high-priced hotel room, and adopt a plausible credit history by stealing the identity papers of a wealthy person who is out of town, staying in his vacation home. The timing of the scam is linked to a variety of temporalities, their victim's vacation practices among others. But the most challenging bit of timing of the scam involves opening several bank accounts and depositing and withdrawing the same amount, ten thousand dollars, several times. These moves are predicated on a knowledge of the timing aspects of banking practices. The Gypsies arrange the car purchases on a Friday so that the banks won't learn that the checks are not backed by sufficient funds until they reopen on the following Monday.

Moreover, and most significant for this analysis, the use of temporally oriented tactics and writing technologies by the Gypsies cannot be easily reciprocated by authorities, because the Gypsies' private spaces are not coded in official documents. Their relationship to the writing practices that organize the modern city are fugitive. For this reason, the repo men, who serve these authorities (in this case, the banks that have been stung), also must function in the domain of the tactic, seizing the right moments. For example, they look for Gypsies at racetracks and at certain bars that they know to be familiar Gypsy haunts. And each "score" involves precise timing, for example, stealing a car back from a Gypsy by bribing the garage man and using his uniform to pretend to be the one delivering the car from the garage to the front of the hotel, where the Gypsy has been staying under an alias.

The various venues of encounter between Gypsies and repo men help ultimately to trace the circuits of the city and, at the same time, to map a social space that is a hybrid composite of the private and public. A certain bar and lounge, for example, is known by the repo men to be a Native American gathering place. Because one Gypsy they are tracking is known to use a false, Native American identity to work a charity scam, they are able to find her stolen Cadillac parked there. Such spaces (bars, hotels, motels, stores, and banks), linked by roads, elevators, and telephones, constitute a structure of relationships among not so much clear separations of public and private spaces as among forces seeking to retain degrees of privacy and those attempting to impose a public mode of control.

The contingencies of these structures—the combinations of surveillance and haphazardness in the forms and timing of their connections—are precisely what determine the tactics of those who seek to profit from others. The various rigidities of the forms in the modern city produce "free spaces": "The combination of formal requirements of a certain order . . . permits all kinds of freedom or disorder within the interstices."[18] Thus the action in *32 Cadillacs* maps the interstices as well as the structures of the city and challenges any view of an orderly structuring of private and public domains.

However, to appreciate the disorder within the order of the modern

city, we must also recognize the historical emergence of yet another domain of technology, one that has reconfigured the interconnections of
the public and private spheres: technologies of the visual associated with
modern architecture. Walter Benjamin and Asja Lacis were among the
first to theorize the "porosity" of the private-public boundary that modern architecture had wrought: "Just as the living room reappears on the
street . . . so the street migrates into the living room."[19]

The ambiguation of the public-private boundary, which Benjamin
and Lacis saw, has become increasingly an effect of the architectural
forms of the modern city. A variety of technologies have enabled these
forms, not the least of which are different forms of lighting and other
media that enhance visibility—for example, the window, which is implicated in the visual porosity of structures, and television, which, as a "window on the world," introduces an even more radical "confusion over inside and out" and thus over the distinction between public and private.[20]

However, technologies alone cannot alter structures of social interaction. Other forces have provided the context for the forces involved in
the management of vision that structures contemporary orders of association. Not the least of these are the commercial forces shaping both class
structures and the modern, bourgeois sphere of consumption. As Habermas noted in his investigation of historical changes in the public sphere,
the prebourgeois, aristocratic order staged its station in public space with
displays of insignia, dress, and demeanor.[21] Although it is certainly the
case that the contemporary bourgeois public sphere involves display,
much of that display is based on a technologically and architecturally
aided display of commodities. Commercial concerns employ "color, glass
and light" to attract a clientele that is driven less by an ascribed status to
which appropriate insignia attest than by rules of normality with respect
to body weight, clothing styles, investment practices, and rules of sociability.[22] And they are impelled by a social logic of distinction, which prescribes different practices for different age groups, genders, and social
"fractions."[23]

While Gypsies operate largely outside the pressures of both the dominant commercial structures and the related normalizing judgments that
help them function, the tactics enabled by modern zones of visibility are
not lost on them. A bank scene in *32 Cadillacs,* in which a Gypsy is
working his loan scam, effectively shows the way in which the architecture of the contemporary commercial bank reflects a set of shaping
forces on and a set of relays between the zones of the public and private.
In a key scene, the aforementioned Rudolph Marino enters the main

branch of "California Citizens Bank at One Embarcadero *(Now Open Nine to Five Every Weekday to Serve You Better)*" and is able to see all his relevant opportunities:

> Since a man was handling New Accounts, Marino scanned the other bank officers behind the metal and Formica railing. He chose a pretty, early-40's, round faced woman with pouty lips. She wore floral perfume and pink-tinted glasses that magnified her eyes into a slightly surprised expression. She did not wear a wedding band. Her nameplate said HELEN WOODING.[24]

The bank, laden with signs and spaces organized to seduce a clientele and governed by a rigid temporal structure (fixed opening hours, consistent durations for check clearing), turns out to be an easy mark for one prepared to be the seducer rather than the seduced. Just as the temporal structure is spelled out, the subordinate-superordinate structure and the personalities and lifestyles of the personnel are available to direct vision. The points and moments of attack are wholly readable (even to one who eschews literacy).

The architecture of commercial and public buildings, which structure much of the public experience of the contemporary city, is only part of the context provided in Gores's novel. The patterns of visibility and concealment in domestic architecture also help to distinguish the functioning and interests of the repo men and Gypsy subjects. As Beatriz Colomina has noted in her analysis of domestic architecture, "Architecture is not simply a platform that accommodates the viewing subject. It is a viewing mechanism that produces the subject. It precedes and frames its occupant."[25]

Colomina's insight about modernity was already evident in the emergence of the private spaces of domesticity in the eighteenth-century Western world. As a bourgeois culture developed, houses were increasingly designed to create an economy of exposure and concealment in which persons sought to "determine when and how much of oneself is to be known by others."[26] Subsequently, much of bourgeois family life has been organized around a designed control of visibility. Apart from the way in which the house has reflected the libidinal economy of family life—maintaining separations (except in appropriate parts of the house) between parents and children, sisters and brothers, and family members and guests—the bourgeois home also became, by the twentieth century, a showcase for consumption. The house as partly a place of exhibition underwent a transformation similar to that in the public domain, as public space, with its store windows and billboards, became increasingly a space for attracting consumption.

However, to appreciate the encounters in *32 Cadillacs* between Gypsies and *gadje* it is important to recognize differences between bourgeois American and Gypsy domestic spaces. While, for example, the modern bourgeois house uses glass to create an ambiguity between the inside and the outside, yet maintaining certain strategic separations within the interior,[27] the Gypsy dwelling, as a space for both work and family life, tends to disguise the inside from the outside and to enact further forms of enclosure and opacity within. Thus, for example, in *32 Cadillacs* the home of the Gypsy palm reader, Madame Miseria, is described as being "in one of the narrow one-block alleys leading up the side of Telegraph Hill from Broadway." And in a section describing a fortune-telling scam worked on a young male client, it is noted that nothing about the interior of Madame Miseria's house is evident from outside. Once one enters, the outside world is wholly shut out. Upon entering, the visitor-client climbs a "narrow ill-lit interior stair" and confronts curtains on runners which, when pulled back, reveal a backlit woman in bright clothes.[28] Almost nothing else about the interior is available to the client's view; he is led along narrow drape-lined corridors with little lighting, and he loses visible access to the entry room where he has left his coat. Meanwhile, Madame Miseria's accomplice searches his coat pockets to obtain information that will allow the palm reader to appear appropriately omniscient (she momentarily disappears behind heavy drapes to be briefed on the information) (24).

Certainly both the bourgeois family and the Gypsy family households are strategic inasmuch as they afford family members a different access to visibility from that afforded visitors. But while domestic architecture helps to organize the bourgeois experience with architecturally designed separations that have defined the bourgeois individual since the eighteenth century, the Gypsy home/business is organized less to define dimensions of individuality within families than to mobilize the family as a collective enterprise and to limit the perceptual capabilities of its clientele. And, revealingly, it is evident that Gypsy practices of solidarity have helped them to maintain vestiges of family life that are no longer the rule among the *gadje*.

There is, for example, an exemplary contrast between repo (and ex-repo) men and Gypsies with regard to their relationship with family life. Most of the repo men are single, and in one case, an ex-repo man is deriving his sex life from, as well as making a living off, the disintegration of the bourgeois family. Trinidad Morales, now a private investigator who helps out with the repossession in this case, specializes in the consequences of family fragmentation. "Divorce work. Insurance frauds. Electronic snooping. Betrayed wives, ready to get even for the husband's infidelities by clocking a little motel time of their own with the investigator who'd wise'd them up to them cheatin' hearts" (20–21). In contrast, the Gypsy Rudolph Marino has sex in a hotel with Marla, a check-in clerk, because she might prove useful to his scam, which requires making use of the hotel. His seduction is, in effect, pro-(Gypsy) family (18).

Once outside the Gypsy domestic space, the action in *32 Cadillacs* is more a free-for-all, in which outcomes are a function of different abilities to manage public space. As the Gypsy rip-off and repo men's counter-attack unfolds, the city's streets, highways, bars, hotels and motels, banks, and car dealerships are described in detail. What on a casual reading appears to be mere background becomes pertinent to a reading of the spaces of modernity when foregrounded. It becomes evident that the city's circuits of exchange function in a built social domain that shapes experience, relationships, and opportunities. The windows, elevators, automobiles, telephones, filing systems, open hotel lobbies, and motel complexes are expressive of technological developments that have increasingly reconfigured the boundaries between public and private space.

Moreover, because the primary personae in the detective story make use of the increased porosity between the public and private domains and, most essentially, use the city's temporal rhythms to make the right moves in the right places at the right times, the moments and venues of their interactions reveal complexities of the public-private relationships that are fugitive in the more abstract genres of social or political theory. Nevertheless, in some ways the staging of the Gypsy–repo-men encounter in this detective story conceals a profound and pervasive incompatibility between the commercial life of the city—the derivative, monetary interests to which individuals and groups are connected—and a deeper set of interests that attach to what might best be termed the ethical life. To treat this second domain of interests, we may appropriately summon Hegel once more, this time for a more appreciative hearing.

Although the later Hegel saw the state as a vehicle of history's ineluctable capacity to reconcile contradictions, an earlier Hegel was convinced of an irreconcilable conflict between the commercial and "ethical life" *(Sittlichkeit)*. He referred to the relationship between the two as "tragic," because, from the point of view of the ethical life, the commercial life is both necessary and destructive.[29] Because Hegel's observation provides a framing for the connection between a spatial practice (the public-private division) and interests, we need to find a story and genre that are even more sensitive than *32 Cadillacs* to the connection between spatiality and interests and that, at the same time, treat the ways in which contemporary technologies affect relations between families and both civic and commercial arenas.

The films of Atom Egoyan provide a genre and set of themes that fulfill these requirements. As one summary treatment of his corpus puts it, "Atom Egoyan's movies show a world where two traditionally incompatible spheres are joined: the private intimacies of family life and sexuality, and the public access allowed by modern media technologies."[30] Effectively, he shows the ways in which contemporary technologies disturb the intimacies of the private sphere. While some of his early films focus on the media-related effects on the libidinal stresses within families (for example, *Speaking Parts* and *Family Viewing*), his 1997 film, *The Sweet Hereafter,* based on Russell Banks's novel of the same name, extends its treatment of the disruption of family to the interaction of small-town families with the outer worlds in which media and capital produce forces that intervene in their most intimate concerns, especially their attempts to achieve solace in the face of an event involving profound loss.

Egoyan's *The Sweet Hereafter* provides an appropriate vehicle to extend the analysis, because, as a filmic story about a town's tragedy (many families have lost children in a school bus accident), it operates within the more pervasive, Hegelian tragedy. Specifically, the carriers of a primarily commercially driven motivation invade the communal space of a small Canadian town, disrupting its enclosed moral order. Moreover, the conjunctures and disjunctures in the film reveal the contingencies of interests. On the one hand, a deep, common interest in protecting children connects the characters—the people of the town and a personal injury lawyer—on different sides of an encounter central to the film. But, on the other hand, this encounter evokes disparate motivations. It pits a mutual support structure of grieving parents (part of the local *Sittlichkeit*) against a lawyer whose interest is in amplifying their anger and muting their grief; he wants to articulate their economic vulnerability and anger to produce a class-action suit, whereas before they had struggled to maintain a community based on the bonds of grief-produced mutual sympathy.

The Sweet Hereafter

The critical insights deriving from Atom Egoyan's treatment of Russell Banks's novel owe as much to his use of the film genre as they do to the story line of the screen play.[31] There is, first of all, a productive relationship between the spatial practices involved in the story and the spatiality of film in general. The story begins when a lawyer, Mitchell Stephens, enters the town of Sam Dent. Whereas Stephens is first shown, with zoom and framing shots, in the confined space of his car, the town is presented continually with a wide-angle lens and with panning and tracking shots that explore the town's extension and boundaries. Sam Dent's surrounding mountains give it, at least physically, a definitive boundary, and the camera leaves viewers with the impression that the life-world enclosed by the mountains is more or less available to direct vision. The spatial mapping supplied by the camera work accords with the social situation. The people of the town "have a sense of community; they know where they're from. They are not lost like urban individuals."[32]

We learn early on that the invading lawyer is a representative of shaping forces outside the town. The story then proceeds in what Noel Burch has identified as the two kinds of filmic space (discussed in chapter 2): "that included within the frame and that outside the frame."[33] A world of predatory commercial interests outside the town has become cognizant of the town's tragedy. Mountains are no barrier to media, and air routes and roads also make the town rapidly accessible. As a result, the sets of parents who have lost children cannot be left to grieve within the isolation of the community. The personal injury lawyers on their way in, seeking to profit from the town's tragedy, are attempting to turn an "accident" into some form of responsible agency. They want to find "deep pockets," belonging either to the town or to the bus manufacturer.

Mitchell Stephens (played by Ian Holm) in the carwash, in *The Sweet Hereafter* (1997), before entering the town of Sam Dent to scout for business as a personal injury lawyer.

Other forces outside the frame are also apparent in the filmic story. The Walkers, the first set of parents encountered by Stephens, run a failing motel that cannot compete with publicly owned motel chains on the same route, which connects the town with several others. There is, therefore, a homology between the structure of the film and the situation of the town. They have the forces of political economy pressing at their frame and boundary, respectively. The duality of filmic space is well suited, then, to represent the "outside" as a set of commercial forces, an outside anonymous public—the aggregated shareholders in motel corporations, who cannot be assembled to effect the management of corporations much less the life spaces on which they impact.[34]

In addition to its treatment of space, however, the temporal structure of cinema contributes to its critical perspective. Egoyan's film thinks with time images as well as with its shot-produced spatiality. Although the camera is often trained on the lawyer, Mitchell Stephens, the implications the film generates are a function of the sequence of shots. As noted in chapter 2, the "time image" constitutes a way of reading events that is more critical than mere perception.[35] As long as the camera merely followed action, the image of time was indirect, presented as a consequence of motion. The new "camera consciousness" is no longer defined by the movements it is able to follow. Now, "even when it is mobile, the camera is no longer content to follow the character's movement."[36] The thinking articulated through a film, whose shots shift among a variety of scenes and alter their depth of focus, constitutes meaning not on the basis of the experiences of individual characters but on the basis of the way an ensemble of shots are connected. As is noted in the discussion of *Dead Man* in chapter 2, a crystalline, or nonlinear, film, which is also true of *The Sweet Hereafter*, provides a critical view of the episodes. In this case, the "non-chronological time" of the film interrupts the model of meaning that would obtain if an "organic narration," composed of movement images, privileged the tensions explicitly acknowledged by Mitchell Stephens and the various persons with whom he interacts.[37] Subordinating movement to his structuring of time images, the encounters Egoyan directs add up to a critical event that illuminates "our-time."

Well aware of the critical resources that derive from a crystalline filmic narration, Egoyan notes that "weaving time" is what most essentially constitutes his direction of a filmic story in which narrative closure is resisted: "There's not a lot left to discover when I feel that the story is unfolding from point A to point B. . . . I find it's more exciting when I'm not entirely sure what the alchemy of it all will be and I have to put them together and find out."[38] Certainly Banks's novel generates critical insight as well. But given the novelistic genre of Banks's version of the story, its insights are a function of the way it composes different voices. Throughout Banks's *Sweet Hereafter,* there are shifts in voice, as different characters take over the narration. In Egoyan's version, narrative voice is displaced by the composition of camera shots. The absence of a narrator's voice is wholly appropriate to Egoyan's demonstration that the tensions produced in encounters of difference are less a matter of the incommensurate forms of consciousness of the various characters than a matter of a difference of spatiotemporal "habitus."[39] Egoyan shows a community whose "horizon of experience" is, at least in part, spatially confined;[40] it is bounded by its physical separation from other places.

In contrast, Mitchell Stephens's domain of experience is shown to be horizonless. When he is not in the town, he spends his time on his cell phone, in his car, and on a plane. And even when he is in the town, he is partly outside it; in one scene, for example, he excuses himself from a face-to-face conversation to answer a call on his cell phone from his daughter. Stephens's horizonless habitus is not a matter of idiosyncracy. He reflects an aspect of modernity—the dissolution of space in favor of a temporal simultaneity—that has not yet dominated the town of Sam Dent. Egoyan's critical mixing of temporal traces (flashbacks to Stephens's past as well as to the pasts of some of the townspeople of Sam Dent) intensifies what is at stake in the encounters between the different types of habitus that emerge out of different temporal traces.

As the quintessential modern person, Mitchell Stephens inhabits the life-world as an information-processing node. In the opening scenes, it is his cell phone that connects him to people, both an impersonal operator, whom he calls when he is stuck in a car wash, and his daughter, Zoe, who calls him frequently to ask for money to manage her drug habit. On the occasions in which he must negotiate space (for example, hurrying from a house in Sam Dent to his car to fetch legal forms), his movements are the awkward ones of persons accustomed to having mechanical and informational prostheses connect them with what is distant.

Stephens's uncomfortable management of space and face-to-face encounters is part of a pervasive aspect of modern life. He is a product of what Paul Virilio calls "the urbanization of time"; his "perceptual faculties" have been "transferred one by one to machines."[41] He is part of a modernity whose most significant alterations are owed to a collapse of local time and space that began perhaps when the first time signal was sent around the world from the Eiffel Tower in 1913.[42] In sum, Mitchell

Stephens walking, temporarily disconnected from his modern communication devices and forced to navigate in a communal, face-to-face reality rather than a virtual reality.

Stephens's bodily gestures have seemingly atrophied through the prolonged use of informational equipment and motorized vehicles. Once unplugged or unseated, he has difficulty transacting in a world of spatial inhibitions and barriers to effortless motion or contact. For example, he resists interacting with his seat mate on a plane by resorting to his headset, which connects him with the plane's entertainment programs. A jumbo jet, as Kittler has described it, is "a multimedia embryonic sack supplied through channels or navels that all serve the purpose of screening out the background," an experience- and memory-effacing set of media deliveries where, for example, "the passengers' ears are listlessly hooked up to one-way earphones. . . ."[43]

The "sack" fits Stephens well. He moves between such spaces in which relationships outside are fed in through his electronic prostheses. As a result, he lacks continuity in an experiential spatial location. His reliance on communication technologies has shattered the coherence of his personal experiences. When he learns that his seat mate on the plane is a childhood friend of his daughter, Zoe (in a conversation that happens only because his headset malfunctions), he is unable to recollect that the woman's father was once his business partner. As Egoyan notes, the character Mitchell Stephens lives in the immediacy of his "satisfying occupation—immersing himself in other people's grief, but without really understanding how to deal with, in the longer term, his profound sense of loss."[44]

Only a switch in genres allows Stephens to refocus on the continuity of his life-world. When he abandons his headset and gets absorbed into the conversation with his daughter's friend, he tells a story about a traumatic episode in the life of his young family. He had to transport his infant daughter from a remote cabin to a hospital after she had been bitten by a black widow spider. As the film through flashback shows his frantic trip to a hospital, during which he had to be prepared to perform a tracheotomy, we see him staring intently at his daughter. If her reaction to the spider's poison were to cause her throat to close, he would have to become an amateur surgeon on the basis of a doctor's instructions over the phone. As it turns out, keeping his daughter alive has been Stephens's lifelong task ever since, although he no longer has her in sight. Indeed, it is the primary "interest" that he has in common with the parental couples of Sam Dent.

However, before exploring that common interest, it is important to note the most significant difference between Stephens's world and that of the community he invades for profit. Unlike Stephens, the residents of Sam Dent exist in a frontier between modern forces of simultaneity and the face-to-face world of spatially enclosed communities. They function in a sphere that has not been fully absorbed by modern, globalized corporations. In some cases, family space and work space coincide (as is the case of the Gypsy families represented in *32 Cadillacs*). For example, Stephens's first visit is to the Walker couple, who have lost a child in the school bus accident and live in a motel they own and manage. Later, he visits the Ottos, who have also lost a child and live primarily off the crafts that Wanda Otto makes in their home.

Nevertheless, the wider world is impinging on Sam Dent. Paul Sarossy, the cinematographer, uses a wide screen format to "connect this story of a small town to the larger world." And this format, which permits close-ups and the wider context in the same frame, allows Egoyan to achieve his plan of fitting "the terrain of the face . . . in the context of the greater geography."[45] A composition of "perception images" within a spatially oriented, filmic enunciation shows how personality is subordinated to a geographically situated habitus.[46]

The life-space of the small town is under a technological assault that precedes Mitchell Stephens, however. Wendell Walker, the motel owner, is first encountered when he is summoned from in front of his television set to converse with Stephens. He is a hockey fan, and it becomes evident that his sports fanaticism has him connected to a global mediascape. It is doubtless not incidental, moreover, that Walker, a virtual recluse, whose sociality is primarily a function of his distant connection with other television viewers, utters disparaging remarks about the other grieving parents, remarks that are a function of his prejudices rather than direct experience. When, for example, he expresses an inference that the Ottos are drug users, his wife, Risa, retorts, "You don't know that."

The town's mountain horizon does not, therefore, constitute the entire horizon of experience. Competing with the "topical" place is the "teletopical" place.[47] This is a more general tendency of modernity, for, as Paul Virilio puts it, "the skyline that once limited the perspective of our movements is today joined by the square horizon of the TV set . . ." (90), with the result that "contemporeity" is privileged over local citizenship, because the "live broadcast" dominates the "geopolitical reality" (47) of much of the town (although the town's annual fair is an instance of reaffirmation of locality). Like Virilio, Egoyan (in most of his films) articulates a continuous fascination with the implications of video and other technologies for social relations. But Egoyan does not share Virilio's dystopic tone. "There's a real ambiguity about the role of technology," he notes while discussing his film *Family Viewing*.[48] He avoids a moralistic posture; instead of demonizing technology, he shows how people resist the kind of predatory insensitivity that modernity has wrought.

Although some couples in Sam Dent succumb to Mitchell Stephens's strategy of amplifying anger (and ignoring the mutual support structure) to collect grievances, some of the parents and one survivor of the accident, Nicole, manage to resist. That Dolores Driscoll, the school bus driver, heeds her husband Abbott's injunction to rely on peers rather than legalities is doubtless a function of her connection with everyone; she saw all the children and their parents almost daily when she did her pick-ups and drop-offs. In addition, the parent most resistant to the class-action suit is Billy Ansell, the widower who followed the school bus daily in his truck, seemingly reluctant to let his children out of sight. It is ultimately his resistance to the suit, expressed to Nicole's parent within her hearing, that makes Nicole resolve to testify in a way that destroys Stephens's litigation (she lies and claims that she saw the speedometer reading seventy miles per hour before the accident).

Indeed, the key encounter of the film is between Stephens and Ansell. When Ansell finds Stephens examining the damaged bus in the yard of his garage, he tries to dissuade him from pursuing the suit and threatens to assault him. In response, Stephens evokes a shared interest; he tells Ansell that he is also a grieving parent. His daughter, he says, is a drug addict. Ansell asks why he is telling him this, but doubtless he knows that it is a gesture designed to unite their concerns. In any case, Stephens is partly correct; he and the parents of the town have had a common interest. Both have striven, largely unsuccessfully, to keep their children alive

(Stephens learns near the end of the film that his daughter, Zoe, is HIV positive). Despite their differences, then—one is connected to his child by phone, and the other tried not to let his children out of sight—they have had a common interest. They are both trying to deal with the presence of death in life. Moreover, both have been defeated by unmanageable contingencies. Like the rest of the bereaved parents, both have struggled with modernity's primary parental ambivalence, holding on to their children's affectionate dependence and, at the same time, qualifying them to survive outside the home.

The ambivalence is most evident in the case of Nicole, whose father had tried to foster her singing career but, at the same time, had drawn her into an incestuous sexual relationship. She is destined to remain at home because she is left paralyzed by the bus accident. Nevertheless, she is given a technology that will provide her with a virtual escape. Mitchell Stephens, the man who lives primarily as a global information node, has given her a computer as a gift. Nicole's situation, along with a number of other examples of troubled families and unhappy interfamilial encounters canvassed during the filmic montage of the story, makes it clear that an enclosed horizon of experience is not an unmitigated advantage for producing a felicitous connection between private and public interests. Technologies, which reinflect the distribution of spaces, operate along with other contingencies to disturb attempts at naturalizing and moralizing modes of social organization.

Accordingly, throughout *The Sweet Hereafter,* Egoyan chooses critical thinking over moralizing. He recognizes that incest is an act of coercion, but violence and domination are not his theme. He treats the incest less as an act of coercion than as "something where distinctions get blurred . . . lines are crossed, and characters find themselves in situations which are just as damaging—or more damaging—than the other kind of incest."[49] After the accident ends Nicole's incestuous relationship with her father, she becomes a redemptive figure rather than a victim. In her act of destruction of Stephens's class-action suit, she restores the possibility of a communal resolution to the town's collective grief.

Conclusion: Ambiguated Spheres and the Fate of the Ethical Life

The genre of storytelling embedded in Egoyan's *Sweet Hereafter* effects an important set of changes in the different characters. Storytelling breaks through the enclosed horizon of experience of the people of Sam Dent and opens up the horizonless world of immediacy of Mitchell Stephens. In particular, two stories told in the film, one read by Nicole and one told by Stephens, are the kind of "heterotopias" (spaces of otherness) to which Foucault refers when he notes that some acts of imagination "create a space of illusion that exposes every real space . . . as still more illusory."[50]

In Nicole's case, her reading of "The Pied Piper of Hamelin" to Billy Ansell's children (a scene repeated throughout the film with flashbacks) has special resonance with her situation. Just as the children in the story (with the exception of the crippled one left behind) are liberated to a "sweet hereafter," a place outside the mean-spiritedness of the town, Nicole is left behind, a cripple now confined to a (formerly) incestuous household. But her acts of imagination, evinced at first in her reading of the story, have liberated her from the enclosed horizon of experience of both her home and Sam Dent. And her ultimate act of imagination, an invention of a speeding bus, saves the children of the town, allowing them to remain in the "sweet hereafter" rather than being brought back for an unseemly litigious encounter. Her participation in spaces of illusion (stories) takes her outside the stifling privacy of her home and also outside legalities that would draw the children into a space of informational immediacy and out of the special place within which they reside in the townspeople's memories.

Nicole's reading of the Pied Piper story turns out to be allegorical. Among other things it fulfills the vocation of the storyteller to which Benjamin refers in his remark, "Death is the sanction of everything that the storyteller can tell. He has borrowed his authority from death."[51] Storytelling allows death a presence. It is the genre of imagination that recognizes the pervasive presence of death in life. Temporally, death is at once contingent and noncontingent. Its ultimate presence is inevitable, but the when of its appearance is a matter of uncontrollable contingencies. For Benjamin, displacement of the death-presencing craft of the storyteller by informational genres constitutes a degradation of experience.[52] Accordingly, we can read Mitchell Stephens's existence in the world of information as intimately tied to his attempt to degrade the experience of death for the people of Sam Dent. Virilio's distinction between the roles of information and memory captures very well Stephens's disposition throughout most of the film. Virilio notes—in a remark that locates Stephens in dramatic contrast with the people of Sam Dent, who enjoy a visible connection with their horizon of experience—that with remote control and long-distance "telepresence," we approach a "transparent horizon" and become a society with "no extension and no duration," only an intense and immediate presence.[53]

Technologies have in effect confiscated Mitchell Stephens's depth of field (an insight that is captured cinematographically throughout Egoyan's *Sweet Hereafter*, for perception shots from Stephens's vantage point rarely achieve a long focus). He lives in a world of instantaneous information, or what Virilio calls "immediate memory" (26). It is therefore not surprising that, at the outset of his conversation with his daughter's childhood friend on the plane, he cannot recall her name or even the name of her father, who was his business partner. Stephens's practice of an immediate, instead of a durational, memory provides the most significant contrast with the bereaved people of Sam Dent. The bus driver, Dolores Driscoll, for example, keeps the dead children in her memory with pictures of them on the wall of her living room and struggles to keep them alive with her grammar. In her conversation with Stephens her choice of tenses waivers between the past and present when she refers to the children individually. Unlike Stephens, whose participation in modernity's destruction of duration has effaced his memory, Driscoll's loss of a sense of time is a result of "grief and shock."[54]

But, again, the strongest contrast is between Mitchell Stephens and Billy Ansell. In a conversation with his paramour, Risa Walker, Ansell speaks about an important episode of duration, "the pleasure of the interval,"[55] that he has enjoyed while waiting (sometimes in vain) for her to join him for their liaisons in a motel room. The period of waiting had created a space for him to recall his past life, to summon in memory how life had been before his wife died. Significantly, motel rooms are neither distinctly private nor public. Foucault includes them among his heterotopias.[56] They are spaces of respite, allowing for contemplation outside life's more familiar, temporally restricted zones of interaction.

Finally, however, Mitchell Stephens's experience of duration/memory does not turn out to be a lost cause. As he tells the story of his frantic trip with his daughter to a hospital, he is extracted from the world of information and absorbed into memory. He has abandoned his headset and has used the duration of his flight to tell a story whose details are aided by camera flashbacks. The filmic montage provides a reinforcement of the time images in the story, as Stephens's predatory commercial aims seem to be temporarily suspended while he tells the personal story of a near-tragedy. Like the assemblage of camera shots from different periods of his life, telling the story locates him in a duration that reminds us what he and the people of Sam Dent have as an ultimate common interest—participating in life and providing each other with solace, in the recognition that everyone's life is ultimately intimate with death.

4. Literary Geography and Sovereign Violence: Resisting Tocqueville's Family Romance

> Democracy loosens social ties but tightens natural ones; it brings kindred
> more closely together, while it throws citizens more apart.
> **—Alexis de Tocqueville, *Democracy in America***

"American" Families

The initial impetus for this chapter is Alexis de Tocqueville's discussion
of the influence of democracy on "the American family," from which the
epigraph on social versus kindred ties is taken.[1] Restricting his observations to a comparison between the traditional aristocratic family in
Europe and white bourgeois families in nineteenth-century America and
perceiving what he regarded as a spirit of equality prevailing "around the
domestic hearth" (2:193), Tocqueville imagined, simultaneously, a breakdown of "all the old conventional rules of society" (2:197) and a closer
family bond (especially between fathers and sons). Such a bond, he
noted, reflects an affection and intimacy not afforded by the patriarchal,
command-based relationships in aristocratic families. Not unlike Hegel,
Tocqueville regarded familial bonds as "natural" and therefore moral.
Within the aristocratic family, which Tocqueville juxtaposes to the American democratic family, relationships were, he states, based on socially induced conventions. Inequalities in the social order impose norms of inequality on the aristocratic family, even forms of vassalage, leaving little
space for "nature" to direct relationships.[2]

However, Tocqueville's sanguine view of democracy's effect on "the
family," especially his celebration of the emergence of a natural atmosphere of "mildness" *(douceur),* because the conventions of the aristocratic, estate-based social order have been abrogated, comprehended
only a small part of the American family scene. An inspection of Tocqueville's travel notes reveals that his remarks about the American family are

based primarily on his encounters with those who hosted him—white, well-to-do families. His initial experiences of American domesticity took place when he and Beaumont went "out into society" in the evenings in New York. Among the "several American families" they saw "fairly often" were the families of Mr. Prime, a banker who, Tocqueville noted, "is the richest businessman in New York," and the family of Mr. Livingston, "the Prime Minister of the United States."[3] The restricted scope of Tocqueville's generalizations about American domesticity becomes evident when one escapes the confines of his narrow gaze at "the American family" and takes an intimate look at the nineteenth-century, antebellum African American family. Although there are abundant images of, for example, African American domesticity in the nineteenth century, which expose Tocqueville's innocence of the variations in the conditions of American domesticity, an imaginary conversation in a piece of contemporary fiction serves the purpose well.

In Russell Banks's novel *Cloudsplitter,* a series of conversations about black families takes place between the abolitionist John Brown's son Owen and three African American men, one fugitive slave and two former slaves. First, Owen engages the free Mr. Fleete:

> "Do you have a wife or children Mr. Fleete?"
> "No, my wife is dead Mr. Brown. She died young. At about the age of that woman yonder. Died without children."
> "And you never thought to marry again?"
> [Mr. Fleete] Sighed and studied the pipe in his brown hand.[4]

Then he engages the free Lyman Epps:

> "I want to ask you about your wife Susan, did you come out of slavery together?"
> "No, she come north alone."
> "You don't have any children?"
> "No, we don't. Susan has children though. Three of them. They got sold off south, sent to Georgia someplace, she don't know where."
> "What about their father . . . who was he?"
> Lyman turned and looked at me, said nothing, and returned his gaze to the ceiling. (220–21)

And finally, he engages the fugitive James Cannon:

> "Do you have a family in Canada who will help you settle there?"
> "Family? No not exactly Mr. Brown . . . "

"What is the name of the man who was your master?"

"His name? Name Samuel . . . Mister Samuel Cannon."

"The same as yours?"

"Yes, Mister Brown, same as mine. Same as his father's too. Same as my mother."

"So you were born a slave to Mister Samuel Cannon, and your mother was born his father's slave?"

"Yes, Mr. Brown. She surely wasn't Mas' Cannon's wife."

"Who was your father then? What happened to him?"

He looked away from me again. "Don't know. Long gone." (222)

After this last conversation, Owen confesses: "I'd finally lost that punishing innocence, and I felt ashamed of my inquiry" (223).

The innocence of which the fictionalized Owen speaks, an innocence shared by Tocqueville (and generations of neo-Tocquevilleans since), has also been evident in policy discourses focused on the African American family. It surfaced famously in the Moynihan Report, published in the mid-1960s, in which the economic inequality between white and black Americans was blamed in part on absent fathers and the resulting matriarchal structure of black families.[5] Among the more or less continuous and largely contentious reactions to the categories and ethnic imaginaries in the report, Hortense Spillers's is the most congenial to what is implied in Russell Banks's representation of the fictional Owen Brown's innocence:

> "Ethnicity" itself identifies a total objectification of human and cultural motives—the "white" family, by implication and the "Negro Family," by outright assertion, in a constant opposition of binary meanings. Apparently spontaneous, these "actants" are wholly generated, with neither past nor future, as tribal currents moving out of time. Moynihan's "families" are pure present and always tense.[6]

As both Banks and Spillers imply, white and black families are neither analytically nor historically distinct. From the initial fracture of black families through enslavement, through the "corporeal domination" that included the submission of black women to "rape and forced reproduction,"[7] to a history of postslavery subjugation by white-controlled institutions, black families have been intimately interconnected with the practices of power, sexuality, and exclusion of whites.[8] There is, therefore, a significant ambiguity in the very reference to either black or white families. And, there are further complications that subvert the application of ethnicity modifiers to "American" families. For example, in a 1928 study of "the ancestry and physical traits of African Americans," of "1551 Howard University students . . . 27.2 percent claimed to have some Native American ancestry."[9] But the discourse of ancestry is only one among many that are applied to family identities. The writer Kathryn Morgan, an African American with both Native and Euro-American family heritage, for example,

> resisted any singular definition of racial identity when she noted that her great grandmother, great uncles, and great aunt were "white by nature, black by law, African and Cherokee by choice." . . . Labeling themselves "African and Cherokee by choice" allowed her relatives to reconstruct for themselves and others the racial categories assigned to them by law. . . . Remembering Native American and African ancestry became part of a way of resisting a simplistic legal definition of themselves as "colored."[10]

African American resistance to identity imposition has been complemented by a more general attempt to maintain family solidarity. Herbert Gutman's historical research has shown that the black family, even under slavery, has operated within a complex normative culture that has helped it to maintain family ties, even during circumstances of forced dispersion.[11] To overcome the innocence within which the black family is simply judged or interrogated on the basis of romantic imagery of the white conjugal family, thought to be historically segregated from the black family, one must recover diverse genealogies. Such a recovery, which is a small part of Banks's project in his historical novel, requires an ethicopolitical will and a perspective on the political that has been largely absent in national and family histories and in the social and political treatises composing both the American literary canon and social science corpus.

The Perspective

Turning first to the issue of a perspective on the political, the approach to democracy of Jacques Rancière supplies an exemplary antidote to Tocquevillean, liberal constructions of "the political." Contrary to Tocqueville, for whom democracy is both a mode of popular sovereignty (ascribed to a homogeneous citizen body) and a supporting system of social mores, Rancière states:

> Democracy is not a regime or a social way of life. It is the institution of politics itself, the system of forms of subjectification through which any order of distribution of bodies into functions corresponding to their

"nature" and places corresponding to their functions is undermined, thrown back on its contingency.[12]

Politics, for Rancière, is not the interaction of the parts of the social order that are already politically qualified. And politics cannot be mapped on the basis of the spaces created by recognized administrative and legal authorities. Politics exists, rather, through "interruption" (13); it takes place when a space for contestatory speech is opened up, when something "incommensurable at the heart of the distribution of speaking bodies" becomes evident (19).

Instead of thinking the political on the basis of the relation of "the social" as a whole to a political order, Rancière sees politics as an event of "subjectification." Subjectification refers not to identities but to the introduction of a new form of political qualification within social space. While identities simply reinforce existing spatial organization and support the existing deployment of policy problematics, subjectification qualifies what has hitherto been unqualified; it points to an antagonism between recognized parts of the community and those parts that have not been legitimate parts of the social body. Contesting a model of "political reflection and action" in which one identifies politics with a generalized citizen identity, with "the *self* of a community,"[13] Rancière speaks of the process of subjectification, which creates new capacities for enunciation that point to the institutionalization of a "wrong."

When he refers to a wrong, Rancière is operating within a logic of identification different from that which is typical of the Tocquevillean liberal discourse. The identification of a political subject marks a "disparity not an identity, " and "politics begins when those who have no share begin to have one."[14] Rather than accepting the known and legitimated set of parties within an order, Rancière insists that no parties exist until a wrong (a situation of inequality) is declared. Politics, accordingly, makes an appearance in the form of events in which people become articulate political subjects by resisting structures of incommensurability that have denied them speaking parts within the order.[15]

Rancière's way of constituting the political accords well with the sentiments of Edward Ball, whose contemporary study of his own family history, which takes him back to his slaveowning and -trading ancestors in antebellum South Carolina, evinces what I have called the necessary ethicopolitical will to reconfigure the politics of "the American family." The initial provocation for Ball is his father's oft repeated "little joke," in which he makes light of his family's slaveowning past: "There are five things we don't talk about in the Ball family . . . religion, sex, death, money, and the Negroes."[16] Seeking to recover the extent to which the family's plantation history is a part of his patrimony, Ball investigates the genealogies of both his white ancestors and the slaves they owned. The implications of the shared history of some of South Carolina's white and black families, disclosed in Ball's text, are treated later in this analysis. At this juncture, I turn to some of the genre-related bases of Tocqueville's perpetuation of innocence in comparison with Banks's and Ball's exposure of it.

Narrative Space and Political Space

Tocqueville's rendering of the American democracy cannot be understood outside the locus of enunciation within which it is generated. His "America" emerges in a convergence of his understanding of America as a unique, spatiotemporal event and his understanding of his own location in space and time, as a citizen of a republican France recently extracted from a monarchy and an estate-based, aristocratic system of privilege. Tocqueville's analysis of the American spaces of association that fell within his observations is based on what he saw as a radical deterritorialization. He attributed the vibrancy of civic activity to America's departure from the ground plan of aristocracy, the estate-based society, under siege but still significant on the European continent.[17]

Bracketing the more carceral dimensions of the United States, for example, plantation space, which imposed on the American landscape, during the period of slavery and subsequently, "a distinct regime of political, economic, and ethnic regulation,"[18] Tocqueville saw mainly "democratic" proclivities that were enabled, he thought, by a more open model of space, an opportunity for circulation and place-making not afforded by the European system of social boundaries, land tenure, and inheritance structures. Tocqueville recognized that the new land entitlement practices contributed to a social egalitarianism (among Euro-Americans) that shaped American civic life. While he displayed significant failures of insight with respect to spaces of otherness, he is justly credited with articulating important insights about the new spaces of sociability and their "political" implications (if one restricts the notion of the political to the legally sanctioned interactions of sovereign citizens).

When it came to analyzing the nonwhite others in America, Tocqueville's "gaze," his epistemic orientation toward what he saw, was organized on the basis of a distinctive "chronotope" (M. M. Bakhtin's term for the way a literary genre organizes the time/space of its articulations).[19]

Temporally, Tocqueville's text (as John Stuart Mill explicitly recognized) is narrative in structure: Democracy is the political form of the future, and the American democracy is emblematic of an inevitable historical tendency, the direction in which society is "irresistibly tending."[20] And as a society that has inherited European civilization, its political institutions represent the inevitable advance of a civilizationally encouraged, republican politics that will displace other modes of political organization—dynastic, tribal, and so on. Democracy for Tocqueville also represents a civilizationally sanctioned mode of political economy, an authoritative model of exchange in which places achieve value on the basis of actions that turn land and "natural resources" into finished, exchangeable goods.

Spatially, while Tocqueville's civilizationally oriented moral geography favored the culture of Europe, his nation state–oriented model of time favored the nation building practices of Euro-Americans. Tocqueville's world is a system of states with no place for the political expressions of nations without states, much less for captive peoples. Indeed, so focused was Tocqueville on America as an exemplar of the political future that he evacuated it of recalcitrant indications, for example, the prior, Native American nations with which Euro-Americans were at war: "One could still properly call North America an empty continent, a deserted land waiting for inhabitants."[21] Tocqueville is speaking not of any inhabitants, of course, but of divinely sanctioned ones. Ultimately, his failure to recognize and sanction the complex social and civic organization of Native Americans derives from his commitment to what William Connolly has called a "civi-theo-territorial complex,"[22] to a civil society organized as a territorial state, with Christian monotheism providing the "cultural glue binding the civi-territorial complex together" (169).[23]

Apart from the civilizational, nationalistic, and religious conceptions guiding Tocqueville's interpretations of the American democracy, his insights and blindnesses are genre related. In particular, his perspective on Native Americans, within which he attributes to them a nobility but not a coherent nationhood or culture, is part of a venerable tradition of romantic travel writing in which "noble savagery alternated with counterimages of ignobility: indigenous peoples as wild, ugly, childlike, irrational, and degenerate, horrific reinventions of classical Christian notions of barbarism and depravity."[24] At the same time, however, Tocqueville's commitment to the European form of the nation-state as the future of political organization constitutes the dominant chronotope of his writing. While his inland travel itinerary was chosen to provide a glimpse of wilderness and its wild denizens (he and Beaumont "were determined

not to miss savages in a purely savage setting" [754]), his movement
through the eastern states was a Euro-American sovereignty-affirming
venture.

The map of Tocqueville's route, taken from a web site that follows
George Wilson Pierson's account of the Tocqueville-Beaumont itinerary,
is a moral geography as well as an itinerary. While recognizing the political and administrative integrity of the various state jurisdictions and effectively incorporating the carceral structures of the plantations and the
on-going war against Native Americans without visible marking, it inscribes Tocqueville's route. In accord with the map, Tocqueville's accompanying text says, in effect, that politically qualified life is a white phenomenon. Other forms of life receive anthropological rather than
political description: "Indians" and "Negroes" are discussed ethnically
rather than politically in his analysis in "The Three Races in the United
States."[25]

The contemporary virtual traveler can follow Tocqueville by clicking

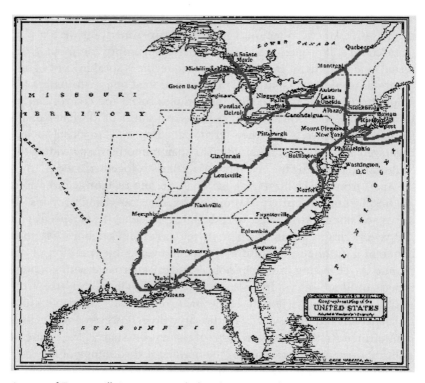

A map of Tocqueville's route traveled with Gustave de Beaumont in 1831.

on various states along his path, retrieving the demographic information about inhabitants, and reading the diary Tocqueville wrote as he traveled. When we arrive in the southern states, for example, we learn (as Tocqueville mentions) that the black population of slaves exceeded the white population. Native American census data are not provided, but, as we know, the various southeastern tribes were on the move. The process of forced removal (a tragedy but an inevitability in Tocqueville's eyes) had been inaugurated under James Monroe's presidency and was being vigorously contested by Cherokees and their supporters, as Tocqueville wrote.

Tocqueville concludes his remarks on "races" with an eye toward the future. His concern with what he sees as an incompatibility among Euros, Indians, and Negroes is bound up with his view of American democracy as the future. Race relations are a "problem" because they threaten the nation segment of the nation-state. They are recalcitrant to the American state's claim to contain a coherent and unified national culture. Tocqueville, like other European nationalists, regarded a homogeneous national culture, with shared mores, as essential to the future of a democratic nation-state. The "Indian" must be a casualty of modernity, and the "Negro," if freed, can never be incorporated successfully within the American society. Neither can ever effectively be part of politically qualified American life.

Given the naive anthropological orientation of his perspective on black Americans, Tocqueville's view of their civic activity was no more acute than his reading of Native Americans (about whose complex organizations, for example, he was virtually clueless). While he construed the Indian as a fiercely proud and independent character type, whom the Europeans had not been able to change (334), he stated that "the Negro makes a thousand efforts to insinuate himself among men who repulse him; he conforms to the tastes of his oppressors, adopts their opinions, and hopes by imitating them to form a part of their community" (334). But what was immediately available to Tocqueville's gaze was misleading. As is evident in the writings of slaves and former slaves, this imitative behavior was one among various modalities of black tactics; it was part of black survival and resistance, a "mask of obedience,"[26] not an essential aspect of "character." Tocqueville's inability to discern a black political struggle, as many were involved in strenuous attempts to retain family attachments and maintain degrees of coherent domesticity, can be attributed to the partialities of his gaze.

Throughout the history of African Americans, from slavery to the present, negotiating an existence in a white-dominated world has required a variety of kinds of role playing, and black society has been more or less continually constituted on the basis of survival and resistance practices. Certainly the spaces of resistant civic association convened by African Americans at the time Tocqueville made his observations were necessarily recalcitrant to the white, sociological gaze. As an extreme but well-known case, Nat Turner's rebellious band met in the woods to plot their insurrection, not only to escape white surveillance, but also because it was the only space not controlled at all moments by their white owners. And Turner's rebellion, which occurred during the summer of 1831, while Tocqueville was making his observations, was not an isolated incident. The bulk of slave testimony indicates that "the slaves were constantly resisting and rebelling."[27]

One need not address the more violent episodes to find active, resistant, black civic action while Tocqueville was in America. In Philadelphia, for example, black abolitionists staged numerous parades when they moved their opposition to slavery "from the pulpit to the street, inventing counter-Independence parades out of the familiar July fourth militia march."[28] It was precisely during the period of Tocqueville's observations that increasingly violent confrontations occurred when white mobs attacked black street demonstrators and civic authorities attempted to curtail the public expression of black community solidarity.[29]

Contemporary black civic association, much of which is organized around familial survival, is also fugitive if one holds out as a model the familiar white spaces of civic assembly (an issue treated below). An inadequate conception of the variety of contemporary social spaces constitutes the primary blindness in the insights of neo-Tocquevillean readings of American civic life. However, before turning to the gap between neo-Tocquevillean discernments and the contemporary black public sphere, we need a deeper appreciation of the differences in the narrative universes within which the Tocqueville, Banks, and Ball texts construct the African American family. It is particularly striking that in Tocqueville's account of the effect of democracy on the American family, he fails to notice the extent to which hybrid families were being produced. He describes Europeans and Negroes as "fastened to each other without intermingling."[30] As a result, unlike Russell Banks and Edward Ball, he offers no effective perspective on the politics of the American family that is sensitive to the structures of domination responsible for producing the configurations of the families of African Americans in the South and the subsequent shared familial histories of Euro- and African Americans. Ultimately, the Banks and Ball texts are accountable to a history of "wrong," while Tocqueville's continues to legitimate that history, through the many valorizing commentaries on Tocqueville and the writings of those whom one could describe as neo-Tocquevilleans. To appreciate the differences among these texts, I turn to a hybrid disciplinary practice and reconstruct them as examples of what Franco Moretti calls "literary geography."[31]

The Narrative Universes of Tocqueville, Banks, and Ball

Moretti's literary geography begins with a mapping of Jane Austen's novels. Locating the venues of interaction of the novels' characters, he shows the immense difference between what the novels were versus what they might have been. For example, there is a glaring cartographic gap between the "industrializing 'Great' Britain of Austen's years" and "the small, homogeneous England of Austen's novels."[32] Austen's "novelistic geography," restricted though it is to the central part of England, reflects an attempt to come to terms with a time of spatial disruption:

> Her plots take the painful reality of territorial uprooting—when her stories open, the family abode is usually on the verge of being lost—and rewrite it as a seductive journey: prompted by desire, and crowned by happiness. They take a *local* gentry, like the Bennets of *Pride and Prejudice,* and join it to the *national* elite of Darcy and his ilk. They take the strong, harsh novelty of the modern state and turn it into a large, exquisite home. (18)

And although romantic alliances are her primary focus, Austen's spatial rendering represents a historical shift from a marriage market restricted to local gentry to one that is more national in scope. There is therefore an interplay between her novels and "the geo-political reality of the nation-state" (17).

Austen's approach to a world of nation-states is not politically acute. For example, characters return from abroad, having magically acquired wealth in the colonies, where "wealth" for Austen is important insofar as it makes a marriage possible, not in relation to the structures of exploitation it may reflect. In such sentimental novels, geography is effectively mythic. As Moretti points out, it is organized to allow for romantic unions. Wealth is simply "found overseas whenever a novel needs it" (27).

The literary geography of Tocqueville's account of the American democracy bears significant comparison with that in Austen's novels. Although his text contains impressive sociological insights, it also resembles a piece of romantic fiction. In addition to its (above-noted) resemblance to his century's romantic travel-writing genre, it has elements of some of the diverse novelistic genres that Bakhtin has differentiated. In places it demonstrates affinities with the "travel novel" in which "the world is a spatial contiguity of differences and contrasts";[33] in places it resembles "the novel of ordeal" in which the hero's adventures constitute a test of his "internal life" and *"habitus"* (13); but Tocqueville's text is closest to the *Bildungsroman* inasmuch as its "organizing force" is held by the future: not "the private biographical future, . . . but the historical future. It is as though the very *foundations* of the world are changing, and man must change along with them" (23–24).

Certainly Austen's texts fit the *Bildungsroman* genre more closely than Tocqueville's. But just as Austen is driven by a sentimental attachment to a future in which "territorial uprooting" is redeemed by marital happiness, Tocqueville is driven by a sentimental attachment to a republican future, in which a homogeneous and democratic national space liberates natural familial relations and redeems the injustices of American justice and the immorality in American morality as they affect the nonwhite segments of the population.[34] However, another literary genre, that of the historical novel, provides a more focused insight into the way Tocqueville's literary geography situates the time-space of his "Indians" and "Negroes." In his analysis of the literary geography of the historical novel, Moretti notes how, in the case of Sir Walter Scott's novels, external borders are political and internal borders are anthropological.[35]

With respect to America's external borders, Tocqueville attributed much of the success of white republicanism in the United States to the "absence of powerful neighbors" sharing borders as well as to the "existence of unexploited lands and resources in the West."[36] The "West" is, for Tocqueville, part of Euro-America's destiny. Like Scott's England, America's internal borders are anthropological. America has "three races" rather than three peoples with alternative territorialized and historical identities. Instead of spaces of national confrontation (Euro- versus Native American), and spaces of national subjugation (Euro- versus African American), America has racial *problems* that threaten its republican and territorial future.

Yet the relationship of time to space works very differently for Tocqueville from how it works for Scott. While Scott read time within space, seeing it in relation to remembrance of a past that contained encounters between family and/or individual biographical time and historical dramas,[37] Tocqueville saw space in terms of its promise for a democratic republican future. His politics was concerned with what he projected as a culturally homogeneous community rather than with, for example, generating the political as an encounter between the forces generating community consent and the history of "wrong" that has attended the violence involved in the forging of the dominant understanding of "community."[38]

In sharp contrast with Tocqueville's chronotope and his politics are Banks's and Ball's texts, both of which are concerned with recovering a history of wrong. As is the case of Tocqueville's report of his American journey, Banks's characters roam across the administrative boundaries of states in antebellum America. And, in addition, the America mapped in *Cloudsplitter* is one in which the routes of fleeing slaves are more clearly defined than the borders of states. Moreover, focused as it is on the abolitionist John Brown's family and the black families with which it collaborates in its war on slavery, the text has a more elaborated treatment of the interplay between political and familial space. As noted in the above-quoted interchange between Brown's son Owen and his black interlocutors, the text treats the articulation of sexual and political domination of whites over blacks. With its focus on the past rather than the future, Banks's text is aimed at overcoming a political innocence. It treats a historical dynamic implicated in the construction of the black family, and by operating within a novelistic genre characterized by heteroglossia (many contending voices),[39] it summons perspectives that challenge an often-unreflected-upon aspect of racism: whites' tendency to regard themselves as colorless.[40]

The political implications of Banks's literary geography—his mapping of white and black family space in the United States—and his treatment of their interaction as he recovers aspects of the antebellum abolitionist movement are developed more elaborately in Ball's *Slaves in the Family*. Ball's literary geography provides a striking contrast with Tocqueville's text. Like Banks's *Cloudsplitter*, Ball's *Slaves in the Family* explores the past. But while *Cloudsplitter* only hints at the historical interrelationships of white and black American families, Ball's text is primarily occupied with them. To explore the consequences of his family's plantation past in South Carolina, Ball interviewed extensively his white relatives and many of the ancestors of the slaves who worked on his family's plantations. He ends up with a comprehensive genealogy of both black and white families (discovering at least one family produced by a Ball ancestor's relationship with a black female slave).[41]

Desiring to depict white and black American families "side by side" (as well as commingled), Ball resists what he refers to as a tendency to "think of American history as a segregated legacy."[42] Temporally, the chronotope of Ball's family biography involves a past that begins in England and Africa in the eighteenth century. Spatially, the plantations of South Carolina are at the center of Ball's family map, but the time-space of his account has trajectories that run from Africa in the eighteenth century to Massachusetts and back to South Carolina in the twentieth (as he traces the ancestries of black families) and from eighteenth-century England to South Carolina and then north on a trajectory from the eighteenth to the twentieth century (as he traces the ancestors of white and white-black families).

Key points on his map include "Sawmill," a town founded by freed slaves in South Carolina (which does not appear on official maps), and Bunce Island in Sierra Leone, where African slave dealers (whose progeny Ball visits) held their captives. In addition, Ball recovers the family genealogies and spatial odysseys of both white (including his own ancestors) and black slave dealers in a quest to face the ethicopolitical implications of a historical wrong with which his family was intimately connected. To appreciate the contrast in political implications between Ball's retrospective journey, driven by a recognition of a history of wrong, and Tocqueville's future-oriented one, we need to understand not only Rancière's construction of the political as a response to the wrongs of exclusion but also alternative topologies of sovereignty.

The Institutional-Juridical and the Biopolitical

As Pierson notes in his summary of Tocqueville's experiences and ideational articulations:

> "Sovereignty of the People." The phrase kept returning with increasing frequency to Tocqueville's pen. However skillfully the fields of sovereignty might be apportioned off between governments, Federal and state, the sovereignty in question was always a delegated power. . . . the ultimate and fundamental authority, remained always the people themselves.[43]

Two aspects of this model of sovereignty stand out. First, who or what are *the* people? Although Tocqueville provided no differentiation when referring to the people as a sovereign body, "the people," as Giorgio Agamben has pointed out, represents a fundamental "biopolitical fracture." On the one hand, it is a figure of inclusion; "the people" refers to "the total state of integrated and sovereign citizens." But, on the other, it is a figure of exclusion, referring to "a fragmentary multiplicity of needful and excluded bodies"—"naked life" as a reality that pulls away from the more integrative concept of political existence.[44] Second, and closely related to the first, Tocqueville's emphasis is on the institutional juridical aspect of sovereignty, specifically on the official territorial administration of the nation-state. As a result, those who are not officially recognized as citizen-subjects become "naked life" rather than politically qualified life. Moreover, a historical process in which blacks, women, and Native Americans have become citizens provides simply a neo-Tocquevillean extension of a moribund, legalistic view of sovereignty. It represents enlarged qualification without providing an appreciation of the violence of disqualification inherent in the institutional-juridical view of sovereignty.

Agamben's introduction of the distinction between naked and politically qualified life into the sovereignty problematic articulates well with Rancière's construction of the political. To relate the issue of sovereignty to a history of wrong, one must appreciate the biopolitical as well as the juridical-institutional aspect of sovereignty. Expanding the idea of sovereignty to treat its productive as well as its legal aspects, Agamben suggests that sovereignty has a complex topology. It exists in "the intersection between the juridico-legal and biopolitical models of power."[45] In addition to its legal supports and legitimations, it is situated in a complex topology of lives, both inside and outside its jurisdiction. Because the deployment of sovereign power is a process of exclusion, acting to locate classes of people outside the law, sovereignty presents a paradox; it "is, at the same time, outside and inside the juridical order" (15). Elaborating Carl Schmitt's emphasis on sovereign power as structured around the making of exceptions, Agamben points out that sovereignty's paradox can be thought of spatially. The law is effectively outside itself inasmuch as sovereignty, as the power to make exceptions, operates outside the law in the process of suspending it. Among the more extreme "exceptions" are, in this century, the Nazi "separation of the Jewish body," legitimated with the view that Jewish life is "life that is unworthy of life" (174), and, in the eighteenth and nineteenth centuries, the separation of the bodies of African American slaves, rendered unworthy of self-ownership.

Tocqueville did not understand this included exclusion on the American scene as part of his celebrated "sovereignty of the people." Slavery, along with the Indian genocide and removal, was certainly an embarrassment to the emerging democratic polity, but it operated outside his notion of the construction of citizen subjectivity. But when sovereignty is understood as functioning in a zone of indistinction between the legal-juridical and the biopolitical, it becomes possible to speak of the violence of sovereignty and thereafter to recover the trace of its biopolitical enactments. In addition to ordering space, sovereignty orders bodies. It segregates bare life from politically eligible life, leaving the former to the vagaries of power while the latter enjoys the privileges of legal protection.

The biopolitics or exclusionary practices of the American union that Tocqueville visited functioned within a kinship discourse. Prior to Tocqueville's visit, the Naturalization Act of 1790, which had added "citizenship to the terms of property and inheritance governed by the patronym," also naturalized "the children of naturalized parents and extend[ed] the (natural) boundaries of the nation to include children born of citizens abroad."[46] By the time of Tocqueville's visit, "the trope of the family connection represents the Union," as Priscilla Wald puts it (84). Tracing the familial tropes generated in various legal decisions, Wald shows how the rhetoric of Justices Taney (in the *Dred Scott* case) and Marshall (in *Cherokee Nation*) evokes a family archetype as their decisions exclude, respectively, African and Native Americans.

The establishment of a Union, symbolically represented as a "white 'family of independent nations'" (85), which was materially realized in the Indian removal and the plantation-based slave economy, is therefore part of the development of the "sovereignty of the people" (to which Tocqueville referred), where sovereignty is a structure of what Agamben refers to as included exclusions. Accordingly, Edward Ball's recovery of the familial after-effects of the Ball family's South Carolina plantations— *their* spheres of included exclusion—whose violent effects are now attenuated but still recordable, constitutes an engagement with part of the history of American sovereignty's biopolitics. It is a history toward which, given his ancestry, he feels accountable. His genealogies provided him and some African American families with a sense of a history of wrong, and they militate against the perspective within which the experiences of African Americans in general can be regarded as a problem peculiar to their "race." Nevertheless, within the dominant liberal political perspective, for example, the one perpetuated by neo-Tocquevilleans, who valorize civic republicanism, the conditions of impoverished African Americans are simply the contemporary version of America's "racial problem." Solving it requires more active citizen participation in *the* public sphere.

The Neo-Tocquevillean Gaze

Like Tocqueville, contemporary neo-Tocquevilleans aggregate "America" within a juridically oriented sovereignty; the United States constitutes one national space for purposes of analyzing the politics of citizenship.

Those invoking Tocqueville of late, for example, regard the problem of inequality as one of a dearth of citizen activism. Effacing spaces of difference and aggregating the social domain within a unifying grammar, they promote inquiry into the relationship of social solidarity and civic-mindedness to a nation's (taken as a whole) democratic performance.[47] This undifferentiated view of political actors, functioning within a homogenized national space (the undifferentiated space of citizenship) conceals specifically situated, historical bodies as sites of the investment of power as well as the ground plan—the organization of social and political space that enables some and disenables others. Instead of treating the political on the basis of enactments that qualify the unqualified, that reconfigure the conditions of possibility for political expression, neo-Tocquevilleans focus on people's participation in traditional civic associations. They judge the level of political engagement on the basis of an extant "propensity to form civil and political organizations," a propensity that the neo-Tocquevillean Robert Putnam, for example, thinks has been lost.[48]

How can we view the social order if we reject Putnam's chronotope, his romanticization of an active civic culture in the past and his model of political action as a set of relays between the home and the PTA organization or the town hall? Putnam's map is effectively a nation dotted with homes where people watch television instead of leaving the house for a collective, politically relevant engagement. However, if we resist the neo-Tocquevillean view that communication technologies are mere diversions from civic life, we can recognize how television (which Putnam blames for the contemporary, civic malaise) and other mass media are used within different social spaces and most significantly are implicated in constituting the spaces within which the political is registered.

An Alternative Mapping of the Political: The Black Public Sphere

As a first approach, it is important to recognize that rather than the "society" unified grammatically within the histories of dominant forms of liberal thinking, what has emerged is a series of fortified enclaves, social spaces differentiated both by their physical barriers and by modes of surveillance. As a result, their modalities of action are affected by the forms of authority and control that differentiate them. Neo-Tocquevilleans fail to recognize both spatial differentiation and spatial interdependence. For example, Putnam wonders about how to solve "the problem of South Central Los Angeles" as if it exists in isolation from U.S. political economy (i.e., from the present forces reproducing inequality among groups and different places) and, more specifically, from the history of wrong involved in helping to create the contemporary situation of urban African Americans. If we heed the forces structuring both national and global economies, the levels of poverty and drug trafficking in South Central Los Angeles are not unrelated to how others live in other places. Income inequality and career choice are produced in relation to the interdependencies involved in national and global political economy. They cannot be understood simply as sets of "data" about various individuals.[49]

The very South Central Los Angeles for which Putnam wishes to provide a solution is a case in point; it is revelatory of the contemporary spatialized mode of control. The state and other powerful economic entities, exercising control over capital investment, play important roles in shaping the terrain within which the African American structures of domesticity and forms of political access or exclusion are constituted. Increasingly, social theorists have recognized that contemporary racism is less a matter of social attitude and explicit legal separation of public services and accommodations and more a system of geographic and economic enclosure. Among the reconfigurations of social space that should attract our attention, then, are what Michael Hardt calls the enclosures that "define the striae of social space";[50] Hardt's insight implies, at a general level, that we can read our epoch in terms of the way it has surpassed the traditional liberal politics of sovereignty. Treating its implications more specifically, we can inquire into the various dimensions of the contemporary black public sphere, which offers a paradigm of politics that cannot be appreciated by taking polls on rates of church attendance and counting bowling league, PTA, and labor organization memberships. Within the traditional models of liberal civil society, recycled by contemporary neo-Tocquevilleans, the black public sphere operates as an "invisible public";[51] it is unmapped in the mainstream, liberal model of American civic space.

Ironically, the chief culprit in Putnam's neo-Tocquevillean lament, television, is a central element in the civic engagement in South Central Los Angeles and other domains of African American domesticity, which have to be regarded as uncivic within his unitary assumptions about society and civic space. Grammatically, and thus analytically, television is not something that a society has as a medium with which to be attuned. Like other forms of technology—writing, paper and electronic money, telephones, virtual communication and interaction—television is part of the social order; it participates in the constitution of space and engagement inflecting the patterns of remote versus local, helping to produce various patterns of use and interaction and, in turn, being shaped by those who use it. Television is part of the structure of association; it has reconfigured the social landscape and, more specifically the relationships between domestic and public space.[52] As a "window on the world," television, like the glass window that preceded it, does more than provide information; it introduces a "confusion over inside and out" and thus over the distinction between the public and the private; among other things, it constitutes neighborhoods electronically.[53] Although some initially saw it in terms of its ecumenical, difference-reducing potential, in some ways it sutures imaginary and real spaces within specific locales.[54]

The black urban experience is a case in point. Like any functioning mode of sociality, black practices of domesticity and public engagement require an effective imaginary, a recognition of the forces constituting the spaces within which one functions and a language that suggests ways both to provoke solidarity within one space and to contest the authoritative forces distributing privileges among social segments. Black music television has been supplying that recognition, and, ironically, it has been enabled by the very commercial forces that are responsible for producing much of the separateness of black living spaces. Although until recently television programing gave relatively little coverage to black music, it is an increasing feature of music television MTV, especially rap. Most significant, since the late 1980s, rap music has created a relay between television and the black ghetto. As Tricia Rose notes, "Nothing is more central to rap's music video narratives than situating the rapper in his or her milieu and among one's crew or posse."[55] Unlike, for example, the heavy metal features, which usually locate the singers in a concert hall, "rap music videos are set on buses, subways, in abandoned buildings, and almost always in black urban inner-city locations" (10). Rap's emphasis on "posses" and on the "hood" constitutes an explicit recognition of the terrain of black habitation (11). While only some of rap evokes aspects of civic engagement, much of it speaks to the situation of a significant portion of the contemporary black urban experience in a politically reflective way. Certainly much of it should be regarded as a music of political critique, for the development of hip-hop was the result of "a concerted effort by young urban blacks to use mass culture to facilitate communal discourse across a fractured and dislocated national community."[56]

If we resist the conceptual tendency to separate social life from civic action, it is possible to recognize that black habitation (for example, the social uses of the home, neighborhood, and city) is a form of political action. Given the discriminatory pressures against the creation of black civil society—through legal manipulation, gentrification, discriminatory criminalization, and various forms of exclusion from mortgage funds, political office, and bureaucracy—"the territorial maintenance and integrity of black settlements" has been a form of civic action.[57] In addition to constituting a civic sphere through the mere fact of managing to continue to live together, African Americans have constituted the black public sphere in part out of distinctive modalities of expression. While liberal political analysts continue to look for civic action—within their homogenizing grammar of "we" Americans—many genres of African American expression represent the disjunctures between white and black American experience. For example, rap musicians acknowledge that black public action is often in the streets. They point out the extent to which the streets are made mean not because of the character of the residents but because of the geographic and economic enclosures to which the residents are subjected.

There is a critical overlap between the thematics of rap music and the work of contemporary black filmmakers. As Michael Eric Dyson has pointed out, both rap music and black film treat a crisis afflicting young black males: their "troubled path to maturity" and their disproportionate participation in and victimhood from violence.[58] In particular, John Singleton's film *Boyz N the Hood,* which features rapper Ice Cube in a major role, "reflects the sensibilities, styles, and attitudes of rap culture" (124). But more important, its focus on the African American family in South Central Los Angeles provides a challenge to the perspectives of those who locate the politics of inequality within the confines of existing policy discourse. The thematics and, most significant, the chronotope of Singleton's film produce a politicized perspective on the relationship between African American family space and political space, one that speaks to the limitations of a generalized model of American civic culture articulated by neo-Tocquevilleans.

Conclusion: "Boyz" and Families in the Hood

John Singleton's film is structured around a spatiotemporal tension represented by the character Tre's parents. After an early scene in which Tre is recalcitrant in his primary school classroom, his mother makes good her earlier threat about the consequences of his failure to clean up his act in school: she sends him to live with his father in a black neighborhood in South Central Los Angeles. Much of the film is aimed at demonstrating the value of male parenting, a presumed lack afflicting young African American males, rendering them susceptible to violence, drug addiction, and a shortened live span. This value is presumably redeemed by the mere fact that, after deciding not to participate in a revenge drive-by killing with his closest friends, Tre, high school age by the end of the film, remains alive.

From the point of view of Tre's father, staying alive while staying in the neighborhood is the essence of black politics. Tre's mother represents a wholly different set of expectations and values, reflecting in a different spatiotemporal practice. She is in school while working and hopes to move up within a white-dominated, meritocractic social and economic order. Singleton's sympathies are clearly on the side of the political commitment of Tre's father, but the filmic chronotope remains divided and ambiguous, reflecting the dividing pressure on African American households. Viewed within a temporal register, the present, for some (those represented by Tre's father), is a time of danger, and the future is simply a matter of having one, of staying alive. Viewed within a spatial register, the political problematic is one of staying in the "hood," of resisting all the pressures that threaten to dissolve neighborhood solidarity. For others (those represented by Tre's mother), the temporal register operates differently. The present is also a time of danger, but staying alive is not enough. Having a future means getting credentials, and within a spatial register, it means leaving the hood behind in order to enjoy prosperity as well as safety. These divisive pressures, a struggle over spatiotemporal commitments, surround the dominant temporal trajectory of the film, Tre's coming of age. He is required to sort through his family's and the hood's strained gender relationships and, most significant, to decide between his father's choice—to remain in the hood but to resist endangering attachments and behaviors—and the choices of his friends, for whom a life-endangering solidarity prevails, driving them toward deadly confrontations.

However, Singleton's film develops a space-time topos that extends well beyond the family dramas central to the narrative. South Central Los Angeles is affected by a future produced by investment decisions made well outside the neighborhood. In a telling scene, Tre's father addresses Tre, his friend Ricky, and a neighborhood crowd in front of a vacant lot with a For Sale sign. Someone else's planned future is afflicting the hood. Tre's father refers to the process of gentrification and its disastrous implications for neighborhood cohesion. And, on the subject of the equally destructive effects of drug use, he maps the trajectories of drug production and distribution, which begin well outside Los Angeles.

Singleton's filmic chronotope is therefore global as well as local. While

Tre's father (played by Lawrence Fishburne) lecturing Tre (played by Cuba Gooding Jr.) and his friend Ricky (played by Morris Chestnut) about political economy, in *Boyz N the Hood* (1991).

forces well outside the hood shape its destiny, more local forces shape its boundaries. While the credits are run at the beginning of the film, the camera pans Stop signs, One Way signs, and police barriers. The signs, representing the forces incarcerating the hood, are complemented by mechanisms of surveillance. A constant buzz of police helicopters is heard throughout the film. Ultimately, the hood is shown as an object of powerful forces that shape the possibilities of existing within it or escaping from it. Key nodes on the map include (implicitly) New Jersey, the home of the Educational Testing Service, which produces the college exams that black athletes must pass to move from the hood to a college campus. And the pervasive television set, which shows college football games under way, indicates how the hood is connected to a national scene, within which athletic aspirations are generated.

Much of the drama in the film takes place within Ricky and Dough Boy's household. Their mother, Brenda, hopes to have Ricky escape the hood with a college athletic scholarship. It is *their* television set that demonstrates the porosity of the hood, its susceptibility to the outside world of athletic recruitment. Moreover, their household, like Tre's, is a divided one, reflecting the divisive ambiguous time-space of the hood. Ricky, his mother's favorite, is aiming to escape, and Dough Boy is a homebody whom his mother reviles.

Ultimately, Singleton's film maps relationships between the space-time of the African American family and the space-time of the United States and beyond. It is clear that the political problematic of staying alive and maintaining a family in the face of almost overwhelmingly threatening local forces and divisive forces with global trajectories remains a central and distinctive aspect of African American existence. It is evident as well that a model of politics focused on generalized citizen participation neglects a historical trajectory of sovereign violence that only a commitment to a politics of equality—of reconfiguring space and qualifying excluded bodies—can redeem. The work of diverse African American artists and intellectuals is important in this version of politics. Thus, for example, focusing on "Afro-modernity" and treating the distinctiveness of what he calls "racial time," Michael Hanchard points to the importance of reconstructions of the past undertaken by African American activists and intellectuals.[59] In addition, Hanchard's recognition of the critical distinctiveness of African American temporality is suggestive of the more general importance of challenges to homogeneous models of nation-state time. Chapter 5 is addressed to those challenges.

5. National Times and Other Times: Rethinking Citizenship

Prelude: Temporal Disruptions

As I noted in chapter 4, Tocqueville's civilizational moral geography was complemented by a commitment to nation-state time. His "America," as an imagined, politically consolidated, democratic union, represented for him an inevitable future. In preparation for this inevitability, Tocqueville conceptually evacuated the American continent of recalcitrant modes of cultural and political organization. Despite Tocqueville's predictions, however, recalcitrance remains. Some people(s) and structures of attachment continue to resist the time of the nation-state. In this chapter, I analyze the disjunctures among alternative temporalities, especially as they bear upon the concept of citizenship. Then I turn to a consideration of the state-resistant aspects of family time.

There is an important philosophical predicate that must be at least implicitly involved in any consideration of citizenship. Although citizenship is a concept that has developed with the modern nation-state and has drawn its primary force as a juridical-territorial phenomenon, its more basic mode of being is intimately tied to the phenomenon of temporal presence. The temporal implication of citizenship becomes evident when one recognizes that its warranting in specific cases evokes attention to persons' trajectory through time, their mode of historical arrival—through birth, migration, legal processing ("naturalization"), and so on. Because being a citizen, like "Being" in general, achieves its (contingent) forms of stability through temporal practices, a critique of contemporary citizenship requires inquiry into a culture's temporal involvements. To approach this involvement, I begin with a fictional conversation that conveys the ontological significance of time, its relationship with individual and collective ways of inhabiting the life-world.

In Thomas Pynchon's novel *Mason & Dixon,* an eighteenth-century exchange of views on calendar reform takes place in an English pub. The conversation is precipitated by one customer's lament that England's head astronomer has stolen eleven days from the calendar. The astronomer's deletion, aimed at rectifying English time with the time in other global venues, has been implemented by an act of Parliament; September 2 is to be followed by September 14 instead of September 3. Although the conversation is a piece of fiction, the episode under discussion has a historical referent. In 1582, a calendar reform commission under Pope Gregory XIII had its recommendations for reform of the Julian calendar realized. October 4, 1582, was followed by October 15. The new calendar, promulgated throughout the Roman Catholic world, was not accepted in England until 1752.[1] By that time, the gap to be reconciled amounted to eleven days. However, the historical backing for Pynchon's vignette is less interesting than the way he evinces an imagination of its significance. As the pub conversation rages on, one speaker reflects on the kind of people who could accept such a change with equanimity. The astronomer, he suggests, would have to hire

> a people who lived in a different relation to Time—one that did not, like our own, hold at its heart the terror of Time's passage, far more preferably, Indifference to it, pure and transparent as possible. The verbs of their language no more possessing tenses, than their Nouns Case-Ending,—for these People remain's as disengaged from Subject, object possession, or indeed anything which might among Englishmen require a Preposition.[2]

Such a people, he adds, would effectively have to displace time with static space:

> Their Commission, that is their Charter if you like, directed them to inhabit Days, yet *not to allow the time to elapse*. They were expected to set up households, Farms, Villages, Mills,—an entire Plantation in Time. (196)

Pynchon's imaginative gloss on the disruptions attending calendar reform provides three insights that I want to extend at the outset of my analysis. First, he recognizes the ontological significance of the way people inhabit time; to disrupt their temporal existence is to disturb their way of being. Second, he understands the ways in which linguistic practices reflect a people's temporal habitus. And third, he recognizes that one strategy by which peoples construct collective coherence involves the dissimulation of temporal contingency; they spatialize temporality, turning a dynamic of existence into a territorial fixity.[3]

With these dimensions of Pynchon's insight into temporality in mind, we are edified by summoning St. Augustine's meditation on time, because his struggle to make sense of his own temporality covers and deepens the intellectual terrain evoked in Pynchon's episode. In his *Confessions*, Augustine poses, implicitly and explicitly, probing questions in response to the disruption that time must present to one's claim to be wholly present to oneself and to the world. His penchant for dwelling on his "past foulness," bringing it "back to mind," is less an apology for past conduct than it is an implicit attempt to be whole in time. Reflection on the past "gathers" him from a "disordered state" of "shattered pieces."[4]

Augustine responds to the ontological challenge posed by the passage of time explicitly by wondering about how to reconcile the nonpresence of past and future states with the unity of one's existence. How, he asks, can "these two kinds of time, the past and the future, be, when the past no longer is and the future as yet does not be?" (288). As is well known, Augustine's solution to these aporias of existence in time is to enlarge the self (or soul). He notes that, in preparing to recite a psalm, "the life of this action of mine is distended into memory by reason of the part I have spoken and into forethought by reason of the part I am about to speak" (301). Augustine's distension effectively extends presence. The past exists through memory, the present through attention, and the future through expectation. Although the three modalities remain in flux during an act (the present continually becomes past, lengthening memory; and expectation becomes exhausted as the act is consummated), Augustine seems to have contented himself with a subjectivist spatial solution. The self is the place that unites the tripartite division of time. Augustine's soul is *his* "Plantation in Time."

Along with his treatment of the ontological paradox of the existence of the past and the future, Augustine, like the characters in Pynchon's English pub, manifests an acute awareness of the grammatical proprieties needed to manage a temporal existence. The use of the future perfect tense, for example, becomes a self-conscious part of his management of a totalized temporal presence as he speculates that a future, "which does not yet be . . . will have become present" (290). Augustine's grammatical calisthenics accompanies his struggle to make a soul, which is "torn asunder by tumult and change, . . . flow together" (302). He recognizes that dealing with time is intimately connected with knowing how to speak. This is as much the case for collective temporalities (for example, how peoples do history) as it is for autobiographical stories of the subject. Reinhart Koselleck has expressed it succinctly: "In the absence of linguistic activity, historical events are not possible."[5]

Whatever may be the shortcomings of Augustine's solution to the on-tological paradoxes of time, his struggle to maintain a unified presence to self and world is exemplary.[6] His drive to dissolve aporia in order to rec-oncile his commitment to the subject's noncontingence in a flux that is the essence of contingency helps inaugurate a tendency in philosophical speculation about the self that runs to Martin Heidegger's monumental effort to locate the totality of Being in relation to time. And for my pur-poses, it illustrates a drive toward the establishment of identity bound-aries that also exist at the level of collectivities—specifically in the at-tempts of nation-states to achieve a grammar that turns the boundaries of states from the arbitrary result of geopolitical forces into the noncontin-gent warrant for the state as a container of a temporally coherent national culture. For Heidegger (whose meditation on time served a violent na-tionalistic project), as for Augustine, time, unless correctly thought and assiduously linguistically managed, is disruptive to a recognition of the essence of Being.[7]

While I want to resist both Augustine's and Heidegger's insistence on the ultimate unity of the self and both of their failures to provide for dif-ferences in people's temporal trajectories (like Augustine, Heidegger, with his concept of *Mitsein,* homogenizes people into a shared temporal habitus), their contributions to locating a person's presence as temporal-ly implicated inspires much of the analysis that follows. To recognize the ontological significance of one's temporal existence and the resulting shattering effect on the self of temporal disruptions and, at the same time, relaxing an insistence on the ultimate unity of the self and the sameness of people's presence in time, I consider a pervasive, contempo-rary form of temporal disruption analyzed by Alexander García Dütt-mann, the situation of people with AIDS. A consideration of Düttman's findings and conclusions provides a conceptual frame for a treatment of collective attachment (for example, a model of citizenship) that resists unifying the national body.

Being "Not at One"

García Düttmann's meditation on the present as "the time of AIDS" ex-plicitly resists the Augustinian and Heideggerian quest for the unity of the subject in time. A reflection on the temporal peculiarity of people who have AIDS provides for García Düttmann more general insights about the ultimate inability to be one-in-time of both individual and collective subjects. People with AIDS have a distinctive relationship with time. The anticipation of "dying before one's time" disturbs the temporal habitus of the AIDS sufferer. The resulting anxiety-driven fluctuations in perspective on their relationship to time constitutes a "Being-not-one-in-time" and a "Being-not-one with AIDS" that "foils the constitution of a coherent time and of the coherence of a life." It is a "collapse of the subject, through and for which the unity of life exists."[8]

In the course of his investigation, García Düttmann encountered some "confessions" of AIDS-infected people that bear comparison with the temporal implications of Augustine's confessional discourse. For Augustine, the confessional mode was an attempt to gather a scattered self. Augustine construed his act of writing the way he understood action in general. The writing of his confessions reproduced the tripartite temporal resolution of past, present, and future that all action enjoys. By confessing, Augustine saw himself as one becoming-one-in-time.

García Düttmann discerns a marked contrast with the Augustinian coherence in time in the confessions of AIDS sufferers. Although, like Augustine, AIDS victims often see their act of writing as a way to gather the self, as an act of "coming to oneself" (14), there is another topos of self-reflection that works against the attempt to become coherent in time through writing. García Düttmann describes it as the topos of "Being-not-one" and Being-not-at-one":

> In the short time left, the sick person who attempts to come to himself through writing must write all the books that remain to him to be written. But time for writing, the time that actually corresponds to these books, is being robbed by death, by the fact that the author will die "before his time." Writing devours the time it no longer has, since it is devoured by time and since Being-not-one threatens to cancel the production of coherence and unity. (15)

Crucially, García Düttmann sees the clash of topoi experienced by the writer with AIDS as reflective of a more general aspect of temporal existence. "The time of life," he states, "never just forms a closed unity and always already exposes itself to Being-not-one" (16). What distinguishes HIV-positive and AIDS-diagnosed people is not, therefore, the circumstance of Being-not-one in time; it is the particular "way that he or she relates to this Being-not-one" (17). Although García Düttmann's discursive approach to the subject-temporality relationship is articulated in Heideggerian language, he rejects Heidegger's position that the recognition of Being's dispersion in time creates the condition of possibility for achieving wholeness or unity. Edified by his observation that the AIDS condition provokes a "flight from death into dispersion" (23), García Dütt-

mann interprets the Being-not-one with AIDS as the sign of an "originary im-pertinence," a sign that one cannot achieve a coherence in the
face of even "the certainty of his (more or less) definite death." In the face
of this originary im-pertinence, García Düttmann proclaims the necessity for exiting from the commitment to the unity of identity at the level of
the subject:

> Perhaps one only has time to live and time to die when one is neither in-
> debted to an identity nor reduced to its opposites, disruption and frag-
> mentation. Perhaps one has this time—without having it at one's beck
> and call—in originary Being-not-one, in originary not-belonging, in
> originary im-pertinence. (25)

The discernment that AIDS provides of the disruption, or "im-
pertinence," of the Being-one-in-time of the subject operates at the level
of collective (and thus historical) time as well. The "time of AIDS" is
more than merely the catastrophe of a spreading disease. The resistance
of AIDS to a cure constitutes a disruption in the story of modern medi-
cine, a narrative organized by the idea of ending *all* disease (27). At this
collective level, AIDS therefore constitutes a "rupture in history" (27).
And because AIDS has not been contained spatially or temporally—it
renders "geopolitical, social, economic, national, cultural, ethnic, sexual
boundaries" permeable (40)—García Düttmann implies that only a
recognition of the "originary im-pertinence" of existence—as a Being-
not-one—to collective foundational temporalities can yield a thinking
"capable of measuring up to the destructive force of the disease" (41).

Heeding García Düttmann's suggestion about the thinking required
to oppose the ontological violence wrecked by AIDS on both individual
and collective subjects, I want to argue that it is also the way to resist the
violent excesses and interpretive monopoly of a statism that manifests itself as resistance to the disjunctures of political time through a spatialization and naturalization of the time of the citizen. Once we allow the stories of states, and their corollaries in stories of national culture, to receive
competition from other times, articulated in other narratives, we can rethink the citizen. It becomes possible to think citizenship as a multiplicity
of different modalities of presence and the politics of citizenship as a continuous negotiation of copresence. This way of thinking citizenship provides an alternative to the new cosmopolitanism that seeks simply to enlarge the *space* of citizenship by extending people's juridical status across
national boundaries. To begin this task of thinking, I want to show the
ways in which the time of the national citizen is always already disrupted.

The Spatiotemporality of Citizenship

Of all the forms of collective affiliation, citizenship would appear to be the one whose constitution is almost exhausted by a model of space: the territorial boundaries of the nation-state system. Given the juridically recognized state's control over global space, citizenship receives most of its practical, legal, and conceptual recognition as a form of licit presence within a state. While ancient citizenship was understood in terms of the topos of affiliational structures, modern citizenship is situated primarily in the juridical network of the (imaginary) international system of state sovereignties.[9] Although recent social movements and theoretical speculations have combined to politicize the concept of citizenship—expanding it to imagine, for example, citizenship under a condition of fractured subjectivity and "cultural citizenship," a vernacular rather than an official collective bonding, based on aspects of participation in the common life[10]—the territorial state remains the dominant frame for containing the citizen body, both physically and symbolically.

Nevertheless, if we heed the problematic linkage between nations and states in the term *nation-state*, we can discern a disjuncture. The spatial discourse of citizenship is uneasily articulated with a temporal one. The state, in its contemporary realization, is understood as a territorial entity, even though it has a history of emergence, having gradually or rapidly, as the case may be, expanded its political, legal, and administrative control by monopolizing violence and incorporating (by statute, by force, and/or by other means) various subunits into a legal and administrative entity with definitive boundaries. The primary understanding of the modern "nation" segment of the hyphenated term is that a nation embodies a coherent culture, united on the basis of shared descent or, at least, incorporating a "people" with a historically stable coherence.

Inasmuch as few if any states contain coherent historically stable communities of shared descent, the symbolic maintenance of the nation-state requires a contentious management of historical narratives as well as territorial space. Effectively, states' aspirations to nation-state existence are realized in various modalities of collective autobiography. The nation-state is scripted (in official documents, histories, and journalistic commentaries, among other texts) in ways that impose coherence on what is, instead, a series of fragmentary and arbitrary conditions of historical assemblage. At the same time, other modalities of writing (e.g., journals, diaries, novels, and counterhistorical narratives) challenge the state's writing performances that impose coherence. As a result, the temporal

NATIONAL TIMES AND OTHER TIMES

identification of the citizen is suspended in a continuing conflict of discourses. Persons and peoples take on different levels of coherence and incoherence in diverse modes of writing. While the clash of writing performances, a shifting terrain of the production and reconfiguration of citizen presence, is the main focus of my analysis, to provide a context, I focus first on aspects of the state's symbolic management of citizenship.

Because a state's performance of its temporal coherence—expressed in constitutions, statutes, official histories, annual national celebrations, and so on—persists alongside its spatial management, nation-state citizens receive what Jürgen Habermas calls a "double coding."[11] Citizenship is located both in a legal, territorial entity, within which it is associated with the privileges of sovereignty and the rights of individuals, and in a cultural community, where it is associated with a history of shared ethnic and social characteristics. The provocation for Habermas's concern with citizenship is a perception of crisis. Like others responding to the effects of an increasingly globalized economy, seen as attenuating state boundaries and producing new immigration flows, which alter the distribution of felt attachments within states, he wants to reconceive citizenship within a cosmopolitan democratic ethos. In search of a broadened democratic frame for communal solidarity, he warns of the dangers of the organic view of the nation, in which national solidarity is predicated on the myth of a "prepolitical fact of a quasi-natural people" (406).

At the same time, however, Habermas contributes to a narrative of contemporary nation-states that encourages such a myth. He suggests that only recently have we experienced pluralistic societies that "are moving further and further away from the model of a nation-state based on culturally homogeneous populations" (408). Moreover, his more general story of how nations became modern states emphasizes a benign process of political integration. Neglecting the reconfigurations of identity spaces associated with a history of imperialism, Habermas's cosmopolitan political ethos is insensitive to the spatiotemporal disjunctures *within* states that have remained in imperialism's wake.[12] His interest in an ethical civic bond fails to register the centrifugal forms of otherness within the modern nation-state.

Habermas's narrative of the integration and recent attenuation of nation-state space has been subjected to considerable criticism, some of it aimed at noting the exclusion of different forms of subjectivity that his commitment to abstract, supranational solidarity entails,[13] and some of it wary of his requirement of equivalent and distinct spaces for identity attachments.[14] My departure from the Habermasian narrative is concerned with addressing a paradoxical connection between national attachments and exclusions from political qualification. Inasmuch as every attempt to achieve a new abstraction within which to unite citizen bodies yields new forms of exclusion, I want to sketch a politics of citizenship that seeks less to bind than to unbind, that constructs the "community" in a way that loosens the demand for a generalized way of being-in-common.

Because I am proposing a model in which community attachments are seen as a dynamic of binding and unbinding, I am attracted to the language of community elaborated in the writings of Jean-Luc Nancy, whose approach (treated briefly in chapter 2) is predicated on a model of the social bond that countenances particularities and eschews generalized communal attributes.[15] Nancy's commitment to community based on the "unworking of communication" is diametrically opposed to Habermas's model of community based on communicative consensus. It accommodates a recognition of incommensurable modes of presence. Community, for Nancy, cannot be based on communicative consensus, because, he maintains, there are no stable spaces and no secure identity boundaries to assure communicative integration. Nancy suggests that the singularities of subjects who find themselves in common cannot be confined within aggregated social identities.[16] To the extent that there is community, it is a being-in-common of "'particularities,' . . . not founded on any autonomous essence" (75). Being-in-common for Nancy involves "only a juncture" (76), the sharing of a space of encounter.

What I want to derive from Nancy's recognition of the absence of a definitive basis for attachment is a politics sensitive to the temporal junctures and disjunctures that every political collective encompasses. In accord with Nancy's insights and idiom, I want to figure the structure of the social bond as a "community of literature," an uneasy and conflictual articulation—"not organization" (77)—of writing performances that challenge the state's autobiographical attempts to perform historical coherence. What Nancy calls a "literary communism," the disjunctive copresence of different forms of writing or "inscription[s] of meaning" (80), is a way of constituting the political domain that resists the closural impulses in "proposing the exemplary (which means also legendary, hence mythic)" (77), as is the case with the texts (e.g., official histories) that invent a singular, prepolitical culture as the legitimating condition of state boundaries.

Within Nancy's frame, community as literary communism (engagements among alternative ways of scripting the meanings of selves) implies a politics that privileges encounters between articulations that issue from different ways of being present within the space of the state rather than a politics that moves toward integration within a unitary national culture. It is a politics within which no way of being-in-common can achieve completion (80–81). To illustrate the kind of encounter that speaks to Nancy's resistance to an integrative politics and to provide a threshold to the specific analysis that follows, I turn here to an encounter that challenges Habermas's claim about what was once an expanding solidarity served by the state system. A personal event reported by the Mexican writer Carlos Fuentes provides evidence of the disjoint presences that have been endemic to nation-states since the colonial period.

Fuentes offers a gloss on the relationship between writing and the imagination of time when, after losing his way on a driving trip, he stopped to ask directions of a Mexican peasant in the Morelos region. When he asked the peasant the name of the village into which he had wandered, the man responded: "That depends, we call the village Santa Maria in times of peace. We call it Zapata in times of war."[17] Stunned by the response, Fuentes ascribes a knowledge to the "old campesino" that "most people in the West have assiduously ignored since the seventeenth century: that there is more than one time in the world, that there is another time existing alongside, above, underneath the linear time of the calendars of the West" (61). Fuentes recognizes that there is always a trace of nonpresence in presence, and he notes, more specifically, that the presence of the West's historical time has debts to other times.[18] He suggests that state control over identity is based in part on a unimodal model of temporality and that, by implication, a critique of Western hegemony must be, among other things, a challenge to the West's monopoly of future orientations and its erasure of alternative pasts.[19]

Two kinds of significance emerge from Fuentes's treatment of his encounter. The first, to which I turn immediately, concerns a nation-state's attempt to colonize time as part of its more general attempt to mythologize a national culture. The second, which occupies much of the subsequent analysis, concerns Fuentes's remarks about the ways in which novelistic fiction can subvert the Western nation-state's monopoly of spatiotemporal presence. The novel, he suggests, is an important locus for the critique of the West's "successive, linear, and positivistic notion of time" (63). It is the place where a challenge can be issued to a modernity in which "the rising industrial and mercantile classes of Europe gave unto themselves the role of universal protagonists of history" (64). Writing, he states, can alter "the spaces of presence" (73). And, I shall be noting more specifically, there is a critical relationship between the spaces of presence and the politics of citizenship.

Managing Disjoint Temporalities

The state's symbolic management of nation-state territoriality is increasingly intense of late. In this age of simultaneity, in which speed dominates transactions, territorial space gives way increasingly to what Paul Virilio calls "chronospace."[20] Informational nodes displace boundaries and frontiers as the zones where practices of exclusion are concentrated. The increasing movement of bodies, a growing global diaspora—of refugees, exiles, illegal aliens, migrant workers, and intellectuals—has encouraged postnational, nonterritorial forms of affiliation and solidarity.[21] Increasingly, populations affiliate themselves translocally: in other places and times. These changes are implicated in attempts, like Habermas's, to rethink citizenship.

Yet because the citizen has always been a subject lodged precariously in time and space, we can amplify Habermas's insight into the double coding of citizenship to appreciate how the state system has continually performed its conceptual hegemony. To do this we need to specify how it has displaced and overcoded competing modalities of affiliation that divide loyalties. Most generally, as states narrate themselves as the ultimate organizational achievement of modernity, they locate themselves in an identity-producing story that replaces the religious story of salvation and the evolutionary biological story of humanity's emergence from the "great chain of being," which have served previous forms of power and authority.

If one holds to the story of the state as the successor of the time of the church and the time of the king, as the heir of earlier "fictitious universalities,"[22] citizenship would seem to be a stable universality and, as Kant would have it in the eighteenth century, a felicitous one, having shucked the tutelage of both religious and political hegemons. The subordinated subject is replaced by the moral, republican citizen. But the citizen-subject has remained a divided one in the discourse of the state. The unstable dialectic of inclusion and exclusion, which haunts citizenship, is evident in the ambiguous concept of "the people" to which Giorgio Agamben refers (as noted in both the introduction and in chapter 4) when he notes the "biopolitical fracture" that the concept entails: "the people" as the totality of citizens versus "the people" as the excluded and "needful" bodies.[23] Because this latter aspect of the people contrasts with aggregative conceptions of politically qualified existence, Agamben's concept of fractured subjectivity, unlike Habermas's "double coding," references forces of exclusion rather than integration.

The state's autobiographical performances, its stories of its founding, legitimacy, and continuity (including Habermas's recent version), are aimed in part at overcoming this biopolitical fracture. The state attempts to write itself in a way that ends the split, creating unity out of constitutive division.[24] Indeed, once we locate the state imaginatively in a theatrical frame, performing its distinctiveness rather than simply existing passively within a naturalized, geopolitical space, the temporal dimensions of its existence become more apparent. As a spatial entity, the state appears, as Homi Bhabha has noted, as mere "crowded spectacle," but diverse cultural movements have served to "disperse the homogeneous, visual time of the horizontal society" and to reveal nations as containers of disjunctive temporal performances.[25] Bhabha speaks of the "double time of the nation" (294). Against the reality of an arbitrary and disjoint present, the state engages simultaneously in two incompatible performances. To produce a coherent people, it produces a national pedagogy, making the people "historical 'objects'" in a story of a pre-founding social homogeneity" (297). At the same time, however, that prior, historical presence is erased in a different kind of performance; the state presents its people as "subjects" in a signifying process aimed at showing the national life as a continuous heterogeneous process of renewal.

The implications of the temporal disjuncture toward which Bhabha points are similar to those deriving from Agamben's analysis. "The national culture" is a "contentious performative space" (307), wherein the problematic of citizenship moves from its framing within a normative territoriality to one of a contested spatiotemporality. To elaborate the relevant contentions and to assess their implications for an approach to the politics of citizenship that transcends the familiar geopolitical or juridicospatial framework, it is necessary to heed additional aspects of temporally related dramas in which both individual and collective national subjects are involved.

Once we recognize the complexities of the within-timeness of citizenship, by supplementing spatial imaginaries with temporalities, a rich array of articulations within various genres of media can be seen to challenge the time of the state. In particular, I shall be arguing that the being-in-common of citizenship need not take the form of finding a common discursive ground within which different interests can be communicated. Indeed, as Nancy has suggested, the sharing of the space of community requires the shattering of the myths of commonality upon which collectives predicate their (imaginary) cohesion. The "community to come" is always at a distance; it is part of an ongoing political process that cannot be completed.[26] If the existence of disjoint forms of presence is recognized, a politics of citizenship will require a continuous renegotiation of the aggregation of difference, based on an appreciation of an uneasy copresence among subjects existing in overlapping but different temporal traces. To move toward such an appreciation, I want to extend the drama of "the people" discussed by Agamben and Bhabha in order to discern additional contestations among disjunctive temporal presences.

Expanding the Struggle over Temporality

The state's attempts at monopolizing the staging of citizenship take a variety of forms. As part of its pedagogy of national unity, for example, it must frame its encounter with the prior inhabitants of its territory in a way that keeps them (indigenes) off the national stage. This is accomplished ingeniously in one case: The Museum of Anthropology in Mexico City devotes considerable space to Mexico's indigenous origins. The rhetoric of its collection admits "that national culture has its source and its axis in the indigenous."[27] But the subversive effect of Mexico's indigenous origins on its claims to a unified national culture is contained by a procedure of "separating ancient culture—the pre-Columbian indigenous—from contemporary culture."[28] The separation is accomplished both architecturally and scenographically; the displays are located on different floors, and they are referenced within different disciplinary practices. The archeological is separated from, even opposed to, the ethnographic.

States have put considerable energy into managing anticipation as well as historical memory. European states, after the establishment of the Westphalian system in the seventeenth century, instituted controls over astrological readings. They sought to maintain their people's focus on national rather than apocalyptic futures.[29] However, since the eighteenth century, with increasingly less competition from the millennial expectations of religious movements, there has been a more pervasive threat to the historical drama of unifying national culture. Economic forces disrupt states' ideational management of their presents and futures. Flows of capital, along with the other dynamics associated with the increasingly global economy, compete with the state systems' production of identity spaces and, more important, challenge the containment strategies, discursive and material, with which states attempt to control allegiances. "Capital times," as Eric Alliez puts it, produce a different drama of the subject, because "money turns value into a *flow* that tends to escape the juridical frame of political territoriality."[30]

To extend Alliez's argument, one could say that the state capture of subjectivities is challenged by a rapid system of circulation that resists the forms of capture by which subjectivity is held in modes of nationally relevant generality. Hegel's version of the state-family relationship, treated in chapters 1 and 2, in which family subjects are captured within a state-oriented mythic history, is a case in point. Since Hegel's treatment, histories, articulated in a variety of forms, reflect attempts at appropriating the traditional family with a traditional libidinal structure—patriarchal, heterosexual, incest-resistant, and erotically monopolistic—to represent the state as the container of a homogeneous national culture. The current proliferation of family values discourses reflects, among other things, an attempt to defend a nationalist narrative of undivided and coherent citizen subjectivity.

One example of the appropriation of the traditional family for state legitimation is a media text issued from the seat of government, a recent series of "public service announcements" sponsored by the Ad Council. President and Mrs. Clinton are featured in a plea for parental involvement with children: "We're fighting for the children. Whose side are you on?" In response to this image, which "coercively shapes the structures within which the 'political' itself can be thought," Lee Edelman criticizes "the politics that informs the pervasive trope of the child as a figure for the universal value attributed to political futurity."[31] The "queer oppositionality" that Edelman summons in his response seeks recognition for a queerness that functions within a different temporal trajectory, a "*vision of futurity*" that does not imagine a heteronormal family with a reproductive agenda (22).

Edelman's evocation of the oppositionality of queer time, like the response of Carlos Fuentes's Mexican peasant to a query about the name of his village, reveals other times, other modes of presence that lie outside the familiar juridical frames for constituting the meaning of citizenship while resisting the absorption of a particular model of family time into national time. Capital time provides a condition of possibility for different family stories to emerge. In capital time, the primary subject is the consumer, not the family member or citizen. Within global commercial media, the family becomes an object of appropriation, responsive to forms of consumer desire that overflow the space of the normative family. Rather than normalizing the family within a story of the state's legal and political monopoly of subjectivity, various media (for example, feature films with global distribution) dwell on the family's inability to manage extrafamilial and illicit forms of erotic energy (for example, the recent remake of the film version of *Lolita*) or dramatize the way that social and economic forces produce alternative or nontraditional family structures (for example, the feature film *Boogie Nights,* treated in chapter 2, which chronicles the familial structure of a pornographic film company, attempting to keep its "family" together as home video technology displaces pornographic movies).

Apart from operating in the time of consumption rather than the imposed and legitimating historical time of the state, such films reflect another countertemporality; they show the ways in which families, far from being foundational to the nation's political and commercial life, are the (often arbitrary) after-effects of political and economic forces. In contrast with the moralizations of the family that integration-oriented state stories tend to offer, in capital time, the family is an object of representation for any consumer whatever, not an exemplary moral unit in a legitimating tale of the state. Capital time—the economically driven, rapid appropriation of social imaginaries—cannot be contained by nationally oriented attempts to manage historical time. Doubtless, for example, the attempts of the family values movement at curtailing the media reflect a losing battle to maintain the illusion of a temporally coherent national culture based on traditional and homogeneous familial structures.

In the domain of discourses on the family as in other domains, the temporalities associated with capital effectively challenge the national presence-in-time. The flows encouraged by capital circulation attenuate as well as transgress the boundaries with which states have sought to spatialize and thereby control time. The family therefore provides an effective locus of enunciation from which to challenge national time, for although it has been an object of appropriation by conflicting political and economic forces, it has also been a site where family members have articulated (or written) their familial affiliations in order to challenge national times with familial and other times. I turn, then, to one sphere within which this challenge has been mounting.

Nation-State Time versus Family Time

Among the diverse aspects of "family time," the most familiar has to do with the time allotted for families to spend together. The contemporary form of this aspect of family time is relatively modern, having taken shape in the 1880s. Early in the nineteenth century, for example, Sundays tended to be a time of communal gathering, while Mondays were a more common day off. However, whatever has been the time families have reserved for themselves, it has not tended to be a result of explicit normative injunctions. A genealogy of family time (over the past two centuries), in the sense of time devoted to within-family interactions, has been primarily a function of the relationship between families and both capital and national times. Thus, as John Gillis points out, to appreciate contemporary family time one must recognize that "[t]he ritualization of family time that took place from mid century onward must be understood in the context of the emergence of the capitalist industrial society organized in the form of the modern nation state."[32] Despite the interdependency of family time with other times, the neoconservative lament about family time as a victim of exogenous forces is inconsistent with the historical record. Contrary to their family-as-victim scenario about the effects of industrialization, for example, the family, as Tamara Hareven points out, has been an active agent in its own transformation. It has played a major role in constructing itself as a constantly shifting entity.[33]

Hareven's inquiry reveals as well a persistence of diverse subcultural modes of family time that have not been wholly suborned by industrial capital time or nation-state time: "'Irish family time' differed in certain respects from 'French Canadian family time,' while both differed from 'Native American time'" (60).

Thus, there has never been a stable national family time in the American case, and the bases for family time have differed across subcultures and through time in the United States and elsewhere. Family time, in the sense of a family member's commitments to his or her familial versus other attachments, national or otherwise, has been quite diverse. The family has been a locus of enunciation of a variety of temporal commitments as different families and different members within families have placed differential value on the family as a source of identity and attachment. As a result, instead of treating the family as "a utopian retreat from the world," which it has never been "except in the imagination of social reformers and social scientists" (69), I treat it as a domain of critical political reflection and initiation, for some family-oriented genres, which heed the disjunctures within family time and between familial and other times (for example, the novel), provide an exemplary political challenge for thinking about attachments in general. To make this case, I turn both to the novel and to a venue within which its personae reflect a struggle between familial and national times.

Another Venue

Violent encounters in the Middle East provide at least as rich a domain for an analysis of the clash of temporalities as for an analysis of the clash of armies. On one side of this clash is the dominant, state-oriented mapping. Constructed from the point of view of the militant national security culture in Israel, the map of Middle Eastern state sovereignties reflects a preoccupation with Arab threats to Israel's "security." One member of this culture, Israeli security analyst Emmanuel Sivan, has recently speculated about the historical failure of Israel's "enemies" (Arab political movements) to achieve an effective pan-Arab solidarity. In an essay organized by a set of nationalist "chronotopes,"[34] he begins with a characterization of the present, stating, "These are not easy times for pan-Arab nationalism, the hegemonic ideology in the Middle East."[35]

Sivan's "Middle East" is more or less exhausted by an Israeli "nation-state" and an outer ring of militant Arab leaders, who, in a series of historical misadventures—represented by the attempts of the Egyptians al-Husri and Nasser, the Libyan Gadhafi, the Syrian Ba'athists, and finally, the Iraqi Hussein—have failed to achieve a unified political movement. The singularity of his state-oriented geographical imaginary aside, what is striking is the selectivity of Sivan's history of "the Arab." The Arab world, for Sivan, is strictly a form of dangerous militance, existing wholly outside the state of Israel, and "Israel" is a single locus of enunciation.

Despite Sivan's attempt at projecting Arabness outside Israel's state boundaries, Arabs are present, in an extended historical sense, within two temporally overlapping Israels. Inasmuch as Arabs trace the genealogy of their peoplehood to Canaanites, there is a radical entanglement between Jews and Arabs in the "land of Israel" that extends backward to biblical times (and is a discursive object in Israeli official history). Although the biblical story, beginning with Jehovah's alleged land grant to Abraham, constructs the "Jewish people" within a story of "how one man, through the generations, gradually becomes a whole nation,"[36] an ethnohistorical treatment reveals a different narrative. Ancient Israelites coalesced in various ways: economically, legally, linguistically, and through inter-marriage with Canaanite tribes. Despite warnings from the prophets about the dangers to the integrity of the people from the Canaanites and their customs, the legal structures invoked to protect "the people" were more or less part of Canaanite rather than Israelite legal culture. The Canaanite codes, based on the practices of an urban and monarchical people in contrast with a patriarchal and tribal people (the Israelites), are what dominate much of Exodus and Deuteronomy.[37] The Canaanite was already deeply imbricated in the culture of the "people of the book."

The legitimating tales of the contemporary state of Israel (the geo-political Israel) are also haunted by the Arab within. Although a dominant narrative of the Israeli state is the "tower and stockade story," which valorizes the heroic acts of settlement in defiance of "the antagonistic policy of the British mandate and armed attacks by Arab gangs,"[38] there is another story within which the Arab cannot be separated from the Jew. This is the story of the Levant, a story of the history of a shared dynamic of cultural coinvention between Jew and Arab. This story continues to have strong resonances for both Arabs and "oriental," or Arab Jews within Israel, so much so that it is not unusual, for example, for an Israeli Jew with an Iraqi lineage to recognize herself better in Palestinian poetry than in the contemporary Hebrew novel.[39] This is the case in part because contemporary Hebrew has been constructed as part of a strategy to create a national culture in which Arab culture is erased. Nevertheless, there are multiple loci of enunciation from which Hebrew is expressed. In some hands, for example, the Hebrew novel has disrupted a nationalist attempt at imposing an exclusively Jewish coherence on the nation-state. It has provided an instrument of recovery of the very Levantine world, a shared Arab-Jewish cultural formation, that modern Hebrew was invented to help erase. I focus, in particular, on a case in which the novel is structured by family time, which is represented specifically in opposition to the time of nation-state, which, in order to achieve a myth of a unitary national culture, denies a history of cultural coinvention.

Specifically, I offer an interpretation of an instance in which an Israeli woman writer has resisted the dominant historical imaginaries that radically separate Jew and Arab, privilege reasons of state, and encourage a practice of both armed and representational violence by denying co-existing temporal presences not encoded in the stories of states. Ronit Matalon's novel *The One Facing Us* treats the genealogy of a dispersed Egyptian Jewish family and allows the Levantine world to reassert itself while allowing us to discern a Middle East not present in discourses of national security.[40] Matalon's novel, which juxtaposes family time with the historical time of the state, restores diverse forms of copresence and exemplifies a politics of inclusion outside both nationalistic and cosmopolitan discourses of juridical citizenship.

Resistance to national historical time in Matalon's novel owes as much to the novelistic form as to her particular thematics. As Fuentes argues, novelistic fiction contributes significantly to the recognition of diverse and contending copresences not afforded in official political discourses. States locate themselves in a historical trajectory within what is a Hegelian model of spatiotemporality, an epochal model of history that "enables the consolidation of the modern nation-state."[41] In contrast with Hegel's model, which offers a progressive history in which signs eventually achieve their objects,[42] the contemporary novel tends to resist an abstract narrative of attunement between discourse and experience. As a distinctive "chronotope" (as Bakhtin terms it), it articulates time-space with a "density and concreteness" absent in a Hegelian epochal narrative.[43] A diverse set of temporalities converge in the novel as biographical and historical time sequences juxtapose "the time of life" with "historical time" (250), allowing for an emergence of diverse presences that were absent in earlier literary genres, for example, the Greek and Gothic, which presented characters unrelated to either biography or history.

The One Facing Us

In *The One Facing Us,* seventeen-year-old Esther, the primary narrator in the novel, is summoned from Israel by her uncle Sicourelle for a visit to her extended family in postcolonial Cameroon. Uncle Sicourelle hopes to have her marry his adopted son, Erouan. Esther resists this planned future and, at the same time, assembles her family's past, revealing, through photographs, letters, and conversations, the history of a dispersed Egyptian Jewish family that was very much a part of the Levantine world that official Israeli national culture has sought strenuously to erase.

Upon her arrival in Cameroon, Esther is greeted in French by her uncle Sicourelle's secretary. Sicourelle himself, who speaks four languages, all of them badly, frequently addresses her in Arabic. And, in general, there is no single language that dominates the novel's conversations. Stylistically, therefore, Matalon's novel instances M. M. Bakhtin's "intentional novelistic hybrid," which assembles different sociolinguistic worlds and "sets them against each other dialogically."[44] This form lends the novel an agonistic temporality; the different languages in dialogue represent "different times, epochs and days" (365). And, most significant for my purposes, the "multi-languagedness" of this novelistic form challenges a dominant aspect of linguistic consciousness; it weakens the "system of national myth" by breaking the association between a language and an ideology (369–70). In this case, the novel breaks the association between Israel's national language and its ideological commitment to being a historically coherent Jewish nation.

In addition to its multilingual character, which reflects the hybridity of tongues spoken by Jews from the Levantine world, the novel functions in a visual as well as a written register. It opens with a photo of Esther's uncle Sicourelle and his workers, accompanied by Esther's reflection on family photography and its relationship with the past, present, and future of selves. Thereafter, additional photographs and the written text, primarily in Hebrew (and translated into English) but containing smatterings of other languages (French, Arabic, etc.), combine to convey diverse layers of time. The photos achieve this diverse set of temporalities by virtue of their varying locations within the family's past, while the writing displays diverse temporalities through shifting verb tenses, shifts of scene, and changes in the historical sites of enunciation. In addition, the interactions between written and visual texts emphasize the disjunctures in the family's story line.

In general, as a genre, the novel is characterized by its varying of the temporal trajectories of its different characters, their different ways of arriving in the plot, and their movements through the narrative. And although novels can halt temporal sequences while focusing on characters' relationships, the overall novelistic structure is temporal, not only because it involves a narration—the description of events unfolding in time—but also because novels (at least the most familiar, realist type) operate within a "genealogical imperative" (as described in chapter 3); they place their acts and images in "a dynastic line that unites the diverse generations of the genealogical family."[45] This is the case in part because many cultures tend to use the genealogical model of family time as a metaphor for chronological time and in part because a patriarchal tradition articulates itself through novels as it does through other cultural forms.

But although Matalon's novel follows a genealogical line (it is focused on the drama of difference across generations of a geographically dispersed and culturally centrifugal family), Matalon achieves a critical distance from the imperatives of a family genealogy by introducing disruptive ambiguities into the dynamics of familial attachments. The primary circuit of interaction between Esther and her uncle Sicourelle is an encounter between a character (the uncle) bent on achieving a continuous genealogy for his Jewish family and one (Esther) whose investigations continually reveal elements of discontinuity and difference that disrupt the genealogical story of the family that her uncle wants her to enter.

Matalon's main strategy for disrupting the genealogy is the interspersing of text and family photos. Her readings of the photos situate the pull of a genealogical drive against an equally powerful pull of disintegrating forces: the dispersal of an Egyptian Jewish family to Israel, other areas of Africa, and America, presented in a series of vignettes about wives, ex-wives, mistresses, and stifling marriages. The effect of the readings is to show not only the sundering forces of time, geography, temperament, and affiliational preference, which combine to defeat a coherent family culture, but also those forces that operate centrifugally against the attempt to forge a national culture in Israel as the legitimation of a Jewish (in the sense of non-Arab) state.

Most essential, for Matalon, "the photograph offers evidence of what is remembered, but it also intimates what might have been."[46] She recognizes the absence that is a necessary part of every presence, and she deploys this recognition at the levels of both individual and nation. For example, while viewing a photo of her father, Esther imagines his sitting for the picture as a momentary arrest of temporal exigencies; her father's plans are momentarily "shunted aside" for the duration of the sitting (24). He is a man who "hated the specifics of place and portrait. In Israel he was constrained to only one place and one portrait. But not in Cairo. In Cairo there were a thousand possible places" (30). The discomfort that Esther perceives in her father's temporary arrest in a photo is an allegory for a more pervasive state-imposed discomfort. As a genre, the photograph is congenial to the state's fixing of citizen identities in that it spatializes time; it halts movement, locating its characters in a single scene. The dramas through which nation-states perform their existence as a coherent national culture are also forms of arrest. But Esther's interpretation of this photo resists its static tendency. She notes that her father finds the constraint of staying in one place and adopting a single cultural identity to be even more intolerable than the duration of stillness demanded of one who sits for a photograph. He and Esther's uncle Sicourelle are men from the Levant, a culture open to hybridity. The Cairo of the 1930s did not demand of them a singularity of identity. When Esther first meets her uncle Sicourelle, he inquires in Arabic rather than Hebrew, "What became of your father?" (16).

Indeed, for centuries, in this part of the Levantine world, the Jews of Cairo did not experience the same demands for cultural singularity exacted in contemporary Israel. For example, the Egyptian Jewish trader Abraham Ben Yiju wrote in Judeo-Arabic back in the twelfth century. Although "he and his friends were all orthodox, observant Jews, strongly aware of their distinctive religious identity . . . they were also part of the Arabic speaking world"; they practiced a Judaism that was strongly inflected by Islamic ideas and practices,[47] and most important, they felt a strong affinity to the world they shared with Arabs. Although Ben Yiju experienced a strong genealogical imperative, seeking near the end of his life to return to the Middle East (from his trading home in Mangalore) to effect a Jewish marriage for his daughter with his brother's son, he manifested no imperative to wall himself off from the Arab dimension of his cultural being.

Eight centuries later, the Levantine Jewish family in Matalon's novel manifests a similar ease within their cultural hybridity. In contrast with the rigid practices of exclusion constituting the drive toward making Israel a "Jewish state," the world of Esther's Levantine relatives resists strict cultural boundaries. One father in the family, for example, would not begin eating until the Arab members of the household were at his table. And although some of the family manifest a strong attachment to lineage, seeking to locate all members of the extended and dispersed Egyptian Jewish family, others wholly distance themselves from it, for example, a *Washington Post* reporter, Zuza, who lives on the run between major capital cities, having a life with no room for a marriage and no interest in going back to her family roots. She lives in a present world of developing information, not a past world to be summoned in memory.[48]

Interpretations of blurry and missing photographs are the primary vehicles for Matalon's representation of the ambivalence of attachments of the Levantine world of her family. Commenting on her image in a photograph with "three blurry figures," Jacqueline Kahanoff (an Israeli writer as well as another narrator in the novel) likens the familiar ambiguity to her Levantine experience: "The photograph resonated within me: after all, the blurring of figures and landscape, of general and specific, is exactly what typified our Levantine experience. The light that floods the photograph, obliterating distinctions, is my light, the light of my Levantine generation" (126).

The missing photographs attest even more strongly to the Levantine-Jewish resistance to a singular identity attachment, whether national or familial. Esther's father seems to will himself to forget, losing the only remaining photograph of a deceased child (179). Like Esther's father, the siblings, who have gone their separate ways and have been divided by "different needs and experiences," have deliberately lost or destroyed many of the family photos (shown as blank photographs on many pages of the novel). It is as if, Matalon writes, "[t]hey were rejecting the burden of proof, denying the need to record who they were and where they came from; as if the very idea were an affront; as if photographs, mere objects, were an insult to their memories and to the boundlessness of the imagination" (113).

The Levantine cultural tendency toward ambiguated boundaries of selves and nations and resistance to constraints on the exercise of imagination (e.g., one character buys electronic gadgets, "finding novel uses for them that allowed her to reinvent herself again and again" [148]) is also manifested as a welcoming orientation to Arab copresence. Some of the novel's characters evince an impatience with Zionism. For example, the character Jacqueline Kahanoff, whose childhood was spent in Egypt, notes that "few of us were Zionists because we believed that for humanity to be free, one had to give up one's narrow individuality" (183). And Grandpapa Jacquo, for whom Cairo was home, is so upset that he begins wheezing when he sees a relative clutching Zionist pamphlets in Arabic and French (114).

In contrast with Ashkenazi-Zionist Jewish nationalism, which locates the Arab outside Israel's boundaries, the Levantine mentality of Esther's dispersed Egyptian Jewish family is deployed at one point with a gardening metaphor. In a conversation with her aunt, who has just spoken of the intimacy of her Levantine family with their Arab servants, Esther's cousin from America, Zuza, objects that some Arabs are anti-Semites. The aunt replies, "Where aren't there? Weeds like that grow everywhere. Don't you have any in your America? Even here in Israel we have some" (74). The gardening imagery here suggests a different mapping of Israel's peoples. Rather than residing on a map that separates them with sharp boundaries, they have grown in the same plots, and each group has individuals who flourish differently.

This imagery resonates well with Ammiel Alcalay's poignant reflection on what he has called "the geography of time." In his lament about the gradual disappearance of the Arab culture that had historically participated with Jews in coinventing the ethnic texture of the city of Jerusalem, he says:

> As the Arab character of the city is continually being eroded, strangling its links to the Levant, Jerusalem encloses the space of yet another incoherence. A complete microcosm of the Levantine Arab Jewry . . . remains effectively cut off from significant access to the texture, substance and wider sphere of determinants that [compose] the world it forms a part of.[49]

In effect, Alcalay is pointing out how one can read, in Jerusalem's cityscape—which has been changed from terraced olive groves and *ruti* trees into "massive residential and institutional structures," fortresslike dwellings "overshadowing rural enclaves with the remaining 'natives'" (507)—how the state's cultural nationalism has reshaped the social body and erased Jewish-Arab copresence.

Toward a Politics of Citizenship

If one is committed to a politics that resists the identity-fixing effect of a state-oriented model of political space and the homogenizing of the temporal presence of citizen-subjects, the domain of the political must articulate itself through a continuous negotiation of copresence among those with diverse ways of being-in-time. This way of construing the political enables a politics that resists state practices (and the conceptual work of state theorists), which seek to contain modes of presence by erasing or conceptually incorporating them. Such a politics becomes evident when one discerns alternative constructions of presence in modes of writing. Different genres, different kinds of texts, bear witness to the struggle in which the state seeks to manage diversity, while those who do fit comfortably within the range of identities supplied by a nation-state imaginary, who occupy other models of time, seek to establish a recognizable presence. A concern with a politics of citizenship that takes cognizance of other times, then, becomes a concern with allowing those who have remained ungrammatical in the dominant policy discourses to achieve status as political subjects. The case of Middle Eastern presences is exemplary. Matalon's novel shows that Israeli nationalism renders Levantine temporalities ungrammatical. Those who emerge from a Levantine past cannot *be* unambiguously because their *having been* has been erased within the language of national cultural coherence.

Matalon's novel challenges a statist narrative of national cultural coherence by mobilizing time images associated with a family genealogy. Her main narrator, Esther, is plunged into the past on her first encounter with her uncle Sicourelle. The experience has the effect, as she puts it, of "forcing on me an intimacy with a world that has never been mine."[50] That world, a hitherto hidden past in her present, is referenced throughout the novel in the grammar of her remarks and in her recovery of the family's heterogeneous cultural trace as she encounters family photos. As the nonverbal time images in the novel, the photographs reflect the different ways family members relate to their past. Some long to recover it, while others, like Uncle Sicourelle "and the few whites he had befriended" (in Cameroon) have "left the past behind" (22). The photographs themselves, in diverse modes—clarity, blurriness, and absence—constitute a rhetoric of temporal difference. They deepen the novel's genre-related challenge to Israel's dominant national time. The photographs with which Esther works, as she reassembles a family history, are therefore unfinished time images; they are open to her renarrativization, which challenges the dominant national story in a state that seeks to invent a singular and coherent national culture.

Although, as chronotypes, novels are especially pertinent counternarratives to texts that narrate national time and reproduce a statist, juridical view of citizenship, I want to conclude my analysis in this chapter by pointing to ways in which even a state's official texts constitute a form of double writing that ultimately imperils the erasures and containments that characterize national time. Producing effects that encourage a diversity they seek to contain, some official texts promise a politics of citizenship that opens a space for more diverse forms of presence based on different ways of being-in-time. The texts to which I turn are civil rights and voting rights acts, beginning in the mid-1960s and culminating with the Civil Rights Act of 1991.

To appreciate the role of the law as a discursive enactment of national cultural coherence, we must recognize that, apart from its particular prohibitions and inhibitions, the law legalizes a recognition of aspects of diversity. In Foucault's words, the set of penalties it prescribes "does not simply 'check' illegalities; it differentiates them, it provides them with a general 'economy.'"[51] More specifically, as Carol Greenhouse has pointed out, the history of civil and voting rights acts in the United States reveals significant changes in the law's practices of differentiation. Whereas, for example, the 1965 Voting Rights Act, like the 1964 Civil Rights Act, "collectivizes 'any citizen' and 'persons' in its guarantee of protection against denials and abridgments of voting rights 'on account of race or color,'" the Civil Rights Act of 1991 produces a more differentiated construction of classes: "There are virtually no references to 'persons' or 'individuals,' as in the older texts."[52] Suggesting a "more complicated world than the earlier ones," the act mentions "women and minorities," and it "gestures toward other venues—negotiation, alternative dispute resolution, and foreign legal systems. The public space is more crowded in this act, not only with more categories of people but also with sources of authority" (228).

This change in the law's discourse of difference is doubtless a reflection of emerging forms of diversity whose venues of expression have been hitherto outside official texts. Greenhouse locates this change in the law's production of difference in the context of a clash of temporalities: "The law positions itself at the juncture where timeless and timely social orders conceptually divide, that is, where the issues of humans' 'natures' (as racial, gendered, violent, weak, and so forth) are separated from the cultural vision of a national story in time" (228). This positioning of the law is intended, according to Greenhouse, to contain the radical political manifestations of diversity. It is, in her words, aimed at "transforming diversity into civility" (229). Lawmakers are attempting to maintain a homogeneous community by manipulating the texts of citizen rights. They seek to colonize the future through a management of diversity.

What I want to note, however, is that the double writing of the law (a simultaneous production and containment of difference) constitutes two conflicting moments. While the law's current rhetoric of differentiation is aimed at containing and managing diversity, it also names and legitimates a diversity that had been confined to extralegal texts. And while some of the identities it inscribes reinforce a commitment to the state's historical time (e.g., the concept of a "minority" belongs to the narrative of state forms),[53] what the law seeks to contain it also enlarges. It thereby opens the way to a future of ways of being-in-common that cannot be contained within the more generalized sense that a sovereignty-oriented political discourse has imposed. It allows for encounters of recognition among persons and groups who have existed outside the traditional juridical discourse of citizenship. In attempting its own spatialization of temporality, in constructing society as a place where community and diversity are dangerous rivals, the law paradoxically helps to produce a diversity that must inevitably endanger its containment strategy.

Rather than speaking in terms of dangers to community, however, I want to argue that the law has been complicit in enlarging the sphere of the political. By positioning itself among conflicting temporalities, it aids and abets other times and thus other presences. Accordingly, it, like other more radically disruptive texts, points to a promise of a new mode of citizenship, a recognition that "community" consists of disjoint presences and requires continual renegotiation of whom it contains; it is "a politics without denouement."[54] Opposing the suppressions inherent in the Hegelian chronotype, official/legal as well as fictional forms of writing are making clear that being-in-common consists of diverse trajectories of arrival and projection. The texts to which I have referred resist the state's staging of a temporally coherent national culture, its production of national politics as a collective's will to realize its essence. Instead, they encourage an approach to the political that is "receptive to the *meaning* of our multiple, dispersed, mortally fragmented existences."[55] The politics of citizenship within this framework accepts disjoint copresence and moves toward a model of community that cannot exist in one coherent temporal trajectory, that cannot found a single "horizon behind us," and cannot anticipate the accomplishment of a unified self-presence.[56]

6. Sovereignty, Dissymmetry, and Bare Life

The Assyrian Home Front

> And the widows of Ashur are loud in their wail,
> And the idols are down in the temple of Baal.[1]

These two lines from verse 6 of Lord Byron's poem "The Destruction of Sennacherib" are spatially disjunctive in the context of his otherwise exclusive focus on the battlefield. Substantively and melodically, Byron's poem celebrates the Israelites' Jehovah-aided victory over their Assyrian enemies, namely, the first two verses:

> The Assyrian came down like the wolf on the foal,
> And his cohorts were gleaming of purple and gold;
> And the sheen of their spears was like stars on the sea,
> When the blue wave rolls nightly on deep Galilee.
> Like the leaves of the forest when Summer is green,
> The host with their banners at sunset were seen;
> Like the leaves of the forest when Autumn hath blown,
> The host on the morrow lay withered and thrown. (180)

Only in the first two lines of verse 6 does Byron's poem acknowledge a domestic Assyrian context. Those lines supply the sole recognition that Assyrian soldiers (for example, "the rider distorted and pale, / with the dew on his brow and the rust / on his mail" [from verse 5]) had a life within a household and a religious community. Byron's emphasis is in accord with his "proto-Zionist" nationalism ("the wild-dove hath her nest, the fox his cave, / Mankind their Country, Israel but the grave"— from "Oh Weep for Those" [138]). "Byron the national melodist" (74), and Western civilizationalist, saw the Hebrew Bible as a prototypical model of the contemporary nationalisms he endorsed. For example, in reaction to a threat to Italy (part of the "West" in Byron's civilizational imaginary) from an Austrian army massed at Italy's northern border, Byron evoked the same biblical story: "O Jerusalem! Jerusalem! The Huns are on the Po; but if they once pass it on their way to Naples, all Italy will be behind them. The Dogs—the Wolves—may they perish like the Host of Sennacherib!" (181). For Byron, unless the Jews occupy the terrain of their original, ancient conquest, it is a place that is historically unfulfilled: where "the godless dwell" (from "Oh Weep for Those" [138]), where "the Arabs' camels stray" and "the Baal-adorer bows" (from "On Jordan's Banks" [143]). Byron read the Hebrew Bible as a heroic national story. Its coherence for him is based on the primary coherence that most commentators have lent to the text, a focus on "the geography of the land to be conquered."[2]

There is, however, another important venue in the Hebrew Bible, the household. In Mieke Bal's feminist interpretation of the Book of Judges, she offers what she calls a "countercoherence" to a nationalist reading. In her approach, the spatial emphasis shifts from the land to be conquered to "the houses to be conquered," the places where, among other things, "[d]aughters . . . meet their undoing," places, moreover, where "the interaction between the political and the domestic is located" (170). Because her concern is with the fate of women rather than with the destiny of a nation, Bal provides a different locus of enunciation. Domestic space looms large as women, who are part of "bare life" but not "politically qualified life," achieve subject positions.[3] While, for example, Byron's poetic version of "Jephthah's daughter" simply perpetuates a heroic, nationalist story in Judges by having a nameless victim give her father permission for her sacrifice, Bal reorders the episode's political significance. She gives Jephthah's daughter a name, "Bath Jephthah," to resist the text's "ideological position" and lend significance and agency to a life that is otherwise rendered passive and instrumental to another's.[4] In effect, she reorders the boundary between "bare life" (that aspect of humanity that is excluded from the determinations constituting the polity) and "politically qualified life."[5] By foregrounding the Book of Judge's basic dissymmetry—"the double opposition between male and female on the one hand, and between victim and killer on the other"[6]—Bal elevates the lives of characters who have been below the threshold of recognition in traditional readings and offers an interpretation that moves the gender relations within the Israelite household into the center of the political order.

Dissymmetries among the cast of characters in and around the old "Holy Land" continue to be perpetuated, in both official discourses and popular culture. If we move from the Book of Judges to the contemporary scene, we can discern alternative ideological positions that are also constructed around the location of the family within the political order. In particular, my focus is on two recent "patriot games," one involving U.S. president Bill Clinton and one involving novelist Tom Clancy's heroic character Jack Ryan as he is constructed in a feature film version of *Patriot Games*. Ultimately, the aim of this analysis is, like Mieke Bal's, a "humanitarian intervention." I want to disrupt the reading of the character of different aspects of humanity in recent "patriot games" by analyzing a recent filmic cultural text, Elia Suileman's *Chronicle of a Disappearance*, with a largely nameless cast of characters, existing within complex family milieux in the same region. In addition, focusing on this region, I want to destabilize and thereby politicize the boundary that sovereignty enacts between bare life and politically qualified life, a boundary that politically differentiates aspects of humanity and operates as a relatively unquestioned predicate of the more explicitly recognized policy problematic known as humanitarian intervention. To appreciate this aspect of sovereignty—its meaning-creating protointerventions—it is necessary to assess the structure of the sovereign gaze and its related enactments, which have been responsible for the ways that politically eligible life is ordinarily conceived in the region.

"Patriot Games"

The *New York Times* reported on August 20, 1998, that "President Clinton . . . ordered U.S. military strikes against terrorist facilities in Afghanistan and Sudan after linking them to the embassy bombings in Africa." Clinton cited "compelling information" that the targets "were planning additional terrorist attacks." The strikes—one on a pharmaceutical company in Sudan, alleged by the "intelligence sources" to be a chemical weapons plant, and one on an alleged terrorist training camp in Afghanistan—resemble an event in the feature film *Patriot Games*. Just as the decision to use overwhelming force against the alleged "terrorist" enemies of the United States was made in the face of conflicting intelligence reports, a strike on an alleged Arab-run North African terrorist training camp in the film is made despite significant uncertainty. When the film's hero, retired intelligence officer Jack Ryan (Harrison Ford), is shown the satellite pictures of the terrorists he wants eliminated, he responds that he is not absolutely certain of what he is seeing. But when his former CIA superior (James Earl Jones) asks him if there is anything in life about which he is absolutely certain, Ryan, after responding, "Only my daughter's love," accedes to the strike decision, and lethal force is employed. The response is telling; it generates complex commitments to interconnected life-worlds—family on the domestic front and dangers to U.S. domesticity abroad in the form of a loose alliance of terrorists from Northern Ireland and the "Arab world."

The justifications for the use of lethal force, in violation of territorial sovereignties, nevertheless illuminate, in both the actual and filmic scenarios, a significant attribute of the contemporary structure of sovereignty. The decisions reflect an aspect of modernity's biopolitical imperatives; they are justified on the basis of models of "life" that provide much of the political basis for contemporary sovereignty. The CIA strike in the film, in a desert thousands of miles from Ryan's home, is carried out to protect Jack Ryan's family from terrorists bent on avenging Ryan's contribution to the death of one of their family members (Ryan's reference to the certainty of his daughter's love reflects both the film's familial theme and the fact that his daughter is recovering from life-threatening injuries inflicted by the vengeful terrorist). Clinton's strikes, also delivered thousands of miles from U.S. shores, were undertaken to defend those at home. Their justification was, in the words of Defense Secretary William Cohen, reported in the *New York Times* on August 21, 1998, "our absolute obligation to protect the American people from terrorist activities."

The decisions, in both cases, to engage in an exceptional violation of the structure of international sovereignties, derive from an aspect of a biopolitical legitimation of violence that Michel Foucault has identified as peculiarly modern. Whereas wars were once "waged in the name of the sovereign who must be defended," now "they are waged in behalf of the existence of everyone . . . the decision that initiates them and the one that terminates them are in fact increasingly informed by the naked question of survival"; killing takes place "in the name of life necessity."[7] Elaborating Foucault's insight about the change in the legitimation of violence from protecting the inviolability of the sovereign to the task of "administering life" (137), Giorgio Agamben points out that modern sovereignty has been reinflected by the "politicization of life."[8] Sovereignty, at the level of executive decision making, he notes, operates in a process of making exceptions in order to use extralegal force in behalf of some aspect of human existence. Rather than functioning wholly within a legal framework, it exists in a zone of "indistinction" between violence and the law (19).

To appreciate what appears to be paradoxical—the sovereignty-affirming significance of a violation of territorial sovereignties—one must recognize that sovereignty-as-enactment exists in "the intersection between the juridico-legal and biopolitical models of power" (6). In addition to its legal supports and legitimations, sovereignty is situated in a complex topology of lives, both inside and outside its jurisdiction. Because sovereignty's biopolitical imperatives, realized in the making of exceptions (for example, the missile strikes in the Sudan or decisions to engage in "humanitarian intervention," also in Sudan of late), are derived from the power to administer life, sovereign power can be deployed to kill without committing homicide (83). The political order, consequently, is constituted as much by an extralegal dimension of power as it is by its networks of legalities and institutions. Sovereign power is continually involved in the specification of a model of "life" that extends well beyond notions of politically qualified life (for example, the lives of state citizens).

Sudan's recent eligibility as a target of exceptional action, for example, has required a specification of the kind of life at stake, at home and abroad, both within and outside Sudan. The decision to perpetuate an "emergency" in Sudan, which, at the same time, produces U.S. humanitarian assistance and a flow of weapons to a Christian-dominated region in the southern portion of the country, is not unrelated to what is seen by many in the United States as the special qualifications of Christian lives: In October of 1998 the U.S. Senate unanimously passed the International Religious Freedom Act, giving power to the president to decide how to react to violations. As noted in the *New York Times,* "The bill grew from an effort more than a year ago by the Christian Coalition and other conservative religious groups to require the government to step up its fight against religious persecution from Sudan to China."[9] The lives of primarily Christian "believers" are seen as imperiled by Arab/Muslim political institutions and initiatives.

In an age in which a number of states have been continually at war with resistant portions of their indigenous populations (for example, Mexico and Guatemala), the substantial death rates among indigenous peoples have not resulted in a discourse of humanitarian emergency in the U.S. Congress, which has been quick to evoke these terms in relation to what is increasingly characterized as a "persecution of Christians" in Sudan. The map of humanitarian concerns, long influenced by a geo-strategic imaginary, is also heavily influenced, of late, by a map of Christendom (although support from the American Jewish Committee as well as a wide range of Christian organizations has also influenced the cartography of religious persecution).

At a minimum, apart from the fate of Christians and Jews, "bare life" in the Middle East and in Islamic Africa has not received a complex coding. The characteristics of life, which sovereignty administers in its decisions about who can be killed without committing homicide in these regions, have been relatively unspecified in comparison to the characteristics of life that sovereignty sees itself as protecting. The feature film *Patriot Games* reflects this dissymmetry in the specification and evaluation of life; it provides a contemporary reflection of the distribution of bare life, with which sovereignty-as-exceptional-enactment has been concerned. And, what is especially timely and revealing about the film's thematic, in this epoch of an increasingly insistent discourse linking "family values" and nationalism, is its construction of the aspect of life specifically threatened by the functioning of Arab-trained terrorism: the American family. Most of the drama of the film surrounds the attempt by a rogue (non-IRA) Irish terrorist, Sean Miller, who is trained at an Arab terrorist camp, to strike at members of Jack Ryan's family because Ryan intervened in a kidnapping in London and killed the terrorist's brother.

The film, not unlike official policy discourses, contains a remarkable dissymmetry. Terrorists' families receive almost no specification, while Jack Ryan's family is richly and elaborately developed in its loving, harmonious, and domestic life-worthy relations. The film opens with an assemblage of panning shots of the Ryans' family home on the Chesapeake Bay in Maryland. The images of family photos, diplomas, and the paraphernalia of daily life indicate a family that is both child-centered and actively professional. We subsequently learn that Jack Ryan is a retired CIA man with a Ph.D. who lectures at the Naval Academy, his wife (Ann Archer) is an eye surgeon, and their daughter is a model child enrolled in a private elementary school. As director Phillip Noyce notes in his comment about the opening "theme shots," in which viewers are "led to Jack Ryan's house. . . . It's the house of a family, because the movie is about family."[10]

The film drama's precipitating incident takes place in London, where the Ryan family is combining business with pleasure (Ryan is in England to lecture to the Royal Navy on Soviet fleet deployment, and the rest of the family is with him to enjoy sightseeing). Just as Ryan is about to meet his wife and daughter, who are watching the guard change at Buckingham Palace, he spots a kidnaping attempt under way. A group of suspected IRA operatives, which includes Sean Miller and his younger brother, are attempting to snatch a member of the royal family from his car. Ryan's

The Ryan household in the film *Patriot Games* (1992), clearly depicted as the home of a child-centered, professional family.

intervention foils the plot and results in the death of Miller's brother. The event establishes two themes: First, it underscores Ryan's character; he is represented as a devoted family man who will nevertheless risk his life (and the possible result—a husbandless/fatherless family) to be a dedicated and heroic antiterrorist. Second, the event results in a dangerous contagion; it brings the deadly virus of terrorism "home" in two senses. It comes to the United States, and it ultimately invades Jack Ryan's home when a Sean Miller–led group launches an assault on Ryan's house, where Ryan, his family, and the grateful English royal he rescued are assembled. By this point in the plot, Ryan has rejoined the CIA in order to become, in effect, a relay of that dimension of sovereignty that can kill. His character serves, ultimately, as a convergence of family protector and sovereign killer.

Sean Miller is also a killer. He kills often and without inhibition. During his escape, he executes those who were guarding him on his way to prison, and subsequently he kills fellow terrorists who seek to turn his attention (unsuccessfully) from his preoccupation with personal vengeance toward the larger political goals of his movement, which aims to free Northern Ireland of British involvement by targeting members of the royal family. However, there are significant dissymmetries between the two killers. While Jack Ryan is a married man, whose sexuality, like his wife's, is contained within the marriage, Sean Miller is single, and his female partner is a lethal lover, who uses her sexuality to lure an antagonist of their rogue movement to a hotel room, where instead of having sex with him, she shoots him. In contrast, the Ryans' sex is aimed both at affirming the marriage bond and at procreation (in one scene, Mrs. Ryan tells Jack that she is pregnant with their second child). While a strong familial commitment characterizes almost every aspect of Jack Ryan's persona, Sean Miller's primary (terrorist) being is in his danger to Ryan's family. He specifically targets the Ryans' daughter, who barely recovers from critical injuries after Miller runs her mother's car off the road with his van.

Ultimately, the film turns a symmetry between Ryan and Miller into a dissymmetry. Both are angry men. When Ryan is asked by one of his Naval Academy colleagues why he intervened in the kidnapping, he says it was because the attack on an innocent victim made him mad. But Ryan's anger is distinguished by its righteousness. It is aimed at protecting state officials and his family. Sean Miller's anger is represented as dangerous and irrational. In fits of rage he kills colleagues who oppose the singularity of his quest for revenge. As director Noyce suggests, the film is about "Sean Miller's family as well,"[11] but through the dissymmetry that the filmic story effects, Jack Ryan gets to kill without committing homicide, while Sean Miller remains merely a killer. In addition to the deaths in the North African desert, for which Ryan is responsible, in the final scene of their confrontation, Ryan, the relay of legitimate sovereignty, confronts Miller, the killer, in a chase scene in boats on a stormy Chesapeake Bay. They end up grappling in the same vessel, where Sean Miller dies when Ryan impales him on an anchor. But long before this death scene, Miller has been impaled on a symbolic anchor. He has run afoul of American intelligence heroics in the form of an exemplary protective husband and father, whose sexuality is strictly marital, who combines the detachment of an intellectual with a Ph.D. with the moral indignation of the righteous, and who, in the last analysis, can kill both because his violence is sanctioned by a recognized state and because he is certain only of his daughter's love.

In comparison, Sean Miller is as good as dead well before the final struggle. His political initiative is criminalized while Ryan's is legitimated; his familial and erotic attachments are impugned (his brother is a misguided young coterrorist and his love interest is a cold-blooded assassin to whom he is not married), and his colleagues, in particular the Arabs with whom he trains for his assault on the Ryan family, are faceless traders in violence. They are represented simply as terrorists who have been continual objects of satellite surveillance. There is no hint that they have any attachments. No other context, historical or political, is supplied for why young Arab men might be engaged in military training in the desert.

The repression of context in representing Arab terrorists is a long-standing tradition in both official political discourse and media dramas. As Edward Said has noted, "'terrorism' as a phenomenon of the public sphere of communication and representation in the West" is characterized by its "isolation from any explanation of mitigating circumstances."[12] The political circumstances abetting the recruitment of terrorists from among historical victims tend to go unacknowledged in the official discourse on terrorism, as well as in popular media treatments (48). Rather, the "rationalized violence" of dominant states is represented in the use of its superior technologies for "controlling, surveying . . . subject only occasionally to the heterogeneous, quixotic, venturesome counter-violence of the outcast, the visionary, the prophet" (53).

This particular dissymmetry between rationalized and justifiable sovereign violence and quixotic counterviolence is realized in *Patriot Games* as a dissymmetry between the Ryan family and the decontextualized Arab terrorists in the desert. The film, in its depiction of author Tom Clancy's preoccupation with a weapon's-eye view of global danger, shows no close-ups of Arabs. They are seen only though the imaging of a spy satellite, while those to whom they are a danger are elaborately contextualized with panning shots of their home and work venues and with framing shots that lend them both depth and agency. The close-ups, or what Gilles Deleuze calls "affection-images,"[13] present them as subjects with complex emotional lives, and the frequent shots taken from their vantage points present their struggle for survival as the privileged moral and political problematic. Deleuze provides a pertinent analysis of the affection image as the close-up, which "is the face" (87). The face, he notes, is the place where the significance of all the bodily movements, as an ensemble of the agency of the self, is registered. It is the face that answers the questions: "What are you thinking about?" and "How do you feel?" (88).

In the deciding scene of *Patriot Games,* while Jack Ryan is sitting with his CIA colleagues, looking at satellite images of the alleged terrorist groups in the North African desert, the contrast between "these fuzzy little shapes on the screen" and the reaction shot of Jack Ryan is striking.[14] The filmic emphasis is not on the experience of the fuzzy shapes, who, Ryan is told, could be wiped out by an SAS team "in under three minutes"; it is on Jack Ryan's morally vexing decision. In contrast with the distance shots of the fuzzy shapes are the close-ups of Jack Ryan's ambivalence-strained face. The film's visual rhetoric constitutes the political problem as the hard decisions that must be made to protect the American family, which has already been located (with the elaborate mapping of familial home, work, and school spaces) in a topology of American life. And it reproduces the decontextualizing effects of the official discourse on Arab terrorism. Arab terrorists are identified first in various paper and electronic files and then as grainy, satellite-eye images. Throughout the film, they are faceless. Moreover, there is no contextualizing narrative of the complexities of the arrival of Arab terrorists in the desert training camp. Among other things, in contrast with the situating of Ryan's career history and family life, the absence of context renders them as unattached killers without legitimate political warrant.

We are left to ponder where the households of Arab "terrorists" fit into the contemporary politics of the region. It would seem on the surface that modern discourses of international conflict have abandoned the household in favor of a purely national imaginary. The discourse of Israeli security, for example, aggregates the people into a state or (in the more long-term historical discourse) a "land." And the Arab/other is not a patriarch or family member but a leader of a "movement." From the perspective of U.S. security analysts, the Arab world is a venue of destabilization and an exporter of violence, primarily through the machinations of Arab "terrorists." Insofar as Arabs have families within this perspective, they are breeding grounds for multiple terrorists. What is endemic is a threat to become epidemic (as it did when Jack Ryan caught the bug and brought it home in *Patriot Games*).

While the terrorist is represented in a decidedly afamilial way, the American family has been recruited as the focal point in the social order in contemporary security discourses. This elaborated political role of the

Ryan (played by Harrison Ford) looking at satellite images of an Arab terrorist training camp in the North African desert.

American family is part of a historical trajectory in which the space of the family has been increasingly connected with the spaces of the political. Once the state began legitimating itself on the basis of its role in preserving social life, the private life of the family became a public good. At the level of domestic politics, the family became an object of symbolic manipulation to protect the "liberal definition of the state" against the more extreme consequences of a free-market economy. As Jacques Donzelot points out, "the discourses denouncing social privilege and class domination had to dissociate themselves gradually from the critique of the family,"[15] which had hitherto been regarded as a competitive venue of social power impeding policy initiatives. To protect itself from various forms of social protest, the state transformed the family into a "positive form of solution to the problems posed by the liberal state rather than [dealing with it] as a negative element of resistance to social change" (53). In the U.S. case, an exemplary discourse on "the Negro family" emerged by the mid-twentieth century, with the suggestion that the high incidence of black poverty could be combated by improving family solidarity.[16]

At the level of interstate relations, the family became the primary unit of national cultural life. As nations became states, nationalist projects aimed at inventing a coherent national culture co-opted the family as part of its primary strategy for symbolically wedding nationalism to sexuality.[17] And as nationalism increasingly required a form of civilizational distinctiveness, norms of decency (as noted in chapter 2), connected to familial sexuality, encouraged Western states to locate the family as the symbolic center of the nation. Since the epoch of state formation, in which codes developed that connect familial structures with national distinctiveness, the civilizational map has served various expressions of domestic anxiety about dangers to the nation and/or to "Western civilization" as a whole.[18]

The relationship of the family to exceptional action in the elimination of global danger therefore has considerable historical depth. Sovereignty's administration of life, enacted in defense of a familial model of domestic life, has a long and complicated historical legacy. And, of late, actor Harrison Ford has been the popular culture avatar of the defense of the current, deeply politicized version of domesticity against what is increasingly seen as the primary post–cold war external danger, terrorism. His Jack Ryan (Alec Baldwin played the parallel role in *The Hunt for Red October*)—heroic father, husband, and intelligence analyst— has been supplemented by another of his characters, President James

Marshall, a two-fisted chief executive who saves himself and his family from a terrorist hijacking of the presidential plane in the feature film *Air Force One.*

Ford's various roles as a heroic family man reflect what Karen Schneider has identified as "a major shift in the narrative and ideological focus of the 1990's action thriller."[19] She, among others, has pointed out that, as "debates about the family moved to the forefront of the American socio-political discourse of the late 1980's, the family began to find its way into the action-thriller" (2–4). A new genre of film, with "elements of the traditional family—heroic father, supporting mother, vulnerable children," came into focus within a narrative in which a variety of threats place "families at risk only to bring about their salvation" (4). And most significant for locating the polarity between the Ryan and Miller families in *Patriot Games,* it fits very well the version of the action-thriller film that focuses on criminal types. This subgenre treats "the potential for the destruction of a large number of people" but focuses its "plot . . . narrative tension and the related spectacular violence . . . on one family and its dark double" (4).

Nevertheless, there are other families and, perhaps most significant, alternative loci of enunciation (treated within other film genres) that challenge the dissymmetries in the representations of U.S. families versus those who allegedly endanger them. To provide a more politicized and less reactive politics of the family, I turn to one of them.

Elaborating Bare Life: Another Locus of Enunciation

While U.S. official discourse and popular culture have rendered Arabs in general and Palestinian families in particular as breeding units for dangerous terrorists, and the Israeli government has enacted this view with repressive policies (for example, ordering the bulldozing of Palestinian houses of the relatives of suspected terrorists), there is another locus of enunciation, from within a Palestinian family, provided in a 1996 film, by the self-exiled Palestinian filmmaker Elia Suileman. His *Chronicle of a Disappearance* (hereafter *Chronicle*) disrupts the U.S. and Israeli constructions of bare life among Arab peoples in general and Palestinians in particular. The first half of the film is situated in Nazareth, primarily in Suileman's family home but also in various other city locations, for example, a cafe and a tourist shop. The second half is located in Jerusalem, where a drama is staged in which Palestinians pretend to be part of a terrorist conspiracy. The film's actions and props in this second half encourage viewers to expect an episode of violence. But the conspiracy scenario turns out to be a parody. For example, what looks like a grenade on the desk of one character in the plot turns out to be a cigarette lighter.

Taken as a whole, *Chronicle*'s depiction of Arabs contrasts sharply with *Patriot Games*'s, in which Arabs are decontextualized both in the structure of the script and in the nature of the distancing camera shots. *Chronicle* provides an elaborate view of Palestinian subjects with close-ups of faces, mappings of family space, and tableaux of the exchanges of recognition involved in friendships. Apart from this stark contrast—a conjuring away of Arab subjectivity versus its restoration and elaboration—the two films, *Patriot Games* and *Chronicle,* have remarkable parallels. First, they both dwell on the space of the family (although they depart dramatically in the ways in which they treat the relationship between local domestic space and the wider global context in which it is shaped). Second, both films treat conspiracies. However, while *Patriot Games* has conspiring Irish and Arab terrorists, *Chronicle* stages a parody of the view of the Palestinian as terrorist, and, most significant, it departs from the allegorical structure that Fredric Jameson has attributed to the way conspiracy films treat the local-global relationship.

One element of the conspiracy film, according to Jameson, is the way "local items of the present" contain individuals who "can add up to more than their sum."[20] Jameson has in mind the way in which local events refer allegorically to an "unrepresentable totality," a "global or world system" (10). In *Chronicle,* however, individuals, ironically, add up to less than they are; they are not part of a global terrorist network that the action in part two seems to be suggesting (until the signs are reversed, late in the film). Yet, there is a way to locate Suileman's characters—family members, friends, and acquaintances—in a wider global context. One needs to lend Israel's Palestinians a history to develop that context. They are a people who have been largely left out of the historical (usually violent) process of state formation. Within this historical process, in which internal forms of resistance were eventually pacified (or expelled), those deprived of their proprietary holdings and spaces of collective attachment were forced into marginalized positions, either outside the borders of their ancestral lands or incorporated within them in a diminished and highly surveilled status.

The latter is the case with Suileman's family, which is living in the town of Nazareth in Israel. After voluntary exile, Suileman returns to participate in the representation of the victims of Israel's state formation. With a series of humorous, ironic, and parodic vignettes, he presents the life of the tightly surveilled and restricted Palestinians in Israel as a habitus of primarily mundane domesticity rather than as a danger to Israel's aspiration to be a Western and Jewish state. Allegorically, the situation of Suileman's Palestinians adds up to both less and more than they are. Although they are less inasmuch as they are not participating in a global network of terrorists that is the preoccupation of the Clancy-Noyce *Patriot Games,* they are much more than the faceless, ahistorical characters in the terrorist training camp of *Patriot Games.*

The economies of the less and more in which Palestinians achieve recognition in Suileman's film are presented by the assemblage of camera shots, which construct the spatiotemporalities of Palestinian daily existence. In terms of the less, whatever may be their aspirations, it is the case that the Palestinians within Israel, like those in (the increasingly autonomous territories) Gaza and Hebron, are without a homeland. But Suileman's film is not simply a lament about the status of the people whom Said, in his more polemical approach, describes as the "victims of victims."[21] Instead, he maps the consequences of resident homelessness with a visual rhetoric. And rather than promoting an identity politics, seeking to define and elaborate an essential Palestinian identity (as a counterimage to the Palestinian-as-terrorist, for example), he plays with ambiguities.

The domestic lives of Suileman's Palestinian family and friends and acquaintances are mundane and indistinguishable from typical forms of domesticity among many peoples. Suileman's opening scene sets the tone of the incessant production of ambiguity throughout the film. A close-up of an indistinguishable shape slowly comes into focus until we see what looks like a barren landscape. As the camera draws back, however, that "landscape" turns out to be the nose of Suileman's sleeping father. If we heed one of Jameson's primary insights in his treatment of the "geopolitical unconscious," we can read this shot as an allegorical moment. As Jameson puts it: "On a global scale, allegory allows the most random, minute, or isolated landscapes to function as a figurative machinery in which questions about the system and its control over the local ceaselessly rise and fall."[22] Suileman confirms the allegorical significance of the nose as "minute landscape" with the on-screen dedication at the end of *Chronicle*: "To my mother and father, my last homeland."

The framing shots of the cramped spaces in the Suileman household, which are explored through the first part of the film, indicate the way in which family space provides an inadequate venue for Palestinian collective realization. Family life confines its members to the rituals of birth, death, and marriage, as is implied in an early scene in which Suileman's aunt, framed in the Suilemans' narrow sitting room (which is further narrowed with the use of a concave lens), is gossiping about various family members as she prepares to visit relatives in order to offer condolences on a death in the family. The confinement of Palestinians in their spaces of domesticity is reflected in diverse allegorical vignettes throughout the film (for example, in scenes in which Suileman shows the family pets, a bird and a dog, in cages).

Yet even within the confined space of the family home, Suileman is able to show the way in which Palestinians are part of a venerable historical trajectory. His assemblage of camera shots has a cut from the scene of his gossiping aunt to one in which his father is smoking a water pipe (hookah) while playing a video game of backgammon. This shot shows how the small family home contains layers of historical time. A Palestinian has entered modernity but has not left his cultural past behind.

What is minimalist in the way Suileman's script treats the practices of historical memory through which current Palestinian culture in Israel is articulated is augmented by his camera shots. In the scene in which his father is smoking a hookah and playing a video game, the juxtaposition conveys a memory effect. In Deleuze's terms, it "makes sheets of past and layers of reality correspond,"[23] thereby indicating how various relationships coexist. The cinematic faculty that Suileman summons here is thus not comparable to a psychological memory. It is, rather, a "strange faculty" that connects the domain of the individual with that of the collective, or "private business" with "the people's business" (221). Suileman's camera effectively makes the household a site in which the pressures and ambivalences of the marginalized Palestinian, situated between cultural memory and modernity, are elaborated. The singularities of cultural practices encounter the generalities of a media-dominated modern lifeworld, which enter the house through a public window, the Suilemans' television set (shown in many scenes).

Suileman's camera also captures this tension between cultural singularity and public life in the world of Palestinian commerce. He visits a friend's tourist shop, which sells religious icons and other paraphernalia to groups of tourists visiting Christ's alleged childhood home in Nazareth. The political economy of tourism, into which the local Palestinians have been drawn, has turned a religious practice among Palestinian Christians into a mundane and deceptive sales practice. For example, we see Suileman's friend preparing for tourist visits by filling bottles labeled as holy water from the tap in the sink, and we see a small statue of the Virgin Mary constantly tipping over. No attempt by the proprietor at

Elia Suileman's father, smoking a
hookah and playing a video game
of backgammon, in *Chronicle of a
Disappearance* (1996).

balancing the statue will make her stand. The shop scene constitutes an effective allegory for the fate of Palestinian cultural practices as they are confronted by a global commercial structure. In a repeated scene, a distance shot shows a bored Suileman and his friend, smoking outside the shop, their bodies conveying a sense of resignation in the face of the way systems of exchange have shaped the life-world of Nazareth's Palestinians. Like the falling statue, they cannot recover a stable place. While the scene is local, the reality is a local-global set of relations. Just as Suileman's camera, deployed in the family home, gives Palestinian life a historical context, his camera inside and outside the shop locates it within an increasingly global political economy. To state the relationship briefly, as structures of exchange value are imposed, the cultural predicates of value are repressed. Reflecting a pervasive tension, cultural practices tend to maintain the singularity of things, while economic practices promote their exchangeability. And, like almost everyone else, the Palestinians in Nazareth confront the historical tendency for commoditization to overwhelm cultural inhibition.[24]

Although the tourist shop, named Holy Land, represents a moment in the relentless commoditization of worship and the summoning of Nazareth's Palestinians into a global economy, it also serves as a venue where a nonverbal aura of friendship persists. Suileman and his friend, the shop's proprietor, are captured at various points in the cinematic (nonlinear) narrative, sitting together in front of the shop, wordlessly smoking. On the one hand, the time of the present, as an epoch of commoditization, constitutes a radical break with ancient times; on the other, the temporality of friendship persists. Suileman's repeated tableau of the two friends,

Suileman and his friend in front of the friend's tourist shop in Nazareth—a framing of their persistent friendship in a world shaped by global tourism.

presented with a series of identical framing shots, offers a "referential montage" in which each succeeding shot refers to a previous one.[25] The reference is to the temporality of friendship, an aspect of persistence in a world of change. As was noted in chapter 1, friendship "never presents itself outside of time"; it becomes stabilized "through an ordeal which takes time."[26]

The "direct image of time" assembled by Suileman's camera shots in his repeated scenes of himself and his friend in front of the Holy Land tourist shop is therefore a critical intervention in the narrative of modernity's incessant commoditization.[27] Suileman displays an aspect of Palestinian life that has resisted the pressures of both the surrounding structure of political hegemony and the system of global exchange. Neither dispossession nor commoditization has sundered the attachments of friendship. Nor have they sundered the bonds of mutuality that constitute community. In another series of repeated scenes, a car keeps stopping in front of a cafe. Each time, when an altercation ensues between the driver and passenger, it is stopped and mediated by the men in the cafe, who rush to placate their friends in the troubled exchange.

Space as well as time is effectively thematized in Suileman's filmic ethnography. At one point, a cut to Suileman's father and fishing companions, who are out on a boat in the Sea of Galilee, enacts a contrast between the cramped spaces of Palestinian homes and some moments of leisure within an open space with a distant horizon. The contrast is deepened when one of the fishermen stands on the deck of the boat and, with arms extended toward the distant horizon, sings the theme song from Rodgers and Hammerstein's *Oklahoma!* (a musical that treats one's territorial

patrimony as expansive rather than confining). Given the spatial con-
striction of Palestinian life, the song about belonging to a land that is
grand is ironic and parodic.

Nevertheless, time is Suileman's primary focus. Many of the vignettes
that show the bonding involved in friendships and community involve
Suileman himself. Back after twelve years away, he finds that his friendships have survived. They have withstood the ordeals of regional history
and separation. The scenes in which Suileman and his friends are smoking together serve as a sign of maintained attachments. These scenes are
repeated in various venues—in restaurants, doorways, and hallways, as
well as in front of the souvenir shop. The referential montage, applied to
the silent bond among Palestinian men, like the repeated scenes that cut
back to the Suileman household, show how Palestinian life exists in complex layers of time. The framings of the encounters with depth-of-focus
shots display a marginalized people who, although left out of the national time of the state in which they dwell, are nevertheless located complexly in moments of time that speak to what remains shared by a people who
must seek collective identity in something other than a territorial sovereignty. And, inasmuch as the domesticated Palestinians cannot effectively
evince a masculine force of arms in behalf of a territorial nation, their
male agon is shown to be confined to episodic contests. For example, in
one scene Suileman's father is shown, ritualistically (and unconvincing-
ly), vanquishing all comers in arm wrestling contests in a local restaurant
hangout.

While the time of historical encounter between Jews and Arabs is, for
Palestinians, a time of disruption and dispossession, a time of centrifugal
pressure on Palestinian collective identity (one character in the film
speaks of the time "after the Israeli invasion"), family and friendship
time, as well as the recent Palestinian historical time, is more centripetal.
This later temporality of relatively contemporary Palestinian history is
also presented through a referential montage. The Palestinian writer Paha
Mohammed Ali is shown on two occasions with a framing shot as he tells
a story told to him on many occasions by his grandfather. In response to
the request "Tell me about Istanbul," what is told instead, in exacting detail, is a personal experience. Beginning with the line "Istanbul is the
flower of cities," the story becomes diverted to a vignette about a meal the
grandfather was able to buy in the market, a delicious lamb's head with
bread, which far exceeded the spartan fare available to soldiers in the
Turkish camps. The repeated telling of the story is more than a humorous insight into a self-indulgence; it reveals the complex assemblage of

diasporic experiences that are turned, through the medium of story-telling, into the kind of collective memory that both speaks to and contains the Palestinian dispersion in the region.

Despite the moments of coherence that Suileman's camera affords a dispossessed, spatially disrupted people, his film does not seek to display an essential Palestinian identity. Instead he stages an ambivalent encounter. While his camera provides intimate portraits and vignettes that challenge the distancing rhetorics of antiterrorism (as well as the visuals provided by the surveillant satellite images of the U.S. Defense Mapping Agency), Suileman's only stable identity is as a son and a friend. His presence in the film supplies distance as well as the close-ups of a filmic ethnography. Indeed, in stark contrast to a geopolitical, state-oriented imaginary (for example, the one presented in *Patriot Games*), Suileman crafts his presence as an outsider as well as an insider. Instead of a gaze based on a stable state citizenship, he brings to his encounters the bifocality of the diasporic artist. He participates in a "cinema of displacement," a genre produced by "liminars" who occupy a "'slippery zone' between two 'structural force-fields.'"[28] And because the diasporic identity he brings to his encounters is, in Salman Rushdie's words (applied to the diasporic writer), "at once plural and partial,"[29] he manifests a pervasive ambivalence toward his experiences back in his old "homeland."

The most telling instance of Suileman's ambivalence is represented in his inability to deliver a talk to an assemblage of Palestinians in a community meeting hall. A combination of severe microphone feedback and the continual ringing of cell phones keeps interrupting his lecture. His inability to give the talk is not unrelated to his inability to have something definitive to say. Like his camera, which jumps among scenes of family and community life that have no overarching and binding political coherence, there is no clear narrative to which his words can be attached. The film must offer an ambiguous politics, because the people on whom it is focused—Suileman himself and his family, friends, and acquaintances—function in life-worlds without a definitive temporal, spatial, or political warrant. Nevertheless, Suileman provides faces and human connections to a world that sits precariously in the interface between the past and present, between the old Palestine and the present Israel, between a sacred past and a commercialized present (the biblical Sea of Galilee is shown now with modern watercraft and is so polluted that, as a Greek Orthodox priest notes, now anyone can walk on that water) and between a mundane life-world and an oppressive atmosphere of surveillance visited by the apparatus of the Israeli security state.

The on-screen presence of the security apparatus occupies most of the second half of the film. Under the rubric of "Jerusalem Political Diary," Suileman produces a parody of the security mentality, as clumsy police teams engage in arbitrary searches, rushing to and fro while Palestinians with walkie-talkies amplify their frantic movements by delivering false reports. In addition, while acting out the features of a terrorist plot with their movements and props, Suileman's Palestinian actors demonstrate the absurdity of Israel's condition of "hypersecurity,"[30] an enactment of a fantasy of control through technologically driven measures of surveillance of a largely quiescent, subordinated population. Through a dramatic change in the operation of his filmic text, Suileman demonstrates the folly of a strategy of total control instead of a peaceful coming to terms with a people who share a Levantine past, in which the culture of Palestine/Israel was largely an Arab-Jewish coinvention.[31]

In contrast with the intense geography of security in which Israeli domestic security forces deploy themselves through the Arab sectors of Jerusalem is a "geography of time."[32] While Suileman's camera displays a quiescent, domestic Arab presence in Nazareth, Arabness alternates between a furtive moving object of surveillance and an absence in his rendering of Jerusalem. Instead of the framing shots and close-ups, Suileman turns to tracking shots to capture the motion of the security system in Jerusalem. The change in camera work begins as soon as Suileman hits the road for Jerusalem. The desert scape become a blur of motion, seen through a car window. Once in Jerusalem, we can read, in Jerusalem's cityscape—which, as noted in chapter 5, has been changed from terraced olive groves and *ruti* trees into "massive residential and institutional structures," fortresslike dwellings "overshadowing rural enclaves with the remaining 'natives,'"[33]—how the state's cultural nationalism has reshaped the social body and erased Jewish-Arab copresence. And that reading is continually interrupted by the blur of motion created by tracking shots aimed at frenetic and clumsy policing agents and their quarry, enacting the Other's fantasy of a conspiracy.

Finally, through an economy of presence and absence, what is on-screen versus what is an off-screen yet pervasive effect, Suileman provides a view of the way Palestinian life in Israel is more a contained and relatively resigned cultural presence than a threat. Noel Burch's identification of two kinds of filmic space (discussed in previous chapters), "that included within the frame and that outside the frame,"[34] speaks to much of the implicit political insight in Suileman's *Chronicle*. Although in Jerusalem, the off-screen Israeli state is represented on screen through the frantic activity of its security personnel, in Nazareth, its off-screen presence rarely intrudes on screen. However, in one poignant moment, as Suileman's camera moves in behind the heads of his parents toward their television screen, the end of the day's programming is followed by the playing of the Israeli national anthem. Shown on their screen is the fluttering Israeli flag. As the camera circles the room, finally stopping in front of Suileman's parents, we see them asleep. At this moment, as in most of the moments of their daily lives, their political subordination is a distant background. Their "bare life" looms much larger than their relatively ineligible political life. The pervasive off-screen presence of the state has a small window of opportunity in their lives, and even that presence is largely ignored.

Conclusion: Sovereignty, Dissymmetry, and Intervention

On the surface, there is a symmetry between the filmic interventions in *Patriot Games* and those in *Chronicle*. Both of them employ a technology that replaces the process of ordinary perception. In the case of *Patriot Games*, the killing scene in the North African desert represents a primary feature of contemporary warfare, a move toward what Paul Virilio has termed "the logistics of perception."[35] It involves "eyeless vision" (2), in which the human vision is displaced by a cinematic apparatus. Substituting for the "homogeneity of vision" in which even adversaries are contextualized within their life-worlds is a heterogeneous perceptual field (20), a global form of vision in which persons are located in a filmic environment. In modern industrialized warfare, according to Virilio, "the landscape of warfare became cinematic" (70).

In *Patriot Games* the cinematic effect is doubled; a film is depicting a filmic mode of perception in which a radically abstracted form of knowing is serving as a relay of the sovereign gaze. The Arab terrorist is "known" only as a target perceived, cinematically through a technological eye that is disengaged from ethnographic contexts. Although the close-ups of *Chronicle* overcome the egregious dissymmetries of *Patriot Games*, restoring a rich life-world to a region that is abstracted in comparison with the elaborated home front of the exemplary and threatened family of the Clancy-Noyce story, it too is involved in replacing ordinary perception. Through the pervasive use of time images, especially in the depth of focus and montage effects, *Chronicle* conveys a more critical perspective than would be allowed within the perceptions of the individuals whose lives are in focus.[36]

Although a time image often operates within *Patriot Games*, in that its construction of danger and the ultimate escape of Ryan and his family form a story that operates outside the perspectives of some of the characters, two particular loci of perception dominate. One belongs to Ryan, whose righteous anger and technologically aided perceptive powers determine the outcome. The other belongs to the surveillance satellite, which locates the terrorist camp as an unambiguous zone for the production of danger. Thus, while *Chronicle* provides a critical view of the politics of constituting "terrorism" by locating the people from whom danger is perceived in a complex, historically deep life-world, using time images that allow for "thinking in cinema through cinema,"[37] *Patriot Games* merely recognizes the same people within the monocular security imaginary of the intelligence community and the related military agencies involved in implementing the state's aspect of sovereignty that permits killing without committing homicide. While *Chronicle* is a critical intervention into this aspect of sovereignty's biopolitics (its administration of life), *Patriot Games* is complicit with it. It aids and abets the discourses of security through which various aspects of humanity are identified and sovereign killing is legitimated.

Ironically, however, even the political discourses that represent a departure from realpolitik and ponder the virtues of "humanitarian intervention" remain conceptually obtuse in regard to the sovereignty's administration of life. For example, in a monograph devoted largely to the "ethical issues" involved in humanitarian intervention, one writer calls attention to "some broad trends" that both "undermine and affirm the idea of national sovereignty as the constituent principle of international society,"[38] and another focuses on the trade-offs involved in what he refers to as "forcible humanitarian intervention."[39] Like other traditional analysts of international affairs, for whom the major issues involve risking American lives to save some within other sovereign jurisdictions or absolutely versus conditionally respecting juridically recognized sovereign jurisdictions, the writers assume that various states are ordinarily radically isolated with respect to the production of the conditions that encourage state domestic violence.

If we heed Agamben's insight into sovereignty's location in a zone of indistinction between the juridical/institutional and the biopolitical (elaborated in chapter 4), we must recognize that, at the level of representation, states are always already involved in a kind of humanitarian intervention. They are constructing models of life inside and outside their jurisdictions and, at the same time, are radically separating politics from humanitarianism.[40] A position critical of states' sovereignty prerogatives is achieved by recognizing states as performative rather than merely juridical entities. From this perspective one can identify the protointerventions involved in the biopolitical acts of sovereignty. In addition to the domestic violence to which states contribute, by supporting government groups or rebels with weapons sales and deliveries or by manipulating other states' economies, the dominant system of global recognition, which is biased toward states rather than nations without states, determines which bodies are politically qualified and thereby contributes to forms of domestic restriction, coercion, and violence.

Those producing the discourse on "humanitarian intervention" are largely reacting to the downstream result. Theorists of "international affairs," for example, weigh the value of a different kind of reactive intervention, such as the sending of their own armed forces. This policy problematic, focused on the *right* to intervene, has been justly criticized because of the way it obscures more determinant processes of intervention that continually shape the violence potential in various global venues.[41] Moreover, because the humanity designated in discourses of humanitarian organizations is the humanity of bare life (for example, "the 'imploring eyes' of the Rwandan child" in the fund-raising advertisements of relief organizations), these organizations function "in perfect symmetry with state power."[42] They serve as a prescription both for saving part of humanity and for affirming the structures of sovereignty that produce an excluded and thus imperiled humanity.

Elia Suileman's *Chronicle* documents rather than prescribes. Instead of pondering "policy," it enlarges the problem of the political. It juxtaposes a complex and ambiguous life-world to a highly abstracted set of global strategic spaces that have become objects of a technologically sophisticated surveillance from a great physical distance, enacted with sanctions that function from a great conceptual distance. *Suileman's* intervention, like the sovereignty-as-killing-without-committing-homicide that Clinton recently enacted, and the one fantasized in *Patriot Games* are aided by a cinematic technology. In Suileman's case, however, the technology is deployed to overcome a representational dissymmetry. His assemblage of camera shots is not followed by weapon shots. They stand as a challenge to a biopolitical order that is at least as oppressive as the juridical order within which questions about the legalities and ethics of humanitarian intervention are framed.

Afterword

Throughout the investigations in this book, I have opposed critical, historically sensitive thought to reactive moralizing about families and about the relationship of families to civic life. I have attempted both to explicate and to demonstrate ways of construing a "politics of the family" that pluralize and open what cultural conservatives would like to close or restrict and that conceptually broaden access to political eligibility (of persons, ideas, and genres). My articulation of a conceptual practice, which has involved both abstract theorizing and applied treatments of genres, with political practice has been aimed at, among other things, displacing certainties with ambiguities and institutionalized forms of coherence with disjunctive differences. I have enlisted approaches to collective modes of being and to "the political" from diverse thinkers: Agamben, Foucault, Deleuze, and Rancière, among others; I have relied heavily on the critical capacities of a genealogical historical sensibility; I have focused especially on diverse genres; and I have emphasized "writing," both mine and that of others, as a way to practice political thinking rather than to merely recognize the range of objects and relationships resident in familiar discourses.[1]

I would like to summarize in a way that articulates cogently the diverse strands of the work of thinking and showing in the preceding chapters. And I would like especially to rearticulate both the ethicopolitical sensibility and the commitment to oppositional writing genres that have directed much of the trajectory of my inquiry. However, instead of moving directly to an attempt at forging a coherence, because I am, at the same time, challenged, edified, and inspired by some of Toni Morrison's reflections on writing versus orality and Fatima Mernissi's account of the power of women's stories in a Moroccan harem, I feel compelled to begin with a detour in which I interrogate and complicate my commitment to writing as a mode of political enactment.[2] Although this move would seemingly take me far afield of the task of summarizing, I think it is more a case of backing up for a better run at it.

Certainly there are many historical instances of oppositional writing that lend support to my reliance on the politics of literary genres. For example, in accord with Jean-Luc Nancy's contemporary critique of universalistic approaches to history (discussed in chapter 2), William Godwin's participation in British literary culture in the late eighteenth century was part of a literary challenge to the "Enlightenment universal history," which Godwin saw as part of the "mystified collective autobiography of Modern Britain."[3] Godwin asserted that

> the writer of romance is to be considered as the writer of real history; while he who was formerly called the historian, must be contented to step down into the place of his rival, with this disadvantage, that he is a romance writer, without the arduous, the enthusiastic and the sublime license of imagination. (147)

Unlike Sir Walter Scott, whose novels (as noted in chapter 4) were complicitous with a British national imaginary, Godwin participated in a writing genre that challenged the mythology of a coherent and undivided British national culture. And, as his remarks suggest, he was attentive to the politics of writing genres. Whatever the impact of his ideas on the British reading public, which was (in a Habermasian sense) an increasingly significant public sphere, his politicizing of the genre of the "republican romance" functioned within an unambiguous commitment to the political significance of writing and to a model of the public as a "republic of letters."[4] However, despite the existence of diverse historical instances of writing genres as counterhegemonic forces, there are instances of politicization to be found in vernacular and largely oral genres, which express peoples' modes of solidarity and their oppositional statuses vis-à-vis dominant groupings within the social order. For this reason, I want to confront the challenge to a reliance on literary forms of opposition provided (ironically) in the *writing* of Toni Morrison and Fatima Mernissi.

Morrison's political challenge to literary culture is explicit. She has pointed to a paradox inherent in her participation as a novelist in a culture of literacy. Although she "participates in the public sphere constituted by print literacy, . . . her fiction strains to constitute itself as anti-literature and to address a type of racial community that she herself recognizes to be unavailable to the novelist."[5] That racial community, moreover, is not simply another America. Like many black writers, artists, and musicians, especially those who preceded her in the twentieth century (and most notably those associated with the Harlem Renaissance), Morrison's audience/constituency takes on its coherence as a protean transnational black culture, forged as much through structures of exclusion and episodes of displacement as through practices of solidarity. And much of the cultural imaginary that forms the implied readership of her novels is "preliterate."[6]

Morrison's ambivalence toward her participation in the literate public sphere is understandable. As she puts it (in an allegorical meditation on Defoe's Friday, who loses his mother tongue in the process of accepting Crusoe's language): "Voluntary entrance into another culture, voluntary sharing of more than one culture, has certain satisfactions to mitigate the problems that may ensue. But being rescued into an adversarial culture can carry a huge debt."[7] To overcome that debt—a loss or surrender of the language of one's culture (xxviii)—Morrison's novels struggle within themselves "between vernacular and literary forms, between oral and written compositions."[8] Her striving to maintain a vernacular language and her recognition of the fragmented nature of public spheres (both black versus white and within each) derive from her commitment to "a conflict between public and private life," which she thinks "ought to remain a conflict."[9]

For Morrison, as for many black intellectuals, artists, and writers, there is no unitary national culture within the United States and no simple set of imperatives to connect spheres of intimacy with civic relations. As a result, in Morrison's understanding, there is no societywide didactic role for the novel (an aim she ascribes to earlier practitioners of the form, such as Samuel Richardson, among others). Of necessity, the novel is situated within (what Rancière calls) a "politics of disparity." Nevertheless, in spite of her ambivalence, Morrison is a public intellectual whose writing not only preserves a black vernacular but also creates a semiosis (an encounter of idioms or systems of meanings) between "black talk" and a white-black culture of literacy.[10]

Because the novel is not the only genre within which such cultural encounters are staged, Morrison's struggle with genre is in evidence in other artistic domains. For example, the striving reflected in the cultural semiosis in her writing is homologous with the cultural struggle evident in some of the jazz compositions of saxophonist John Coltrane. In contrast with the Euro-American tradition, in which composition is an autonomous activity, Coltrane's jazz performances are enactments of composition. They reflect what Christopher Small calls a "struggle between freedom and order," in that the playing of free jazz involves a movement back and forth between the spaces of black vernacular orality and the values and assumptions of the white social order.[11] Rather than a musical fusion, Coltrane's playing performs a *musical* semiosis, an encounter enacted between a production of meaning characteristic of African American culture and the institutionalized referentiality of the dominant white culture. Coltrane's composition-performances typically begin with a musical fragment from a Euro-American piece of music (for example, the Rodgers and Hammerstein song "My Favorite Things," from the Broadway musical *The Sound of Music*) and repeat it several times in different keys and with different chordal arrangements. This practice of repetition is an enactment of an African American mode of meaning production, a "signfyin' on," which, as Henry Louis Gates Jr. notes, involves a doubleness: "assertions and counter-assertions" with strong resonances in "the African American discursive forest."[12] Effectively, Coltrane's music exemplifies the relationship between jazz performance and "the play of black language games" (52), a "telling misuse inflicted on English, an abuse which brings the referent more explicitly to light."[13]

These tensions inherent in some African American approaches to the encounter between writing (whether in novels or musical compositions or other genres) and black orality reflect not only a history of the African American experience but also the fragmentation of public spheres to which much of chapter 4 is addressed. Moreover, and most significant for my concern here, it complicates both the issue of writing and the related problem of "the political," both of which have pride of place throughout my investigations. There are two intimately connected implications deriving from my examples of the way that some African American literary and musical compositions reinflect their genres of expression. First, the examples take the issue of genre beyond an apolitical hermeneutics. They speak to the political practice I have undertaken in this book in that they indicate how a genre does more than prescribe ways to infer meaning or how, more generally, to discern a particular lesson. In many instances, a genre is an arena of political struggle that reflects a broader domain of political encounter among perspectives and life-worlds that admit of no simple resolution.

Second, the political tensions exhibited in these genres complicate the issue of subjectification I have addressed in connection with my explication and appreciation of Jacques Rancière's approach to democracy. Slavoj Zizek's summary of the distinction between Rancière's and Habermas's

AFTERWORD

models of democratic discursive events provides an apt way to reintroduce the purport of subjectification à la Rancière:

> The basic aim of anti democratic politics always and by definition is and was depoliticization—that is, the unconditional demand that things should go back to normal, with each individual doing his or her particular job. . . . And, Rancière proves against Habermas, the political struggle proper is therefore not a rational debate between multiple interests, but the struggle for one's voice to be heard and recognized as the voice of a legitimate partner.[14]

As I noted in chapter 1, for Rancière "the political" is not the implementation of the system of recognized dimensions of existing political qualification—those "interests" that are identifiable within the official political terrain. Rather, politics makes a rare appearance in instances of subjectification, episodes of the appearance of new voices, which are at once expressive and disruptive. However, as the struggles of Toni Morrison and John Coltrane (with novelistic and musical genres, respectively) demonstrate, the problem of warranting a democratic multiplicity, of moving beyond the normal politics of the blending of recognized interests, requires an appreciation of the modalities of the "new voices." Toni Morrison's voice is an uneasy amalgam of black vernacular orality and "Western" literary culture. Similarly, John Coltane's is expressed as a continually modifying repetition of sounds that combine aspects of the Western musical canon and "black talk" as it has been articulated in an African American musical trajectory from blues through jazz.

If we bring Morrison's and Coltrane's struggles to incorporate, without merely synthesizing, writing/composition and black vernacular orality into the conceptual space of Rancière's approach to democracy, the concept of voice requires elaboration beyond Rancière's distinction between mere noise and meaningful articulations, beyond the dichotomy of qualified versus unqualified voices. The voices in Morrison's novels and Coltrane's compositions are certainly instances of subjectification, for they bring new voices into the midst of a literate and musical public, respectively. But, in addition, those voices function with distinctive styles and reflect the history of distinctive *modes* of enunciation that cannot be separated from dynamic *loci* of enunciation. African American styles of enunciation (oral, literary, musical, and so on) are intimately related to a diaspora from Africa to the North American continent during the period of slavery and within the continent, from the South and Southwest northward in the postslavery period. Those styles have been, of necessity, heavily coded. They reflect a history of improvising ways of maintaining solidarity in the face of divisive and oppressive forces and ways of negotiating meanings in the process of participating in a white-dominated national arena.

The consequences of the domestic part of the black diaspora and the subsequent genre-related disjuncture between white and black modes of political articulation are exemplified in Robert Altman's 1994 feature film, *Kansas City*. The venue of Altman's filmic story (Kansas City, Missouri, in the 1930s) was a crossroads of diasporic African American musicians as well as of diverse Euro-Americans involved in national election politics. Although the film's drama has only a two-day duration, situated during the 1934 presidential campaign, the black nightclub and music scene it features reflects a key moment in the movement of much of the African American population from the South and Southwest to the major urban areas of the North and Midwest. And, in the particular case of Kansas City, it shows the result of an in-migration of scores of talented black musicians who shaped the Kansas City version of jazz.

While most of the major American cities were still reeling from the Great Depression, Kansas City was relatively prosperous, in large because of the political influence of the boss of the local Democratic machine, Thomas J. Pendergast, whose delivery of Missouri votes in national elections was redeemed in the form of federal money for local projects. Pendergast created an economic oasis in Kansas City by attracting New Deal labor-intensive public works programs. As a result of the Pendergast-sponsored availability of jobs, Kansas City became a mecca for black jazz musicians, among whom were Benny Moten, Count Basie, Lester Young, Eddie Durham, Jesse Stone, Walter Page, Oran "Hotlips" Page, Mary Lou Williams, Eddie Barfield, Henry "Buster" Smith, Ed Lewis, and Charlie Parker.[15]

Altman's film takes place during the 1934 election campaign, eventually resulting in Franklin Roosevelt's reelection. Although Roosevelt's policies are usually associated with a reduction of the power of privilege in the United States, their racial implications are less benign. The agricultural policies developed under Roosevelt's New Deal provided inducements for white southern planters to demote their workers to the status of casual laborers, employed only seasonally. "Eventually millions [of African Americans] drifted out of the South all together, probably the largest government-impelled population movement in all our history," according to historian Donald Grubbs.[16] This situation, along with other, more violent white practices that made the South increasingly inhospitable to African Americans, led to the diaspora northward.

The African American movement to northern and midwestern urban centers is intimately connected with Afro-American musical developments. Instead of a state-oriented, nation-building geographical dynamic, African American music articulates a musical geography that reflects the black diaspora. The music in Altman's *Kansas City* therefore speaks to developments well outside the particular vignettes in the film's story line. While virtually all the action within the camera's frame takes place in Kansas City, the film makes extensive use of the two dimensions of cinematic space, discussed in various chapters: "that included within the frame and that outside the frame."[17] Because what is taking place in Kansas City in 1934 is, among other things, the preparation for a presidential election, the city's main train station appears in several scenes, as white power brokers and shipped-in voters connected with national politics head in and out of the city while black clients, musicians, and refugees head in.

Briefly, the action in *Kansas City* is generated by an episode taking place over a two-day period. The husband, Johnny, robs a black tourist-gambler headed for Seldom Seen's black Hey Hey Club while wearing black face to make it appear to be a black-on-black crime. After he is found out and apprehended by Seen's henchmen, Johnny's scrappy and resourceful wife, Blondie, kidnaps Carolyn, the wife of Henry Stilton, an influential politician who has connections with boss Pendergast, the governor, and the local Italian crime syndicate and who is headed to Washington, D.C., to confer with President Roosevelt. Blondie's plan is to coerce Stilton to use his connections to rescue Johnny. Stilton is telegraphed at an intermediate station and tries to meet Blondie's demand. But the "rescue" ultimately fails; Johnny comes home mortally wounded, and Carolyn ends up shooting Blondie to death as she lies prostrate over her dying husband. Moreover, the kidnaping drama is less significant than the way Johnny and Blondie's story illuminates the disjunctures between white and black Kansas City.

The film narrative provides a mapping of white election politics as it traces the influence peddling and corruption that attend contests for national, state, and local offices. The Pendergast machine is shown in operation, employing political and criminal connections and violence to steal the forthcoming election. But, at the same time, the film depicts the black music scene enacted within Seldom Seen's Hey Hey Club. Through the cuts and juxtapositions, Altman's film inscribes the separations and encounters that constitute the exemplary racial-spatial order of Kansas City in the 1930s: on the one hand, a white society caught up in an election contest and, on the other, what LeRoi Jones/Amiri Baraka has called the black "meta society" articulating its within-group solidarity and its highly coded relationship with white society through its music.[18]

As the film narrative develops, the pervasive historical doubleness that Kansas City represents is shown to persist. Missouri contained both sides of the slavery conflict in the nineteenth century, and in the twentieth, its most vibrant city contained a juxtaposition of two exemplary racial orders. It is important to note, however, that the form of *Kansas City*'s film narrative is the primary way in which the film speaks of a politically divided American nation. *Kansas City* tells a double story, cutting back and forth between Johnny's and Blondie's participation in the events; it tells, in the words of one critic, "two meandering, sometimes violent stories that finally come together near the end of the picture."[19] By employing multiple camera positions, Altman—as was the case in his filming of *Nashville*, which also explores a racial-spatial order in an American city—Altman resists what his *Nashville* editor, Sid Levin, calls "the classic style . . . the conventional use of master, medium and close-up shots." Rather, there are "three or four different master angles of the same sequence, each with a slight variation in camera angle."[20]

Altman's approach to sound and meaning produces a multiplicity that is of a piece with his approach to the pluralistic situating of angles of vision. In a seemingly trivial yet exemplary moment of filmic and aural montage in *Nashville*, for example, the scene cuts from a hospital, where a husband weeps over the news that his wife has just died, to a festive gathering in which someone is laughing in precisely the same rhythm. In *Kansas City*, Altman produces a similar double resonance. In a scene in which Seldom Seen's henchmen are knifing to death the cabdriver (who had conspired in the robbery of Seen's black gambling customer) in an alley, the film narrative cuts to the Hey Hey Club, where "at the same time the two saxophonists try to outdo each other with a rapid exchange of short phrases. [Coleman] Hawkins and [Lester] Young engage in a cutting contest of their own,"[21] and their intensity produces the same rhythm as that of the killing.

As was the case in his *Nashville*, Altman's focus in *Kansas City* is on encounters between two systems of meaning-making, two domains of discourse—economy and music—that distinguish the white and black ethnoscapes of an American city. In *Nashville*, Altman achieved an improvisatory climate for his filmic narrative by letting his actors function without a fixed script and by complementing the multidimensional ethnoscape he achieved in the visual register with a plurality of camera angles by using many microphones placed to pick up peripheral conversations (a technique used in *McCabe and Mrs. Miller* to convey the complex cacophony of voices structuring the turn-of-the-century West).[22] But Altman's approach to the complexity of voices is deeper in *Kansas City* than it is in *Nashville*. The film as a whole is structured like jazz. While the surface plot maps the Kansas City–Washington, D.C., connection and provides insight into the white election politics of the corrupt, Pendergast-run Democratic machine, the aural rhythms of the film provide a glimpse of another America with a politics coded in sound. Simply put, the voices of *Kansas City*'s characters double the voices of the performing jazz musicians.

Aware of both the history of jazz and its central role in the highly coded (musical) languages with which much of African American political culture expresses itself, Altman creates an effective interarticulation between African American "spatial history" (the historical emergence of the Kansas City style of jazz as black musicians migrated into the city) and a distinctively African American approach to musical intelligibility: Elements of the blues emanating primarily from the Mississippi Delta but also from the distinctiveness of the southwestern bands that had remained true to the old blues tradition,[23] ragtime developed in the Midwest, and New Orleans jazz are fused in the Kansas City style of jazz. However, in addition to its complex spatial history, the music reflects a history of an emergence of "black talk,"[24] which, as noted above, is a form of counterintelligibility on the American scene that is owed in part to its African discursive heritage and in part to the necessarily coded form of discourse that developed among people who have not, in varying degrees and at different historical moments, been free to express themselves directly and, as a result, have been excluded in varying degrees from participation in mainstream forms of Euro-American civic expression.

The complex interrelationships between voice and genre in situations of inequality, demonstrated in Altman's *Kansas City*, are evident in other venues that speak more directly to the central concern in this study, the politics of the family. A case in point is provided in Fatima Mernissi's autobiographical ethnography of the harem in which she grew up in the Moroccan city of Fez.[25] As Mernissi points out in her opening meditation on frontiers, the Moroccan harem is a quintessential realization of patriarchal power, implemented in the form of boundaries and enclosures that confine women to a walled-in and highly surveilled mode of domesticity.

Nevertheless, what appears at first to be a world in which women are wholly disempowered by being quarantined from the domain of civic affairs is shown to be a complex micropolitical universe in which women use the privacy afforded by their confinement to develop an articulate discourse on power, which helps them to enact forms of resistance to the patriarchal structure.

The first hint of female power that Mernissi supplies is in a character sketch of her aunt Habiba, whose husband has sent her out of his household, consigning her to a marginal existence in the harem of her relatives. Mernissi writes that "her husband had kept everything from their marriage" but adds that, according to Aunt Habiba, "he can never take the most important things away from me . . . my laughter and all the wonderful stories I can tell when the audience is worth it" (17). Aunt Habiba's remark is one among many clues that female power in the harem is manifested in the genre of storytelling. And, most important, in response to children's queries about the meaning of such "dangerous words" as *harem,* the mothers and aunts provide a critique of masculine power in the form of stories about the origin of harems or, more generally, about the impetus for powerful men to "collect women."

While some of the women in Mernissi's harem support the male-authored and Islam-sanctified notion that confining and concealing women as well as allowing polygamy is both "natural" and "sacred," others treat it as an exercise of power. For example, in a politically empowering story about the evolution of the practice of collecting and confining women, Mernissi's aunt Chama supplies an important political pedagogy that energizes much of Mernissi's critique of the harem. According to Chama, who provides a "theory" of the harem in the form of a narrative, the collecting and confining of women dates back to a time of bloodshed and the need for distinctive signs in order to appoint a sultan to reestablish order. After consultation, the men decided that "the sultan should have something the others do not have," and, as Chama's story goes:

> They reflected some more [until one of them suggested,] "We should organize a race to catch women . . . and the man who catches the most women will be appointed Sultan. [Moreover,] We need a way to paralyze the women once they're caught, so we can count them, and decide who is the winner." And that is how the idea of building houses started. Houses with gates and locks were needed to contain the women. (43)

The politicizing implications of Chama's fable are evident to Mernissi; the harem is denaturalized, and its female captives are able to see it as an arena of raw power, a venue of male dominance with no transcendent warrants. Mernissi makes it clear, in addition, that such stories, which were part of an ongoing women's discourse on power, encouraged a variety of acts of resistance and ultimately helped to create the ideational conditions of possibility for women's participation in their liberation from patriarchal power. There is an additional implication, which serves my project of theoretical coherence. Chama elaborated her story of the collection and confinement of women beyond the domain of domestic politics. The sign-function value of capturing women, which was allegedly used to distinguish among sultan candidates within Arab countries, extended to the sign-function value one could attribute to Islamic performances of nationhood vis-à-vis other nations. In Chama's tale, the race to collect women took place all over the world until a change in international relations took place: "While the Arabs were busy locking women behind doors, the Romans and other Christians got together and decided to change the rules of the power game in the Mediterranean. Collecting women, they declared, was not relevant anymore," but they kept the change a secret, so the Arabs were stuck with an anachronistic policy—they "went to sleep thinking that they knew the rules of the power game" (44–45).

To place this part of Chama's story within the theoretical frame developed in chapter 6, the disempowering of women with the harem structure, as Chama's story explicates it, is part of what is, in Giorgio Agamben's terms, a biopolitical enactment of a (male-dominated) national sovereignty. As I noted in chapter 6, sovereign power functions, according to Agamben, within a complex topology, a zone of indistinction between juridical power and biopower. Sovereignty territorializes its collective being with legal boundaries, but it also realizes itself in productive, biopolitical enactments. In addition to maintaining juridical authority, sovereignty functions through "decisions" that determine the distribution of dependent, independent, dangerous, friendly, and irrelevant bodies.

There is therefore a critical articulation between Rancière's concept of subjectification and Agamben's concept of sovereignty. Agamben elaborates a politics of nation-state domination, treating especially the extrajuridical determinations through which states locate bodies in political space and determine their relationship to both domestic orders and a state-dominated international order. Rancière's specification of instances of subjectification refers to irruptions of resistance to the biopolitics of order. For Rancière, such irruptions are the essence of a democratizing multiplicity, for, in his terms, they are instances in which the "order of distribution of bodies into functions corresponding to their 'nature' and places corresponding to their functions is undermined, thrown back on its contingency."[26]

Within this articulated frame of the political, the story of the origin of the harem told by Mernissi's aunt Chama, which substitutes historical contingency for a naturalized structure of domination, is a democratizing political act. While, as I have shown, it provides me with an exemplary instance to rearticulate a genre-sensitive politics of the family, it also opens the way to what can be called an ethical questioning.[27] By demoralizing the autocratic world of sultans and their harems (i.e., by showing its contingency as historically specific practices of power and authority), Chama effects a Nietzschean critique; she turns what for many is a "true world" into a fable, and as a corollary, she substitutes a mobile human subjectivity for a fixed human nature. Having thus raised the issue of the ethical, I want to treat three interrelated dimensions of my investigation that complement my concern with a model of the political: my commitments to theory, to moral ambiguity, and to disjunctures and incoherences within individual and collective bodies. These dimensions are best addressed with attention to what I will call the ethics of the critical interpretive work throughout my diverse inquiries into the politics of the family.

In chapter 5, in my treatment of citizenship, I introduced a broadened, multiplicity-accepting model of political eligibility (beyond traditional motions of citizen subjects) by showing how national communities contain disjunctive forms of presence, some of which are made evident by women's voices, articulated from the spatiotemporality of the family. And, through my discussion of Duttmann's philosophically oriented ethnography of people with AIDS and my discussion of Nancy's model of community as a being together of what is uncommon, I suggested that, at both individual and collective levels, there are ambiguities afflicting one's coherence and presence—to oneself as well as to others. I went on to suggest that there is no unambiguous way to establish a basis for "community." To make matters worse (even from the point of view of enlightenment humanists, let alone reactive moralists), by chapter 1, I had already displaced the humanist subject of consciousness with a clash of conflicting and irreconcilable codes. In short, I have divested myself of virtually all the conceptual commitments that provide the traditional bases of an ethically committed, solidarity-promoting form of interpretation. As those (like Rorty, with whom I deal in chapter 1) who disparage much of posthermeneutic critical theory are prone to put it, the incessant historicizing and ironic distancing in this mode of critical theorizing deprives one of the ability to have an "ethics of critical interpretation," indeed, to have any recognizable ethicopolitical position.

Thus, while cultural conservatives constituted my primary antagonists at the outset of my investigations, I have doubtless collected liberal humanist ones as well. While my quarrel with moralistic "family values" cultural conservatives took the form of displacing moral certainties with historically situated contingencies, a treatment of my differences with liberal humanists requires some reflection on the ethics of critical interpretation. Although liberal humanists hold diverse positions, I will focus on Idelber Avelar's characterization of one version, which has emerged in liberal humanists' charges about the absence of ethics in much literary theory, as an exemplar. Avelar describes the position this way:

> The displacement of the sovereign humanist subject and its inscription in a textual/political/libidinal field . . . by "subordinating selfhood to linguistic structure" . . . equals the demise of the ethical. If one can no longer think of "responsibility" and "moral decision" in the terms one once did, it follows that a new theoretical barbarism has replaced our good old ethics.[28]

This so-called theoretical barbarism is far from new; it goes back to the dawn of *theoria,* for it is resident in the spirit of Greek tragedy (in which individuals are subordinated to codes). I want to suggest, in agreement with the initiating predicate of Avelar's approach to the ethics of interpretation, that there are ways to articulate an ethical sensibility without ceding authority to the traditional humanist discourse on subjects and their participation in "public reasoning" as they make choices among competing "moral virtues." Instead of locating ethics as a practice of making choices on the basis of an extrinsic set of criteria, I locate ethical sensibility not simply as historically variable and contestable (i.e., contingent) sets of commitments but also as an attitude toward conflictual encounters—a hospitable commitment to "the other" as both enigmatic and incommensurate (as Emmanuel Levinas has put it) but within the assumption of an instability in the identification of both self and other, whose identities are as much at stake as are the meanings and values resident in the issues involved (as Jacques Derrida's neo-Levinasian ethics would have it).[29]

"The ethical" within this frame is not a search for an enduring human essence but a way of coding the events of encounter and of being open to difference. It accords with the basic attitude (if not the philosophical basis) of Immanuel Kant's hope for "perpetual peace."[30] Relying on a model of discourse as a mode of communication with a growing global reach, Kant was instrumental in the development of an enlightenment humanism. His optimism about the emergence of a peaceful global epoch was based upon a narrative of enlightenment that begins at the level of the subject's enlarging structure of apprehension and proceeds to an intersubjective ethos that would be encouraged by the publicity attending such global events as the French Revolution. Resistant to Kant's transcendental model of critique but, at the same time edified by Kant's attention to his own historical period, Foucault has offered a different way of treating events. As he noted, Kant's specific question about the significance of his time and place (in his text on enlightenment)

> entails an obvious consequence: that criticism is no longer to be practiced in the search for formal structures with universal value, but rather as a historical investigation into the events that have led us to constitute ourselves and to recognize ourselves as subjects of what we are doing, thinking, saying.[31]

Like Kant, Foucault is concerned with events, but rather than relying on "public reasoning" to spread the significance of events, Foucault regards discourse itself as an event. In contrast with rationalistic approaches to public interchange, framed within representational approaches to language that concern themselves with the reliability of speaking *about* events, Foucault's emphasis is on the power of the signifier and on the historical conditions giving rise to discursive events. To exemplify the Foucauldian discursive event, we can revisit Jacques Donzelot's Foucauldian history of modernity's emerging surveillance of the family, focusing this time on its ethicopolitical import. Within Donzelot's investigation, the politics of the family is not a position on its proper role vis-à-vis governance or its civic responsibilities; it is an analysis of the moral and political and economic pressures placed on families, which are reflected in a history of the discourses within which families have been variously problematized. Implicit in Donzelot's genealogy of the family is a critique of the modes of identity subjection that have attended the shifting governmentalities within which the family has been an object of political surveillance.

Thus, the mode of analysis opened up by a Foucauldian recognition of discourse as an event rather than simply a mechanism of publicity and communication involves an important shift in Kant's critical attitude and its ethical implications. For the Kantian concern with knowledge and legitimation (exemplified, for example, in Habermas's contemporary, neo-Kantian approach to public reasoning), Foucault substitutes questions of "power and eventualization."[32] His critical attitude encourages exploration of alternative forms of intelligibility, especially those that are part of a domain of administered silence, as diverse historical forces engender particular discursive objects and particular modes of subjectivity.

Foucault's ethical problematic remains Kantian insofar as he is interested in freeing subjects from their self-incurred tutelage, as well as from the forms of power producing the pedagogies of that tutelage, but his solution is not a move to a transcendental mode of critique. Instead of raising questions about the conditions of possibility for the apprehension of experience in general—the Kantian mode of questioning—he treats the specific historical emergences of the discourses within which subjects and things become potential objects of experience and within which some loci and modes of enunciation are privileged while others are excluded. Accordingly, the "rarity" of discourse for Foucault (that is, the economy of presence and absence it contains, entitling some speakers while silencing others and enabling some identities while disabling others) requires a Kantian style of reflection, but one that focuses on the economies of discourse rather than on the epistemic conditions of possibility for shared experience. This kind of reflection encourages inquiry into the specific historical moments and encounters that challenge the distribution of assets and liabilities resident in official or prevailing discourses (for example, the emergence of a discourse on masculine power among the women in Mernissi's Moroccan harem).

This kind of reflection on the discourse-power relationship is also evident in Jean-François Lyotard's neo-Kantian insights on "the ethical," which, like Foucault's, gesture toward the plurality of voices and perspectives that cannot be accommodated within a Kantian model of a global *sensus communis.* But while Foucault's neo-Kantian departure is precipitated by his reading of Kant's text on enlightenment, Lyotard's position springs from his reading of Kant's political rhetoric in his three major critiques, where Kant refers to the separate domains of governance of the faculties.[33] Like Foucault, Lyotard shifts the emphasis from Kantian mental faculties to language and resists the Kantian commitment to a public use of reason that Kant thought would yield a world increasingly and freely shared. Instead of presupposing a subject with faculties, Lyotard's unit of analysis is the phrase, and instead of a contest of faculties (the idiom for Kant's staging of a conflict between reason and imagination), Lyotard's ethics and politics posit a clash of phrases that has no transcendental basis or other foundation through which different articulations can be rendered commensurable.[34]

In contrast with Habermas's attempt to fashion a neo-Kantian discourse ethics based on a metalevel and universal feature of discourse, Lyotard's ethics seeks both to respect the experience of linguistic incommensurability and to create a frame through which it can be articulated and conflictually staged. Like Kant, Lyotard suggests that philosophical discourse should enable reflective judgment, but within Lyotard's philosophical imaginary, the figure of the tribunal (central to Kant's) is absent. Reflective judgment does not submit disputes to a law internal to subjectivity; rather, it recognizes incommensurabilities and licenses combat among phrases: "Is it the only purpose of the reflective function which is ours to transform, as Kant thought, dispute *(differend)* into litigation, but substituting the law court for the battle field?"[35]

Yet despite his opposition to the figure of the court, Lyotard is inspired by Kant's treatment of the event. The signs of history, about which Kant was so sanguine, do provoke judgments. However, because Kantian judgment is part of a process of litigation *within* the subject with an aim toward "subjective finality,"[36] Lyotard shifts from the space of the subject to the spaces of discursive encounter. He seeks to achieve a recognition of the plurality of modes of expression, which cannot be submitted to arbitration within a moral law accessible to a free exercise of a faculty.

One aspect in particular of Lyotard's approach to plurality is similar to that deriving from Foucault's treatment of the events of discourse— his concern with discursive exclusions. Specifically, Lyotard's notion of the *differend*, or phrases in dispute, is focused on systems of justice that exclude persons who function within different frames of meaning. However, in contrast with Foucault's approach, Lyotard's approach to recovering plurality is ahistorical. Operating within a philosophical rather than a historical idiom, his emphasis is on the contingencies afflicting linguistic encounters. However, if we heed Foucault's analyses of the history of a discourse's rarity, we can locate Lyotard's emphasis on the incommensurability of phrases in dispute in a structure of historical repression. Then the normative implication of the Lyotardian clash of phrases goes beyond the suggestion to simply exacerbate encounters (a primary mechanism of Lyotard's way of doing ethics) and implies instead that they should provoke inquiry into those historically produced discursive formations that are disempowering through their production of structures of nonrecognition.

Finally, however, having outlined an ethicopolitical sensibility that articulates an ethics of interpretation with a politics of democratic multiplicity, I want to emphasize that my assemblage of excluded voices, enunciated from spaces and within genres that tend to be neglected as sources of political thinking/theorizing, is not an implicit polemic in behalf of an identity politics or even a "politics of recognition," aimed at simply adding certain types of people or collectives to the domains of civic identification and political eligibility. Rather than seeking, for example, to valorize the family as a privileged locus of political initiative or to exemplify the identities of particular kinds of individuals as especially worthy of moral solicitude and critical attention, I have stressed the ambiguities attending the genre-mediated articulations I have recruited into my collection of political scenarios, and I have foregrounded the disjunctions within the collective attachments of those whose voices are a part of those articulations.

Elia Suileman's abortive attempt to address an assemblage of his Palestinian neighbors (in his *Chronicle of a Disappearance,* treated in chapter 6) dramatizes the kind of moral ambiguity I see as central to a democratizing approach to "the political." As I noted in chapter 6, Suileman's inability to deliver his address to a Palestinian community assembly (because of interruptions from severe microphone feedback and the continual ringing of cell phones) is symptomatic of his fundamental situation; he does not have anything definitive to say. His identity lacks coherence, and he is not addressing a coherent civic collective. Indeed, perhaps "disappearance" has an ambiguous referent. It may refer not only to the loss of a Palestinian territorialized nationhood but also to the loss of the illusion of both Suileman's and Palestinian identity coherence in general. As I noted in chapter 6, despite the moments of coherence that Suileman's camera affords a dispossessed, spatially disrupted people, his film does not seek to display an essential Palestinian identity. Instead he stages an ambivalent encounter.

A similar sense of moral ambiguity can be derived from some of the other genres I have analyzed. Hanan al-Shaykh's novel *Beirut Blues,* for example, does not simply promote familial intimacy and attachment against the bellicosity of the various factional militias fighting during the Lebanese civil war. The voices from the space of her family reflect different positions on warring violence. As I noted in chapter 1, the ironies disclosed in al-Shaykh's *Beirut Blues* constitute, at once, a moment of ironic detachment and a political statement about the contingencies afflicting all attachments. Family life is shown to have an ambiguous relationship to civic-life-as-war. I should add that "family life," however construed, is contingent as a condition of possibility and has an ambiguous relationship with civic life in general. And, to locate my place within the moral and political ambiguities, I want to close by identifying with Peter Henisch's dual commitments, evinced as he interrogated his father's past: He wished, on the one hand, to have the investigation serve an ethical and political sensibility but, on the other, to "avoid the deceit implicit in a false sense of historical closure."[37]

Notes

Introduction

1. The emergence of the discourse on family values has been traced to both empiricist social science, where it was found to be correlated with Catholic education, and to political campaigning, having surfaced in the Republican Party platform in 1976. See Brent Darryl Lollis, "The Political Dialectic of Family Values," Ph.D. dissertation, University of Texas, Austin, 1999, 23.

2. See, for example, Gertrude Himmelfarb, *The De-Moralization of Society* (New York: Alfred Knopf, 1995); and William Bennett, *The Book of Virtues* (New York: Simon and Schuster, 1994), a sound recording in four cassettes.

3. C. Wright Mills, "Situated Actions and Vocabularies of Motive," in Michael J. Shapiro, ed., *Language and Politics* (New York: New York University Press, 1984), 19; originally published in 1940 in the *American Sociological Review.*

4. Hegel's statement is in G. W. F. Hegel, *Phenomenology of Spirit,* trans. A. V. Miller (Oxford: Clarendon Press, 1977), 288. See Kelly Oliver's feminist treatment of Hegel's argument in *Family Values: Between Nature and Culture* (New York: Routledge, 1997), 48. And for one of the most important and influential feminist critiques of Hegel, see Luce Irigaray's discussion of Hegel's dialectically influenced view of women as a negation of the masculine: *This Sex Which Is Not One,* trans. Catherine Porter (Ithaca: Cornell University Press, 1985).

5. It should be noted, however, that despite his qualms about the influence of domestic life on the public sphere, Hegel conceded that it was impossible to draw an "objective line" between them. See G. W. F. Hegel, *Philosophy of Right,* trans. T. M. Knox (London: Oxford University Press, 1967), 146. That line became increasingly difficult to draw, for as Slavoj Zizek has pointed out when he refers to Hegel's "triad of family, civil society and state," the separations are no longer as distinct because of a "progressive *'familialization'* of public life itself," in which institutions that had formerly functioned "as an antidote to the family, start to function as surrogate families." See Slavoj Zizek, *The Ticklish Subject* (New York: Verso, 1999), 343.

6. Among the canonical theorists receiving the most criticism for promoting the segregation of family life from public or civic life is John Locke. See, for example, Jean Bethke Elshtain, *Public Man, Private Woman* (Princeton, N.J.: Princeton University Press, 1981); Zillah Eisenstein, *The Radical Future of Liberal Feminism* (New York: Longman, 1981); and Carole Pateman, *The Sexual Contract* (Stanford, Calif.: Stanford University Press, 1988). However, one can read Locke's "liberal distinction" between private and public spheres as avoiding the sharp separation with which he has been charged and instead as providing a model of interaction between the spheres that does not wholly depoliticize women and the family. For this argument, see Mary B. Walsh, "Locke and Feminism on Private and Public Realms of Activities," *Review of Politics* 57, no. 2 (spring 1995): 251–77. It should also be noted that the relationship between feminist theory and civic life becomes complicated when one compares gender-oriented movements in different venues. As one feminist theorist has noted, feminism has an ambiguous relationship with such state-oriented problematics as "national sovereignty," especially because there are conflicting ways of appropriating gender and family categories as various movements challenge structures of state hegemony. See Daiva K. Stasiulis, "Relational Positionalities of Nationalisms, Racisms, and Feminisms," in Caren Kaplan, Norma Alarcón, and Minoo Moallem, eds., *Between Woman and Nation* (Durham, N.C.: Duke University Press, 1999), 182–218.

7. Lauren Berlant, "Intimacy: A Special Issue," *Critical Inquiry* 24, no. 2 (winter 1998): 283.

8. Lauren Berlant and Michael Warner, "Sex in Public," *Critical Inquiry* 24, no. 2 (winter 1998): 562.

9. Quoted phrase, ibid., 563.

10. Examples include Jean Elshtain, ed., *The Family in Political Thought* (Amherst: University of Massachusetts Press, 1982); and Christopher Wolfe, ed., *The Family, Civil Society, and the State* (Lanham, Md.: Rowman & Littlefield, 1998).

11. See Jean-François Lyotard's discussion of philosophical discourse and genre in "The Sign of History," trans. Geoff Bennington, in *The Lyotard Reader,* ed. Andrew Benjamin (Cambridge, Mass.: Basil Blackwell, 1989), 395.

12. James Redfield, "Homo Domesticus," in Jean-Pierre Vernant, ed., *The Greeks* (Chicago: University of Chicago Press, 1995), 153–83.

13. See Johannes Pederson, *Israel: Its Life and Culture,* vol. 1–2 (London: Oxford University Press, 1926).

14. Don DeLillo, *White Noise* (New York: Viking-Penguin, 1985).

15. Nancy Armstrong, "Semiotics and Family History," *American Journal of Semiotics* 10 (1993): 135.

16. Ibid.

17. The quoted phrase is from Walter Benjamin, *The Origin of German Tragic Drama,* trans. John Osborne (New York: Verso, 1998), 28–29.

18. See Himmelfarb, *The De-Moralization of Society.* I call her investigation "pseudo," because it is self-validating. Ultimately, her argument is that Victorian virtue caused Victorian virtue. For example, even when those whose virtue she wants to valorize are shown to have strayed from virtuous conduct, she saves their virtue by showing that they are embarrassed by their shortcomings. No evidence is allowed to impeach her claim that Victorian society was an ideal historical exemplar of *the* moral way. For her, all the evidence militates on behalf of a Victorian moral homogeneity. That society, she claims, adhered to "virtues" that "were fixed and certain" (12).

19. Robert Mighall, *A Geography of Victorian Gothic Fiction: Mapping History's Nightmares* (New York: Oxford University Press, 1999), 14.

20. Tzvetan Todorov, *Genres in Discourse,* trans. Catherine Porter (New York: Cambridge University Press, 1990), 18. I want to note, however, that the boundaries of genres are not firm and are historically contingent. As Jacques Derrida has pointed out, "[T]here are no arch-genres that can totally escape historical contingency *while preserving a generic definition.*" See "The Law of Genre," in *Glyph 7* (Baltimore: Johns Hopkins University Press, 1980), 209.

21. David Michael Hertz, *The Tuning of the Word: The Musico-Literary Poetics of the Symbolist Movement* (Carbondale: Southern Illinois University Press, 1987), 13.

22. I am indebted to the ethnomusicologist Ricardo Trimelos for these insights into Debussy's liberties with tonality.

23. The quotation and material on Bruneau's reaction to Debussy's music are from Jane F. Fulcher, *French Cultural Politics and Music* (New York: Oxford University Press, 1999), 44.

24. See Walter Benjamin, "N [Re The Theory of Knowledge, Theory of Progress]," trans. Leigh Hafrey and Richard Sieburth, in Gary Smith, ed., *Benjamin: Philosophy, History, Aesthetics* (Chicago: University of Chicago Press, 1989), 47. My prior evocation of the influence of this sentiment of Benjamin's on my writing is in Michael J. Shapiro, *Cinematic Political Thought: Narratives of Race, Nation, and Gender* (New York: New York University Press, 1999), 6.

25. Janet Maslin, "'Happiness': Music Is Easy Listening and Dessert Is Hard to Take," *New York Times* (on the web), October 9, 1998.

26. Geoffrey Hartman, *Saving the Text: Literature/Derrida/Philosophy* (Baltimore: Johns Hopkins University Press, 1981), 119–20.

27. Norman Podhoretz, "'Lolita,' My Mother-in-Law, the Marquis de Sade, and Larry Flynt," *Commentary* 103, no. 4 (April 1997): 35.

28. This way of characterizing the narrative is borrowed from Neil Hertz,

"Two Extravagant Teachings," in *The End of the Line: Essays in Psychoanalysis and the Sublime* (Baltimore: Johns Hopkins University Press, 1985), 145.

29. Samuel Weber, *The Legend of Freud* (Minneapolis: University of Minnesota Press, 1982), 54.

30. On Sade's apologists, see Podhoretz, "'Lolita,' My Mother-in-Law, the Marquis de Sade, and Larry Flynt," 31; on his buggery focus, see 30.

31. See Hitchens's review of Podhoretz's *Ex-Friends* in Christopher Hitchens, "Unmaking Friends: Norman Podhoretz as Crumb," *Harper's*, June 1999, 73–76.

32. For a treatment of the cultural anxieties associated with historical changes in the construction of personhood, see Priscilla Wald, *Constituting Americans: Cultural Anxiety and Narrative Form* (Durham, N.C.: Duke University Press, 1995).

33. The quotations are from William Connolly's critique of William Bennett in "Drugs, the Nation and Free Lancing," *Theory & Event* 1, no. 1 (1997), on the web at http://muse.jhu.edu/journals/tae/.

34. Lauren Berlant, "Live Sex Acts (Parental Advisory: Explicit Material)," in Nicholas B. Dirks, ed., *In Near Ruins* (Minneapolis: University of Minnesota Press, 1998), 173.

35. See "Declaration Concerning Religion, Ethics, and the Clinton Presidency" (released to the press on November 13, 1998): http://www.moral-crisis.org/declaration.html.

36. Giorgio Agamben, "The People," *Public* 12 (1995): 10.

37. Berlant, "Live Sex Acts," 175.

38. The quotation is from Marvin L. Moore, "The Family as Portrayed on Prime-Time Television, 1947–1990: Structure and Characteristics," *Sex Roles* 26, nos. 1–2 (January 1992): 41–61, quotation on 56.

39. Elisabeth Beck-Gernsheim, "On the Way to a Post-Familial Family: From a Community of Needs to Elective Affinities," *Theory, Culture & Society* 15, nos. 3–4 (1998): 57.

40. Ella Taylor, *Prime-Time Families: Television Culture in Postwar America* (Berkeley: University of California Press, 1989), 126.

41. I owe these observations on *Roseanne* to Kathleen K. Rowe, "Roseanne: Unruly Woman as Domestic Goddess," *Screen* 31, no. 4 (winter 1990): 408–19.

42. Lynn Spigel, "'From the Dark Ages to the Golden Age': Women's Memories and Television Reruns," *Screen* 36, no. 1 (spring 1995): 16–33, quotation on 20.

43. Vivian Sobchack, "Bringing It All Back Home: Family, Economy and Generic Exchange," in Barry Keith Grant, ed., *The Dread of Difference: Gender and the Horror Film* (Austin: University of Texas Press, 1996), 156.

1. Resisting Resolution

1. Pierre Vidal-Naquet, "The Shields of Heroes: Essay on the Central Scene of *Seven against Thebes*," in Jean Pierre Vernant and Pierre Vidal-Naquet, *Myth and Tragedy in Ancient Greece,* trans. Janet Lloyd (New York: Zone Books, 1990), 273. The quotation within Vidal-Naquet's quotation is from Gilbert Murray, *Aeschylus: The Creator of Tragedy* (New York: Oxford University Press, 1940), 140.

2. Aeschylus, *Seven against Thebes,* trans. A. W. Verrall, in A. W. Verrall, *The Seven against Thebes of Aeschylus* (London: Macmillan, 1887), 147.

3. Vidal-Naquet, "The Shields of Heroes," 275–77.

4. I make a similar point in a reading of DeLillo's *White Noise*: Michael J. Shapiro, "The Politics of Fear," in *Reading the Postmodern Polity: Political Theory as Textual Practice* (Minneapolis: University of Minnesota Press, 1992), 131.

5. Tom LeClair, "Interview with Don DeLillo," in Tom LeClair and Larry McCaffery, eds., *Anything Can Happen: Interviews with Contemporary American Novelists* (Urbana: University of Illinois Press, 1983), 83.

6. Bruce Bawer, "Don DeLillo's America," *New Criterion* 3 (April 1985): 37.

7. Don DeLillo, *Players* (New York: Vintage, 1984), 104.

8. DeLillo, *White Noise.* The reference is to Christopher Lasch, *Haven in a Heartless World: The Family Besieged* (New York: Basic Books, 1977).

9. Vernant and Vidal-Naquet, "Preface," in *Myth and Tragedy in Ancient Greece,* 14.

10. Jean-Pierre Vernant, "The Historical Moment of Tragedy in Greece: Some of the Social and Psychological Conditions," in *Myth and Tragedy in Ancient Greece,* 24.

11. Ibid., 26.

12. Ibid., 25.

13. In referring to the shield's emblems as devices, I am following the usage in Vidal-Naquet's analysis of the shields in "The Shields of Heroes."

14. Ibid., 296–97.

15. Froma I. Zeitlin, *Under the Sign of the Shield: Semiotics and Aeschylus' Seven against Thebes* (Rome: dell'Ateneo, 1982), 49.

16. On this point, see ibid., 29.

17. *Njal's Saga,* trans. Magnus Magnusson and Hermann Pálsson (Baltimore: Penguin Books, 1960), 115.

18. D. A. Miller, "Fathers, Sons, Brothers and Others: Family Solidarity in the Thought-World of the Sagas," *Mankind Quarterly* 29, no. 3 (spring 1989): 238.

19. Pierre Bourdieu, *The Middle Brow Art,* trans. Shaun Whiteside (Stanford, Calif.: Stanford University Press, 1990), 26.

20. Alan Trachtenberg, *Reading American Photographs* (New York: Hill & Wang, 1989), 33.

21. See Sally Mann, *Immediate Family* (New York: Aperture, 1992); and Jim Goldberg, *Rich and Poor: Photographs* (New York: Random House, 1985).

22. Craig Decker, "Photographic Eye, Narrative I: Peter Henisch's *Die kleine Figur meines Vaters," Monatshefte* 83, no. 2 (summer 1991): 147.

23. Ibid., 150.

24. Peter Henisch, *Negatives of My Father,* trans. Anne Close Ulmer (Riverside, Calif.: Ariadne Press, 1990), 3.

25. Decker, "Photographic Eye, Narrative I," 156.

26. See Decker's remarks on history versus biography, ibid., 154.

27. Henisch, *Negatives of My Father,* 116.

28. See Art Spiegelman: *Maus* (New York: Pantheon, 1986); and *Maus II* (New York: Pantheon, 1991).

29. The quoted phrase, which is applied to Spiegelman's text, is from Robert S. Leventhal, "Art Spiegelman's *MAUS: Trauerarbeit* and Trau-Ma of the Holocaust," http://www.bitlink.com/~rsl/responses/spiegelman.html.

30. This argument is indeed made by Ian Gordon, *Comic Strips and Consumer Culture 1880–1945* (Washington, D.C.: Smithsonian Institution Press, 1998).

31. This characterization of Kafka's use of personified animals belongs to Marthe Robert. See her *As Lonely as Franz Kafka,* trans. Ralph Mannheim (New York: Harcourt Brace Jovanovich, 1982).

32. See Franz Kafka , "Investigations of a Dog," trans. Tania and James Stern, in *Franz Kafka: The Complete Stories,* ed. Nahum Glatzer (New York: Schocken, 1946), 278–310.

33. See Franz Kafka, "Report to an Academy," trans. Willa and Edwin Muir, ibid., 250–62.

34. Art Spiegelman, "Drawing Pens and Politics: Mightier Than the Sorehead," *Nation* (January 17, 1994): 46.

35. For similar insight see Marianne Hirsch, "Family Pictures: *Maus,* and Post-Memory," *Discourse* 15, no. 2 (winter 1992–93): 11.

36. See Art Spiegelman, *Breakdowns: From "Maus" to Now: Anthology of Strips by Art Spiegelman* (New York: Belier Press, 1977). See also James F. Young, whose critical essay called the breakdown imagery of Spiegelman to my attention: "The Holocaust as Vicarious Past: Art Spiegelman's *Maus* and the Afterimages of History," *Critical Inquiry* 24, no. 3 (spring 1998): 673.

37. See Hirsch, "Family Pictures," 15, on this point.

38. The "collaborative autobiography" designation for Spiegelman's text is suggested by Rick Adonisi in "Bleeding History and Owning His [Father's] Story: *Maus* and Collaborative Autobiography," *CEA Critic* 57, no. 1 (fall 1994): 11–26.

39. Sarah Maza, "Only Connect: Family Values in the Age of Sentiment: Introduction," *Eighteenth Century Studies* 30, no. 3 (1997): 208.

40. See Michel Foucault, "Governmentality," in Graham Burchell, Colin Gordon, and Peter Miller, eds., *The Foucault Effect* (Chicago: University of Chicago Press, 1991), 87–104.

41. For a treatment of the historical connection between economy and moral discourse, see Joyce Oldham Appleby, *Economic Thought and Ideology in Seventeenth Century England* (Princeton, N.J.: Princeton University Press, 1978).

42. Quoted in Eve Tavor Bannet, "The Marriage Act of 1753: 'A Most Cruel Law for the Fair Sex,'" *Eighteenth-Century Studies* 30, no. 3 (1997): 240.

43. Thomas O. Beebee, *Clarissa on the Continent* (University Park: Pennsylvania State University Press, 1990), 73.

44. Terry Eagleton, *The Rape of Clarissa* (London: Methuen, 1982), 51–52.

45. Maza, "Only Connect," 211.

46. For a similar conclusion, see Terry Castle, *Clarissa's Cyphers* (Ithaca, N.Y.: Cornell University Press, 1982), 29.

47. Samuel Richardson, *Clarissa, or The history of a Young Lady: Comprehending the Most Important Concerns of Private Life* (New York: AMS, 1990), 863. And see Beebee, *Clarissa on the Continent,* 125–26.

48. Paula W. Sunderman, "Between Two Worlds: Interview with Hanan al-Shaykh," *Literary Review* 40, no. 2 (winter 1997): 303.

49. Julia Kristeva, "Women's Time," trans. Alice Jardine and Harry Blake, *Signs* 7, no. 1 (spring 1981): 18.

50. Hanan al-Shaykh, *Beirut Blues,* trans. Catherine Cobham (New York: Doubleday, 1995).

51. On *chronotope,* see M. M. Bakhtin, "Forms of Time and of the Chronotope in the Novel," trans. Caryl Emerson and Michael Holquist, in Michael Holquist, ed., *The Dialogic Imagination* (Austin: University of Texas Press, 1981), 84.

52. *Heteroglossia* is a translation of M. M. Bakhtin's term for the many contending voices characteristic of the novel. See his "Discourse in the Novel," in Holquist, ed., *The Dialogic Imagination,* 259–422.

53. The periods of time represented in her novel, according to al-Shaykh, are as follows: "It covers the year 1985 when the two Shi'a militia, Hezbollah and Amal, fought each other. The actual period in the novel is twenty days, although my flashbacks go back to the mid-fifties, sixties, seventies, and early eighties"; see Sunderman, "Between Two Worlds," 305.

54. Al-Shaykh, *Beirut Blues,* 3.

55. Jacques Derrida, *The Politics of Friendship,* trans. George Collins (London: Verso, 1997), 5.

56. Al-Shaykh, *Beirut Blues,* 4–5.

57. The term *chronotype* derives from the anthology by John Bender and David Wellbery, *Chronotypes* (Stanford, Calif.: Stanford University Press, 1991).

58. Al-Shaykh, *Beirut Blues*, 67.

59. Richard Rorty, *Contingency, Irony, and Solidarity* (New York: Cambridge University Press, 1989), 87.

60. Jacques Rancière, *Disagreement*, trans. Julie Rose (Minneapolis: University of Minnesota Press, 1999), 29.

61. Michael Dillon, *Politics of Security* (London: Routledge, 1996), 142.

2. Contingency, Genealogy, and the Family

1. Erich Auerbach, "Odysseus' Scar," in *Mimesis*, trans. Willard R. Trask (Princeton, N.J.: Princeton University Press, 1953), 10.

2. The Palestinian filmmaker Elia Suileman appreciates this aspect of old men's stories. In his *Chronicle of a Disappearance*, there is a comparable story, told by an old grandfather. His story about his life in the Turkish army frustrates his listeners, who want to learn something about what Turkey was like at the turn of the century. Instead, his narration is a wholly self-absorbed account of how one day he avoided the bad army food and ate a satisfying meal he bought from a street vendor. Each time the story is solicited—with the hope of more local detail—the narration remains focused on the details of his meal.

3. The expression is the title of Jean-François Lyotard's *Libidinal Economy*, trans. Iain Hamilton Grant (Bloomington: Indiana University Press, 1993). While the English translation of Freud's concept of *Besetzung* is "cathexis" in the Standard Edition, in French, it has been translated as *investissement*, doubtless encouraging French critical thinkers to interarticulate economic and sexual discourses.

4. See Jonathan Rosenbaum, "A Gun up Your Ass: An Interview with Jim Jarmusch," *Cineaste* 22, no. 2 (1996): 23.

5. This remark is made by Jonathan Rosenbaum, ibid., 20.

6. Gilles Deleuze, *Cinema 2*, trans. Hugh Tomlinson and Robert Galeta (Minneapolis: University of Minnesota Press, 1989), 24.

7. As Richard Slotkin has pointed out, by the eighteenth century more regionally developed stories displaced the biblical version of America's expansion. The significant icons were no longer virtuous, self-sacrificing Puritans but heroic adventurers and Indian fighters. Summarizing this shift, he says: "In the American mythogenesis the founding fathers were not those eighteenth century gentlemen who composed a nation at Philadelphia. Rather, they were those who . . . tore violently a nation from the implacable and opulent wilderness—the rogues, adventurers, and land-boomers; the Indian fighters, traders, missionaries, explorers, and hunters who killed and were killed until they had mastered the wilderness." See Richard Slotkin, *Regeneration through Violence: The Mythology*

of the American Frontier, 1600–1860 (Middletown, Conn.: Wesleyan University Press 1973), 4.

8. Gilles Deleuze and Félix Guattari, *A Thousand Plateaus,* trans. Brian Massumi (Minneapolis: University of Minnesota Press, 1987), 385.

9. The quotation belongs to Partha Chatterjee, whose treatment of civil society in the thought of Hegel has influenced my discussion here: Partha Chatterjee, "A Response to Taylor's Modes of Civil Society," *Public Culture* 3, no. 1 (fall 1990): 123.

10. Hegel, *Philosophy of Right,* 148.

11. Etienne Balibar, "Ambiguous Universality," *Differences* 7, no. 1 (spring 1995): 56.

12. See Jean-Luc Nancy, *The Birth to Presence,* trans. B. Holmes et al. (Stanford, Calif.: Stanford University Press, 1993), 143–66.

13. Friedrich Nietzsche, *The Genealogy of Morals,* trans. Francis Golffing (New York: Doubleday, 1956), 165.

14. Offering a similar insight, Peter Sloterdijk says that Nietzsche offers "a theory of drama that then expands into a protohistory of subjectivity" (Peter Sloterdijk, *Thinker on Stage: Nietzsche's Materialism,* trans. Jamie Owen Daniel [Minneapolis: University of Minnesota Press, 1989], 16).

15. See especially, Friedrich Nietzsche, *Ecce Homo,* trans. Walter Kaufmann (New York: Random House, 1969).

16. Michel Foucault, "Nietzsche, Genealogy, History," trans. Donald F. Bouchard and Sherry Simon, in Donald F. Bouchard, ed., *Language, Counter-Memory, Practice* (Ithaca, N.Y.: Cornell University Press, 1977), 139.

17. Michel Foucault, "The Thought from the Outside," in *Foucault Blanchot,* trans. Jeffrey Mehlman and Brian Massumi (New York: Zone, 1990), 18.

18. Alan Ryan, "Elusive Liberalism," *New York Times Book Review,* July 7, 1996, 8.

19. Michel Foucault, *Discipline and Punish: The Birth of the Prison,* trans. Alan Sheridan (New York: Pantheon, 1977), 192.

20. Foucault, "Nietzsche, Genealogy, History," 140.

21. Foucault, "Governmentality," 100.

22. Ibid., 95. It should be noted that the family-state relationship has functioned, historically, in different ways from the European and, more specifically, French case that is Foucault's focus. In the nineteenth and early twentieth centuries in Peru, for example, the state helped powerful regional families maintain their local hegemonies in return for their participation in the state bureaucracy. Rather than being objects of control or coercion, they were recruited to manage economic tribute, which was returned to the center, and to maintain local peacekeeping. This structure, a form of "clientelism," reflects a different "governmentality." See

David Nugent, "Building the State, Making the Nation: The Bases and Limits of State Centralization in 'Modern' Peru," *American Anthropologist* 96, no. 2 (June 1994): 333–69.

23. Jacques Donzelot, *The Policing of Families,* trans. Robert Hurley (New York: Pantheon, 1979), 7.

24. See, for example, Michel Foucault, *The History of Sexuality,* trans. Robert Hurley (New York: Pantheon, 1978).

25. See George Mosse, *Nationalism and Sexuality* (New York: Howard Fertig, 1985).

26. William Bennett and C. Deloris Tucker, "Smut-Free Stores," *New York Times,* December 9, 1996, A15.

27. Katha Pollit makes a similar argument in her analysis of Dan Quayle's attack on the *Murphy Brown* television sitcom: "Why I Hate 'Family Values' (Let Me Count the Ways)," *Nation* 255 (July 27, 1992): 94.

28. On this issue see Mosse, *Nationalism and Sexuality.*

29. This process is described by Norbert Elias, *The Civilizing Process,* trans. Edmund Jephcott (New York: Blackwell, 1994), 22 ff.

30. Mosse, *Nationalism and Sexuality,* 53.

31. Noel Burch, "Spatial and Temporal Articulations," in *Theory of Film Practice,* trans. Helen Lane (New York: Praeger, 1973), 17.

32. Even the L. L. Bean catalog, for example, romanticizes an American home that is "cozy and unbroken," a place with people who are "mostly married, with car pools and mortgages and aging parents"; it is a world with "no room for the confusion about sex roles that currently besets the rest of our society." Holly Brubach, "Mail-Order America," *New York Times Magazine,* November 11, 1993, 58.

33. Nancy Fraser, "After the Family Wage: Gender Equity and the Welfare State," *Political Theory* 2, no. 4 (November 1994): 591.

34. Sade was of course much more doctrinal than Jack Horner. This is not the place to map the positions and enigmas in Sadean thought and stagings. The primary parallel is their shared resistance to official strictures regulating sexuality and their encouragement of singularity (best articulated in Sade's "Philosophy in the Bedroom") (Marquis de Sade, "Philosophy in the Bedroom," in his *Justine, Philosophy in the Bedroom, and Other Writings,* trans. Richard Seaver and Austryn Wainhouse [New York: Grove Press, 1965]). I address myself to Sadean thought more extensively in Michael J. Shapiro, *Reading 'Adam Smith': Desire, History and Value* (Newbury Park, Calif.: Sage, 1993), 116–32.

35. Jonathan Crary, "Unbinding Vision: Manet and the Attentive Observer in the Late Nineteenth Century," in Leo Charney and Vanessa R. Schwartz, eds.,

Cinema and the Invention of Modern Life (Berkeley: University of California Press, 1995), 46–71.

36. Jean-Luc Nancy, *The Sense of the World*, trans. Jeffrey S. Librett (Minneapolis: University of Minnesota Press, 1997), 93.

37. For an elaboration of this position see Jean-Luc Nancy, *The Inoperative Community*, trans. Peter Connor, Lisa Garbus, Michael Holland, and Simona Sawhney (Minneapolis: University of Minnesota Press, 1991).

3. Families, Strategies, Interests, and Public Life

1. Walter Benjamin, *Charles Baudelaire: A Lyric Poet in the Era of High Capitalism,* trans. Harry Zohn (New York: Verso, 1997), 40.

2. Tom T. Gunning, "Tracing the Individual Body," in L. Charney and Vanessa R. Schwartz, eds., *Cinema and the Invention of Modern Life* (Berkeley: University of California Press, 1995), 20.

3. Joe J. Gores, *32 Cadillacs* (New York: Time Warner, 1992), xi.

4. Foucault, *Discipline and Punish,* 277–79.

5. Michel de Certeau, *Practices of Everyday Life* (Berkeley: University of California Press, 1984), 35–36.

6. Bakhtin, "Discourse and the Novel," 293.

7. Gores, *32 Cadillacs,* 25.

8. These insights are drawn from Isabella Fonseca, *Bury Me Standing* (New York: Vintage, 1995).

9. Patricia Drechsel Tobin, *Time and the Novel: The Genealogical Imperative* (Princeton, N.J.: Princeton University Press, 1978), 6.

10. Marleen Sway, *Familiar Strangers: Gypsy Life in America* (Urbana: University of Illinois Press, 1988), 53.

11. Anne Sutherland, *Gypsies: The Hidden Americans* (New York: Free Press, 1975), 13.

12. Henri-Jean Martin, *The History and Power of Writing,* trans. Lydia G. Cochrane (Chicago: University of Chicago Press, 1994).

13. Benedict R. O'G. Anderson, *Imagined Communities: Reflections on the Origin and Spread of Nationalism* (New York: Verso, 1991), 19.

14. Blackstone, who was instrumental in providing the rhetorical resources of authorial proprietorship in the eighteenth century, explicitly likened literary composition to private property and authors to owners of landed estates. See Mark Rose's commentary on the emergence of the legal author: "The Author as Proprietor: *Donaldson v. Beckett* and the Genealogy of the Modern Author," *Representations* 23 (summer 1988): 51–85.

15. See Deleuze and Guattari, *A Thousand Plateaus,* for a discussion of striated space.

16. Foucault, *Discipline and Punish*, 197.

17. Fonseca, *Bury Me Standing*, 11, 53.

18. The quotations are from Fredric Jameson's discussion of Koolhaas's treatment of the structures of New York; see Jameson's "Postmodernism and Space" (a conversation with Michael Speaks), *Assemblage* 17 (1992): 32–37.

19. Susan Buck-Morss, *The Dialectics of Seeing* (Cambridge, Mass.: MIT Press, 1989), 26.

20. Tom Keenan, "Windows of Vulnerability," in Bruce Robbins, ed., *The Phantom Public Sphere* (Minneapolis: University of Minnesota Press, 1993), 130.

21. Jürgen Habermas, *The Structural Transformation of the Public Sphere*, trans. T. Burger and F. Lawrence (Cambridge, Mass.: MIT Press, 1989), 8.

22. The quoted phrase is from William Leach, *Land of Desire* (New York: Pantheon, 1993), 39–70.

23. For an analysis of the social logic within which such "fractions" function, see Pierre Bourdieu, *Distinction: A Social Critique of the Judgment of Taste*, trans. Richard Nice (Cambridge, Mass.: Harvard University Press, 1984).

24. Gores, *32 Cadillacs*, 34.

25. Beatriz Colomina, "The Spilt Wall: Domestic Voyeurism," in Beatriz Colomina, ed., *Sexuality and Space* (New York: Princeton Architecture Press, 1992), 83.

26. Christina Marsden Gillis, *The Paradox of Privacy* (Gainesville: University of Florida Press, 1984), 7.

27. See Colomina, "The Split Wall," 86.

28. Gores, *32 Cadillacs*, 21.

29. G. W. F. Hegel, *Natural Law*, trans. T. M. Knox (Philadelphia: University of Pennsylvania Press, 1962), 94–95.

30. Carole Desbarats, "Conquering What They Tell Us Is 'Natural,'" in Carole Desbarats, ed., *Atom Egoyan* (Paris: Dis Voir, 1993), 9.

31. See Russell Banks, *The Sweet Hereafter* (New York: HarperCollins, 1992).

32. Atom Egoyan, in an interview conducted by Richard Porton in the journal *Cineaste*, reproduced as "The Family Romance," on the web at http://members.cruzio.com/-akeyche/fr1.html, part 2, 2.

33. Burch, "Spatial and Temporal Articulations," 17.

34. For a good statement of the way that public ownership of corporations depoliticizes and renders ethically obtuse the management of enterprises, see Hillary Smith Ripley's recent letter to the magazine *Harper's* 296, no. 1774 (March 1998): 4.

35. Deleuze, *Cinema 2*, 24.

36. Ibid., 23.

37. For the term *non-chronological time*, see ibid., 129.

38. Egoyan in Porton, "Family Romance," part 4, 2.

39. The concept of the habitus is used by Pierre Bourdieu (e.g., *Distinction*) to refer to the way people are oriented to their social world, not as a form of consciousness, but, in a Heideggerian sense, as a set of involvements. They have their world through various practices of space, time, distinction, and so on, and how they are so disposed is not by acts of will but by various contextually influenced social logics.

40. The expression "horizon of experience" is taken from Oskar Negt and Alexander Kluge's treatment of the public sphere: Oskar Negt and Alexander Kluge, *The Public Sphere and Experience*, trans. Peter Labanyi, Jamie Daniel, and Assenka Oksiloff (Minneapolis: University of Minnesota Press, 1993). Sensitive to mass-mediated forms of public life, they resist the traditional Frankfort school emphasis on the culture industry and treat instead the dynamics of the public sphere.

41. Paul Virilio, *Open Sky*, trans. Julie Rose (London: Verso, 1997), 10.

42. Stephen Kern, *The Culture of Time and Space 1800–1918* (Cambridge, Mass.: Harvard University Press, 1983), 14.

43. Friedrich Kittler, "Gramophone, Film, Typewriter," in *Freidrich A. Kittler Essays: Literature, Media, Information Systems*, ed. John Jonnston (Amsterdam: OPA, 1997), 34.

44. Egoyan, in Porton, "Family Romance," part 3, 2.

45. The quotations are from "Film Notes" on the web at http://www.flf/sweet/cmp/fil-top.html.

46. On the perception image, see Gilles Deleuze, *Cinema 1,* trans. Hugh Tomlinson and Barbara Habberjam (London: Athlone, 1986), 67.

47. Virilio, *Open Sky*, 26.

48. Egoyan in Porton, "Family Romance," part 3, 2.

49. Ibid., part 2, 1.

50. Michel Foucault, "Of Other Spaces," trans. Jay Miscowiec, *Diacritics* 16 (spring 1986): 26.

51. Walter Benjamin, "The Story Teller," in Hannah Arendt, ed., *Illuminations,* trans. Harry Zohn (New York: Schocken, 1969), 94.

52. As Benjamin puts it, "By now, almost nothing that happens benefits story telling; almost everything benefits information" ("The Story Teller," 89). And he adds, apropos of the loss of the experience of death in life: "In the course of modern times dying has been pushed further and further out of the perceptual world of the living" (93–94).

53. Virilio, *Open Sky*, 25.

54. The quotation is from Egoyan, in Porton, "Family Romance," part 1, 2.

55. Virilio, *Open Sky,* 55.

56. Foucault, "Of Other Spaces."

4. Literary Geography and Sovereign Violence

1. Alexis de Tocqueville, *Democracy in America,* trans. Henry Reeve (New York: Vintage, 1990), 2:197.

2. This aspect of Tocqueville's approach to the family is comprehensively explicated in Pierre Mament, *Tocqueville and the Nature of Democracy,* trans. John Wagonner (Baltimore, Md.: Rowman & Littlefield, 1996).

3. George Wilson Pierson, *Tocqueville and Beaumont in America* (New York: Oxford University Press, 1938), 85.

4. Russell Banks, *Cloudsplitter* (New York: HarperCollins, 1998), 219.

5. Daniel Patrick Moynihan issued his report on "the Negro family" in 1965. For a review of its implications and the controversy it attracted, see Lee Rainwater and William L. Yancey, *The Moynihan Report and the Politics of Controversy* (Cambridge, Mass.: MIT Press, 1967).

6. Hortense Spillers, "Mama's Baby, Papa's Maybe: An American Grammar Book," *Diacritics* 17, no. 2 (summer 1987): 60.

7. The quotations are from Lauren Berlant, "The Queen of America Goes to Washington City: Notes on Diva Citizenship," in Lauren Berlant, *The Queen of America Goes to Washington City: Essays in Sex and Citizenship* (Durham, N.C.: Duke University Press, 1997), 229.

8. The intimate connection between white and black families, which has always been part of African American oral history, achieved national publicity in May of 1999 when DNA tests confirmed that there are descendants of the relationship between Thomas Jefferson and Sally Hemings, one of his black slaves. As a result of this virtually irrefutable evidence that "Jefferson had a hidden family with Sally Hemings" (quoted from Nicholas Wade, "Taking New Measurements for Jefferson's Pedestal," *New York Times* [on the web], March 7, 1999), the Jefferson-Hemings descendants attended the eighty-seventh Jefferson family reunion at Monticello (see "Jefferson Reunion Adds Slave's Kin," *New York Times* [on the web], March 6, 1999).

9. Laura L. Lovett, "'African and Cherokee by Choice': *Race and Resistance under Legalized Segregation,*" *American Indian Quarterly* 22, nos. 1–2 (winter/spring 1998): 203.

10. Ibid., 205.

11. Herbert G. Gutman, *The Black Family in Slavery and Freedom 1700–1925* (New York: Vintage, 1976).

12. Rancière, *Disagreement,* 101.

13. Jacques Rancière, "Politics, Identification, and Subjectification," *October* 61 (summer 1992): 59.

14. "Interview with Jacques Rancière: Democracy Means Equality," *Radical Philosophy* 82 (March/April 1997): 31.

15. Rancière, *Disagreement*, 39.

16. Edward Ball, *Slaves in the Family* (New York: Ballantine, 1998), 7.

17. As Donald Lowe notes, the estate-based society was organized on the basis of a set of formal prerogatives, authorized by God. Estate society was thus ascriptive; statuses were hierarchically fixed, and "the major concerns within that formalized hierarchy were precedence, honor, and territoriality." Donald Lowe, *History of Bourgeois Perception* (Chicago: University of Chicago Press, 1982), 63.

18. The quotation is from Clyde Woods, *Development Arrested* (New York: Verso, 1998), 41. Treating, among other things, "the social-spatial construction of the Mississippi Delta," Woods argues that "blues epistemology," an African American mode of being/knowing constitutes a resistance to "plantation bloc explanation," which still characterizes the perspective of much of white society.

19. Bakhtin, "Forms of Time and the Chronotope in the Novel," 84–258.

20. John Stuart Mill, "M. de Tocqueville on Democracy in American" (first published in 1840), in *Dissertations and Discussions*, vol. 2 (New York: Henry Holt, 1874), 85.

21. Tocqueville, *Democracy in America*, 1:25.

22. William E. Connolly, *The Ethos of Pluralization* (Minneapolis: University of Minnesota Press, 1995), 170.

23. Tocqueville was not a simplistic moralizer, however. Allowing in his model of cultural encounter a degree of cultural pluralism, he lamented the demise of the "noble savage," feeling that Native Americans were undeserving of the destruction of their way of life that the European invasion had wrought. Nevertheless, as Connolly puts it, "the historical consolidation of the civil-territorial complex requires the elimination of the Indian" (170). Tocqueville, despite his qualms, is able to "come to terms with violence that is undeserved" (171). The European habitation is a form of justice sanctioned by history. In comparison, the "injustice in justice" (171) cannot be as telling for Tocqueville as was, for example, the injustice of slavery. And, most essentially, contrary to the many readings that locate Tocqueville as a sophisticated sociologist, the myopic gaze he trained on Native American social organization constituted a continuation of European violence by other means, what Jacques Derrida has called a "violence of representation." Jacques Derrida, "Violence and Metaphysics," in *Writing and Difference*, trans. Alan Bass (Chicago: University of Chicago Press), 79–153.

24. Harry Liebersohn, "Discovering Indigenous Nobility: Tocqueville,

Chamisso, and Romantic Travel Writing," *American Historical Review* 99, no. 3 (June 1994): 746.

25. Tocqueville, *Democracy in America*, 1:331–434.

26. For a historical treatment of the various masks that slaves employed to survive not only in the face of the dangers from punishment by their owners but also from the shame among those who shared their behavioral dilemmas, see Bertram Wyatt-Brown, "The Mask of Obedience: Male Slave Psychology in the Old South," *American Historical Review* 93, no. 5 (December 1988): 1228–52.

27. Mike Thelwell, "Back with the Wind: Mr. Styron and the Reverend Turner," in John Henrik Clarke, ed., *Turner: The Black Writers Respond* (Boston: Beacon Press, 1968), 87.

28. Susan G. Davis, *Parades and Power: Street Theater in Nineteenth-Century Philadelphia* (Berkeley: University of California Press, 1986), 46.

29. Ibid.

30. Tocqueville, *Democracy in America*, 1:356.

31. Franco Moretti, *Atlas of the European Novel 1800–1900* (New York: Verso, 1998).

32. Ibid., 14.

33. M. M. Bakhtin, "The *Bildungsroman* and Its Significance in the History of Realism (toward a Historical Typology of the Novel)," in Caryl Emerson and Michael Holquist, eds., *Speech Genres and Other Late Essays*, trans. Vern W. McGee (Austin: University of Texas Press, 1986), 11.

34. The injustice in justice and immorality in morality remarks here reflect William Connolly's contrast between Tocqueville and Nietzsche. See William E. Connolly, "Tocqueville, Territory, and Violence," in Michael J. Shapiro and Hayward Alker, eds., *Challenging Boundaries* (Minneapolis: University of Minnesota Press, 1996), 147.

35. Moretti, *Atlas of the European Novel 1800–1900*, 37.

36. Pierson, *Tocqueville and Beaumont in America*, 121.

37. Bakhtin, "The *Bildungsroman* and Its Significance in the History of Realism," 53.

38. This notion of wrong and of the political as an encounter between the production of community consent and the violent production of political inequality is taken from Jacques Rancière's discussions in both "Politics, Identification, and Subjectivization" and *Disagreement*.

39. See M. M. Bakhtin's explication of the heteroglossic structure of the novel in his "Discourse and the Novel," 257–422.

40. See Banks, *Cloudsplitter*, 423, for an explicit treatment of this dimension of racism.

41. Contemporary with Ball's investigation is a similar one by Macky

Alston. His film documentary *Family Name* is another autobiographical story of a great grandson exploring the connections between his family genealogy and those of the black families whose ancestors labored in servitude on his family's plantation (in North Carolina). Like Ball's, Alston's investigation is aimed at recovering the intimate interconnections among the white and black families who share a plantation past. For a comparison of the two investigations, see Ashraf H. A. Rushdy, "Seeking Forgiveness: The Memoirs of Slaveholders' Grandsons," *Southern Review* 35, no. 4 (autumn 1999): 789–805.

42. From "Inheriting Slavery," interview with Katie Bacon, in *Atlantic Unbound* (on the internet): http://www.theatlantic.com/atlantic/unbound/bookauth/eballint.htm.

43. Pierson, *Tocqueville and Beaumont in America*, 606.

44. Agamben, "The People," 10.

45. Giorgio Agamben, *Homo Sacer: Sovereign Power and Bare Life*, trans. Daniel Heller-Roazen (Stanford, Calif.: Stanford University Press, 1998), 6.

46. Priscilla Wald, "Terms of Assimilation: Legislating Subjectivity in the Emerging Nation," *Boundary* 2 19, no. 3 (fall 1992): 83–84.

47. Exemplary of an investigation guided by this perspective is Robert Putnam's study of "civic traditions" in contemporary Italy: *Making Democracy Work* (Princeton, N.J.: Princeton University Press, 1993).

48. See Robert Putnam, "Bowling Alone: America's Declining Social Capital," *Journal of Democracy* 6, no. 1 (January 1995): 65–78, for his original statement. In his elaborated one in *Bowling Alone* (New York: Simon and Schuster, 2000), Putnam moderates his claims about decline and about the role of television in deterring civic participation.

49. The best-known study that treated the issue of inequality on the basis of individual life trajectories is Christopher Jencks et al., *Inequality: A Reassessment of the Effect of Family and School in America* (New York: Basic Books, 1972). For a critique of this orientation in the liberal theory approach to inequality, see Alan Garfinkel, *Forms of Explanation* (New Haven, Conn.: Yale University Press, 1981).

50. Michael Hardt, "The Withering of Civil Society," *Social Text* 45 (winter 1995): 34.

51. The expression is from Houston A. Baker, "Critical Memory and the Black Public Sphere," *Public Culture* 7, no. 1 (fall 1994): 10.

52. See, for example, John Fiske's analyses in *Television Culture* (New York: Routledge, 1987), which, in contrast with simplistic treatments of television as a social narcotic, show the many ways it is implicated in sociality.

53. On the expression "confusion over inside and out," see Thomas Keenan, "Windows of Vulnerability," in Bruce Robbins, ed., *The Phantom Public Sphere* (Minneapolis: University of Minnesota Press, 1993), 130.

54. For more on this point, see Lynn Spigel, "The Suburban Home Companion: Television and the Neighborhood Ideal in Postwar America," in Colomina, ed., *Sexuality & Space*, 185–217.

55. See Tricia Rose, *Black Noise: Rap Music and Black Culture in Contemporary America* (Hanover, N.H.: Wesleyan University Press, 1994), 10.

56. Mark Anthony Neal, *What the Music Said* (New York: Routledge, 1999), 136.

57. This point is made in Stephen Haymes, *Race, Culture, and the City* (Albany: State University of New York Press), 70.

58. Michael Eric Dyson, "Between Apocalypse and Redemption: John Singleton's *Boyz N the Hood,*" *Cultural Critique* 21 (spring 1992): 124.

59. Michael Hanchard, "Afro-Modernity: Temporality, Politics, and the African Diaspora," *Public Culture* 11, no. 1 (winter 1999): 245–68. Quoting Frank Kirkland, Hanchard explicitly evokes the redemptive significance of reconceiving the African American past (250).

5. National Times and Other Times

1. For a review of this history, see David Thibault, "The Story of the Calendar," *Journal of Calendar Reform* 3 (1933): 139–43.

2. Thomas Pynchon, *Mason & Dixon* (New York: Henry Holt, 1997), 195.

3. For an extended treatment of the critical implications of temporality, see Gilles Deleuze, *Bergsonism,* trans. Hugh Tomlinson and Barbara Habberjam (New York: Zone Books, 1991).

4. St. Augustine, *The Confessions,* trans. John K. Ryan (New York: Doubleday, 1960), 65.

5. Reinhart Koselleck, *Futures Past: On the Semantics of Historical Time,* trans. Keith Tribe (Cambridge, Mass.: MIT Press, 1985), 231.

6. For a good summary of Augustine's analysis of time, see Paul Ricoeur's treatment, where he notes: "Augustine's inestimable discovery is, by reducing the extension of time to the distension of the soul, to have tied this distension to the slippage that never ceases to find its way into the heart of the threefold present of the present. In this way he sees discordance emerge again and again out of the very concordance of the intentions of expectation, attention, and memory" (Paul Ricoeur, *Time and Narrative,* vol. 1, trans. Kathleen McLaughlin and David Pellauer [Chicago: University of Chicago Press, 1984], 21).

7. Heidegger's approach to time diverges radically from Augustine's. For Augustine, beings must come to terms with time in order to understand how the temporal modalities of their actions render their existence wholly present in time. Heidegger, resisting a metaphysical model of consciousness, distinguishes

Being from beings, where Being, as a structure of involvement in the world, is fundamentally temporal. Heideggerian Being is a being toward the future, as the anticipation of one's death. See Martin Heidegger's most elaborate, initial construction of Being in his *Being and Time,* trans. John Macquarrie and Edward Robinson (San Francisco: Harper, 1962), where he argues that Being as the fundamental aspect of human involvement, when authentically heeded (by avoiding absorption into what is present-to-hand), shapes the significance of the past and present. The "I am" is made whole by the way in which Being toward the future integrates the past, present, and future. The "I am" is, in effect, inseparable from the "I am" as "having-been" and "I am" as "will-have-been." Heideggerian temporality articulates, ultimately, the unity of existence. Only the vulgar exigencies of time as calculation are disruptive to the self's reflection on the ontological within timeness, for they lower one's focus to the banalities of everyday existence.

8. Alexander García Düttmann, *At Odds with AIDS,* trans. Peter Gilgen and Conrad Scott-Curtis (Stanford, Calif.: Stanford University Press, 1996), 3–4.

9. This point is made by Etienne Balibar, "Is European Citizenship Possible?" *Public Culture* 8, no. 2 (spring 1996): 358.

10. For the orientation of citizenship under a condition of fractured subjectivity, see Toby Miller, *The Well-Tempered Self* (Baltimore: Johns Hopkins University Press, 1993). The concept of cultural citizenship is described this way in Renato Rosaldo, "Cultural Citizenship and Educational Democracy," *Cultural Anthropology* 9, no. 3 (summer 1994): 402.

11. Jürgen Habermas, "The European Nation-State: On the Past and Future of Sovereignty and Citizenship," *Public Culture* 10, no. 2 (winter 1998): 404.

12. Reminding us that imperialism was not incidental to state formation and that "modern nationalism was not simply a process of integration" but a continuing process of inclusion and exclusion, Timothy Mitchell turns his attention to orders of representation, which are dominated by the state. See Timothy Mitchell, "Nationalism, Imperialism, Economism: A Comment on Habermas," *Public Culture* 10, no. 2 (winter 1998): 418.

13. See Mitchell, "Nationalism, Imperialism, Economism," 417–24; and Liisa Malkki, "Things to Come: Internationalism and Global Solidarities in the Late 1990s," *Public Culture* 10, no. 2 (winter 1998): 431–42.

14. See Arjun Appadurai, "Full Attachment," *Public Culture* 10, no. 2 (winter 1998): 443–49; and Wendy Brown, "Democracy's Lack," *Public Culture* 10, no. 2 (winter 1998): 450–56.

15. My reference to binding and unbinding, a concept I also used in chapter 1, is influenced by Jean-Luc Nancy's reference to being-in-common as a dynamic of tying and untying. Predicated on the view that there are ways to be-in-common

without foundational guarantees, Nancy rejects a "truth of a common subject" or a general model of sense, outside of the "numerous singularity of each of the 'subjects of sense.'" The social bond, for Nancy, is an unending process of tying and loosening: See Nancy, *The Sense of the World*, 93.

16. Nancy, *The Inoperative Community*, 41.

17. Carlos Fuentes, "Writing in Time," *Democracy* 2, no. 1 (winter 1962): 61.

18. See Derrida for a discussion of how the presence of the present is dependent on a nonpresence, in *Speech and Phenomena: And Other Essays on Husserl's Theory of Signs*, trans. David B. Allison and Newton Berber (Evanston, Ill.: Northwestern University Press, 1973), 65 ff.

19. Fuentes, "Writing in Time," 62, 63.

20. See Paul Virilio, *Pure War* (New York: Semiotext(e), 1983).

21. This point is elaborated by Arjun Appadurai, *Modernity at Large* (Minneapolis: University of Minnesota Press, 1996), 165.

22. Etienne Balibar, "Ambiguous Universality," *Differences* 7, no. 1 (spring 1995): 48–74.

23. Agamben, "The People," 10.

24. There are, of course, other mechanisms. J. G. A. Pocock focuses, for example, on the acts of repetition by which societies produce continuity through tradition. See his *Politics, Language, and Time* (Chicago: University of Chicago Press, 1989).

25. Homi Bhabha, "DissemiNation: Time, Narrative, and the Margins of the Modern Nation," in Homi Bhabha, ed., *Nation and Narration* (New York: Routledge, 1990), 293.

26. On the "community to come," see Nancy, *The Inoperative Community*, 71.

27. Néstor García Canclini, *Hybrid Cultures*, trans. Christopher L. Chiappari and Silvia L. Lopez (Minneapolis: University of Minnesota Press, 1995), 129.

28. Ibid., 129–30.

29. Koselleck, *Futures Past*, 10–12.

30. Eric Alliez, *Capital Times*, trans. George van den Abbeele (Minneapolis: University of Minnesota Press, 1996), 6.

31. Lee Edelman, "The Future Is Kid Stuff: Queer Theory, Disidentification, and the Death Drive," *Narrative* 6, no. 1 (spring 1998): 19.

32. John Gillis, "Making Time for Family: The Invention of Family Time(s) and the Reinvention of Family History," *Journal of Family History* 21, no. 1 (January 1996): 10.

33. Tamara K. Hareven, "Family Time and Historical Time," *Daedalus* 106 (spring 1977): 58.

34. The "chronotope" is M. M. Bakhtin's term for the way a literary genre

organizes the time-space of its articulations. See his "Forms of Time and the Chronotope in the Novel," 84–258.

35. Emmanuel Sivan, "Contending Arab Visions," *Macalester International* 4 (1997): 59.

36. Johannes Pederson, *Israel: Its Life and Culture* (London: Oxford University Press, 1926), 1:12.

37. Ibid., 26.

38. Tamar Katriel and Aliza Shenhar, "Tower and Stockade: Diabolic Narration in Israeli Settlement Ethos," *Quarterly Journal of Speech* 76, no. 3 (fall 1990): 361.

39. Ammiel Alcalay, *After Jews and Arabs: Remaking Levantine Culture* (Minneapolis: University of Minnesota Press, 1993), 25.

40. Ronit Matalon, *The One Facing Us,* trans. Marsha Weinstein (New York: Henry Holt, 1998).

41. Bender and Wellbery, eds., *Chronotypes,* 9.

42. This point is made well by Gayatri Spivak, "Time and Timing: Law and History," in Bender and Wellbery, eds., *Chronotypes,* 101.

43. On density and concreteness, see Bakhtin, "Forms of Time and the Chronotope in the Novel," 250.

44. Bakhtin, "Discourse in the Novel," 360.

45. Tobin, *Time and the Novel,* 6.

46. Matalon, *The One Facing Us,* 4.

47. Amitav Ghosh, *In an Ancient Land* (New York: Vintage, 1994), 261.

48. Matalon, *The One Facing Us,* 272.

49. Ammiel Alcalay, "The Geography of Time," *Michigan Quarterly Review* 31, no. 4 (fall 1992): 505.

50. Matalon, *The One Facing Us,* 16.

51. Foucault, *Discipline and Punish,* 272.

52. Carol J. Greenhouse, *A Moment's Notice: Time Politics across Cultures* (Ithaca, N.Y.: Cornell University Press, 1996), 228. I am indebted to Jon Goldberg-Hiller for calling the relevance of Carol Greenhouse's study to my attention.

53. Balibar notes that the traditional conception of the cultural minority is becoming anachronistic. As he puts it, "The very existence of minorities, together with their more or less inferior status, *was a state construct,* a strict correlate of the nation-form. Under current conditions there are *minorities without stable or unquestionable majorities*" ("Ambiguous Universality," 55).

54. Nancy, *The Sense of the World,* 111.

55. Nancy, *The Inoperative Community,* xi.

56. Nancy, *The Sense of the World,* 9.

6. Sovereignty, Dissymmetry, and Bare Life

1. All the source citations for Byron's *Hebrew Melodies* pertain to Thomas L. Ashton, *Byron's Hebrew Melodies* (Austin: University of Texas Press, 1972); quoted lines are from 181.

2. The quotation is from Mieke Bal's critique of the conventional biblical narrative from a feminist perspective. See her *Death and Dissymmetry: The Politics of Coherence in the Book of Judges* (Chicago: University of Chicago Press, 1988), 169.

3. The quoted expressions are from Agamben, *Homo Sacer*.

4. On the text's ideological position, see Bal, *Death and Dissymmetry*, 43.

5. Agamben, *Homo Sacer*, 7.

6. Bal, *Death and Dissymmetry*, 29.

7. Foucault, *History of Sexuality*, 137.

8. Agamben, *Homo Sacer*, 119–25.

9. Eric Schmitt, "Bill to Punish Nations Denying Religious Freedom Passes Senate," *New York Times*, October 10, 1998, 1.

10. Jim Emerson, "Noyce's On," *Film Comment* 28 (July–August 1992): 73.

11. Ibid.

12. Edward Said, "Identity, Negation and Violence," *New Left Review* 171 (1988): 47.

13. Deleuze, *Cinema 1*.

14. For the quoted phrase, see Emerson, "Noyce's On," 74.

15. Donzelot, *The Policing of Families*, 53.

16. For a critical analysis of the policy focus on "the Negro family," see Rainwater and Yancey, *The Moynihan Report and the Politics of Controversy*.

17. See Mosse, *Nationalism and Sexuality*.

18. See Samuel Huntington's *The Clash of Civilizations and the Remaking of World Order* (New York: Simon and Schuster, 1996) for an example of the contemporary commitment to an entity known as Western civilization.

19. Karen Schneider, "With Violence: Rearticulating the Family in the Contemporary Action-Thriller," *Journal of Popular Film & Television* 27, no. 1 (spring 1999): 2.

20. Fredric Jameson, *The Geopolitical Aesthetic: Cinema and Space in the World System* (Bloomington: Indiana University Press, 1995), 10.

21. Edward Said, "Fifty Years of Dispossession," *Harper's*, October 1998, 22.

22. Jameson, *The Geopolitical Aesthetic*, 5.

23. Deleuze, *Cinema 2*, 207.

24. The tension between cultural singularities and tendencies toward commoditization are treated by Igor Kopytoff, "The Cultural Biography of Things:

Commoditization as Process," in Arjun Appadurai, ed., *The Social Life of Things* (New York: Cambridge University Press, 1986), 64–91.

25. The expression "referential montage" is used by John Engell in an analysis of the repeated kissing and dueling scenes in Stanley Kubrick's film *Barry Lyndon*: "*Barry Lyndon*, a Picture of Irony," *Eighteenth Century Life* 19 (1995): 83–88.

26. Derrida, *The Politics of Friendship*, 15.

27. For "the direct image of time," see Deleuze, *Cinema 2*.

28. Bishnupriya Ghosh and Bhaskar Sarkar, "The Cinema of Displacement: Towards a Politically Motivated Poetics," *Film Criticism* 20, nos. 1–2 (fall/winter 1995–96): 104. The internal quotations and the concept of the liminar are from the work of Victor Turner.

29. Salman Rushdie, *Imaginary Homelands* (New York: Viking, 1991), 15.

30. On the concept of hypersecurity, see Michael Dillon, "Becoming Dangerous," paper delivered at the British International Studies 23d Annual Conference, University of Sussex, December 14–16, 1998.

31. Alcalay, *After Jews and Arabs*.

32. Alcalay, "The Geography of Time."

33. Ibid., 507.

34. Burch, "Spatial and Temporal Articulations," 17.

35. Paul Virilio, *War and Cinema: The Logistics of Perception*, trans. Patrick Camilleri (New York: Verso, 1989).

36. Again, as Deleuze points out in his analysis of the time image, contemporary cinema is based on the discovery that the time image constitutes a way of reading events that is more critical than mere perception (*Cinema 2*, 24). And, as I noted in chapter 2, when, in earlier films, the camera merely followed the action, the image of time was indirect, presented as a consequence of motion, and the perceptions of the actors governed the meaning of the narrative. In contrast, the new "camera consciousness" is no longer defined by the movements it is able to follow: "Even when it is mobile, the camera is no longer content to follow the character's movement" (ibid., 23).

37. Ibid., 165.

38. Michael J. Smith, "Humanitarian Intervention: An Overview of Ethical Issues," *Ethics and International Affairs* 12 (1998): 65.

39. Oliver P. Ramsbottom, "Islam, Christianity, and Forcible Humanitarian Intervention," *Ethics and International Affairs* 12 (1998): 81.

40. Agamben, *Homo Sacer*, 133.

41. See, for example, David Rieff, "The Lessons of Bosnia: Morality and Power," *World Policy Journal* (spring 1995): 76–88.

42. Agamben, *Homo Sacer*, 133.

Afterword

1. On the distinction between critical thought and mere recognition, see Gilles Deleuze, *Difference and Repetition*, trans. Paul Patton (New York: Columbia University Press, 1994), 133.

2. Most of what I have to say about the implications of Morrison's reflections relies on an excellent essay on Morrison and the politics of genre by Madhu Dubey: "The Politics of Genre in *Beloved*," *Novel: A Forum on Fiction* 32, no. 2 (spring 1999): 187–206.

3. The quotations are from Jon Klancher, "Godwin and the Republican Romance: Genre, Politics, and Contingency in Cultural History," *Modern Language Quarterly* 56, no. 2 (June 1995): 147.

4. Klancher refers to Godwin's genre as a "republican romance" (ibid., 148), and, inspired by Thomas Paine's expression, he refers to Godwin's reading audience as a "republic of letters" (145).

5. Ibid., 188.

6. Ibid.

7. Toni Morrison, "Introduction: Friday on the Potomac," in Toni Morrison, ed., *Race-ing Justice En-gendering Power: Essays on Anita Hill, Clarence Thomas, and the Construction of Social Reality* (New York: Pantheon, 1992), xxvii.

8. John Brenkman, "Politics and Form in *Song of Solomon*," *Social Text* 39 (1994): 63.

9. Toni Morrison, "Rootedness: The Ancestor as Foundation," in Mari Evans, ed., *Black Women Writers 1965–1980* (New York: Doubleday, 1984), 339.

10. My use of the term *semiosis* is influenced by Walter Mignolo's discussion of the semiotic interaction between diverse meaning systems and their material realizations during the Euro- and Meso-American encounter in the Renaissance, in *The Darker Side of the Renaissance: Literacy, Territoriality and Colonization* (Ann Arbor: University of Michigan Press, 1995), 7–9. On the distinctiveness of a black vernacular, see Ben Sidran, *Black Talk* (New York: Da Capo, 1971).

11. The expression is from Christopher Small, *Music of the Common Tongue: Survival and Celebration in African-American Music* (New York: River Run Press, 1987), 382.

12. See Henry Louis Gates Jr., *The Signifying Monkey: A Theory of Afro-American Literary Criticism* (New York: Oxford University Press, 1988), 52.

13. This quotation is from Nathaniel Mackey, "Other: From Noun to Verb," in Krin Gabbard, ed., *Jazz among the Discourses* (Durham, N.C.: Duke University Press, 1995), 83.

14. Zizek, *The Ticklish Subject*, 188.

15. See Nathan W. Pearson Jr., "Political and Musical Forces That Influenced

the Development of Kansas City Jazz," *Black Music Research Journal* 9, no. 2 (fall 1989): 182.

16. Quoted in Woods, *Development Arrested*, 3.

17. Burch, "Spatial and Temporal Articulations," 17.

18. LeRoi Jones (Amiri Baraka), *Blues People* (New York: Morrow, 1999), 57.

19. Robert Sterritt, "Director Builds Metaphor for Jazz in *Kansas City*," in David Sterritt, ed., *Robert Altman: Interviews* (Jackson: University of Mississippi Press, 2000), 211.

20. Connie Byrne and William O. Lopez, "*Nashville*," ibid., 20.

21. The quotation is from Krin Gabbard's review of the film: "*Kansas City*," *American Historical Review* 102, no. 4 (October 1997): 1274–75.

22. See the Altman interview in Byrne and Lopez, "*Nashville*," 21.

23. My reference to spatial history is taken from an analysis of the encounter between Europeans and Aborigines on the Australian continent. Paul Carter contrasts "imperial history," which is based on a "theatrical assumption that historical individuals are actors, fulfilling a higher destiny," with "spatial history," which, instead of treating historical spaces as "natural, passive and objectively there," focuses on the journeys through which spaces are shaped (xxi). And, he notes, in addition, that "spatial history . . . does not organize its subject matter into a nationalist enterprise (294). See his *The Road to Botany Bay* (Chicago: University of Chicago Press, 1987). On the blues fidelity in southwestern jazz bands, see Jones, *Blues People*, 167.

24. See Sidran, *Black Talk*.

25. Fatima Mernissi, *Dreams of Trespass: Tales of a Harem Girlhood* (Reading, Mass.: Addison-Wesley, 1995).

26. Rancière, *Disagreement*, 101.

27. See Joanna Hodge's elaboration of a Heideggerian ethics, which she derives from Heidegger's critique of metaphysical thinking: *Heidegger and Ethics* (New York: Routledge, 1995). Working with what she calls a "repressed ethical dimension in Heidegger's enquiries" (18), she argues that "Heidegger's enquiries are . . . ethical in the sense that they put humanity in question" (23). It is in this sense that I am deriving an ethical impetus from the power-deconstructing effects of the stories of women in Mernissi's harem.

28. Idelber Avelar, "The Ethics of Interpretation and the International Division of Intellectual Labor," *SubStance* 29, no. 1 # 91 (2000): 81–82. Much of what I have to say in these reflections is edified by Avelar's thorough and effective discussion of the issues.

29. See Emmanuel Levinas: *Totality and Infinity,* trans. Alphonso Lingus (Pittsburgh: Duquesne University Press, 1969), and *Otherwise Than Being or Beyond Essence,* trans. Alphonso Lingus (The Hague: Martinus Nijhoff, 1981);

and see Jacques Derrida: "Violence and Metaphysics," and *Adieu to Emmanuel Levinas*, trans. P. A. Brault and M. Naas (Stanford, Calif.: Stanford University Press, 1999). I have treated the implications of both Levinas's and Derrida's approaches to ethics in chapter 6 of Michael J. Shapiro, *Violent Cartographies: Mapping Cultures of War* (Minneapolis: University of Minnessota Press, 1997).

30. See Immanuel Kant, *Perpetual Peace*, trans. H. B. Nisbet, in *Kant: Political Writings*, ed. H. Reiss (New York: Cambridge University Press, 1991).

31. Michel Foucault, "What Is Enlightenment?" in Paul Rabinow and William Sullivan, eds., *Interpretive Social Science: A Second Look* (Berkeley: University of California Press, 1987), 159.

32. Michel Foucault, "What Is Critique?" trans. Lysa Hochroth, in Michel Foucault, *The Politics of Truth*, ed. Sylvere Lotringer and Lysa Hochroth (New York: Semiotext(e), 1997), 59.

33. Kant's philosophical geography is state- and government-oriented. Concepts are referred to as objects and the conditions under which one can have knowledge of them is dependent on which concepts *govern* within particular domains of apprehension. As he put it in his third critique: "The part of the field in which knowledge is possible for us is a territory *(territorium)* for these concepts and the requisite cognitive faculty. The part of the territory over which they exercise legislative authority is the realm *(ditio)* of these concepts, and their appropriate cognitive faculty." See Immanuel Kant, *The Critique of Judgement*, trans. James Creed Meredith (Oxford: Clarendon Press, 1952), 12.

34. See Jean-François Lyotard, *The Differend: Phrases in Dispute*, trans. G. van den Abbeele (Minneapolis: University of Minnesota Press, 1988).

35. Lyotard, "The Sign of History," 109.

36. Kant uses the expression "subjective finality" in his discussion of the analytic of the sublime, in *The Critique of Judgement*, 101.

37. Henisch, *Negatives of My Father*, 150.

Index

Michael J. Shapiro is professor of political science at the University of Hawai'i and coeditor, with David Campbell, of the book series Borderlines, published by the University of Minnesota Press. His recent books include *Violent Cartographies: Mapping Cultures of War* (Minnesota, 1997) and *Cinematic Political Thought: Narrating Race, Nation, and Gender.*